IMAGES
of Modern America

New York State Pavilion

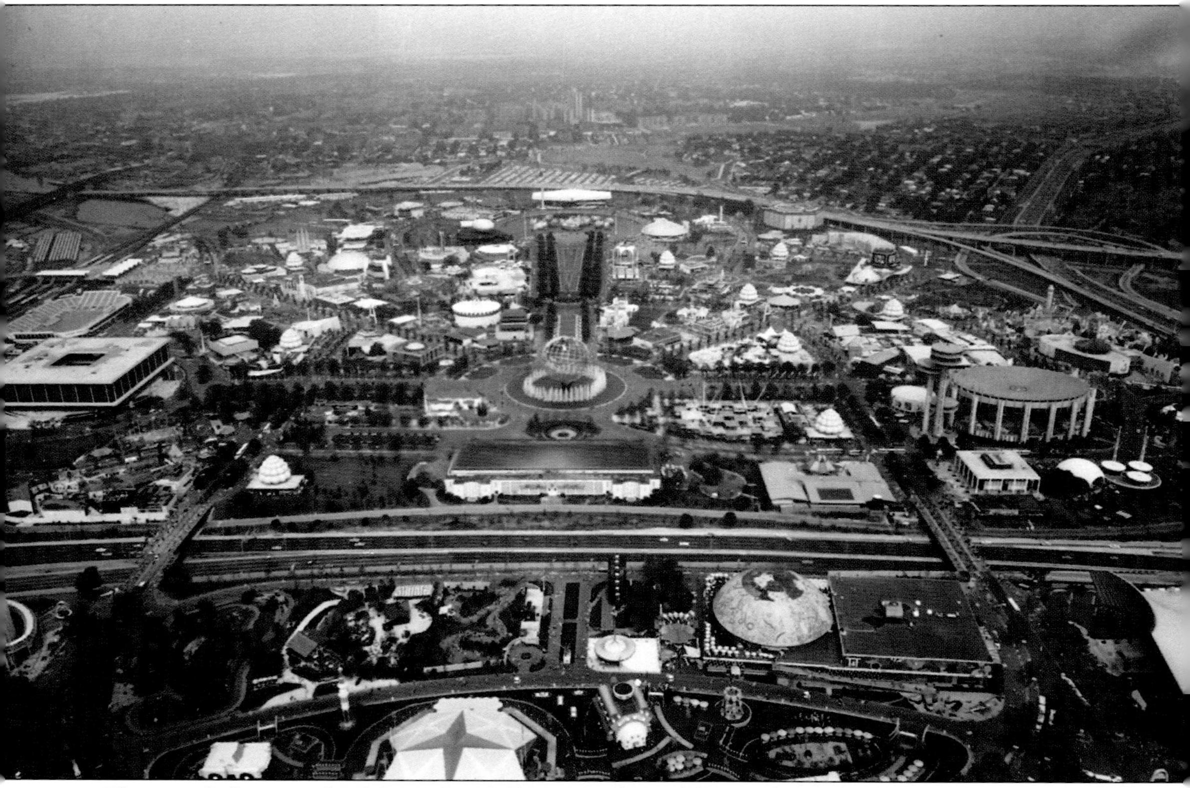

This aerial photograph of the 1964–1965 New York World's Fair shows the New York State pavilion on the right. (Author's collection.)

On the Front Cover: Clockwise from top left:
Tent of Tomorrow (Copyright Christian Kellberg; see page 81), Sky-Streak elevator (Author's collection; see page 52), observation towers (Author's collection; see page 49), aviation warning light (Author's collection; see page 55), the cover of Roy Lichtenstein's *Art in America* (Copyright the Sterling and Francine Clark Art Institute with permission from the Estate of Roy Lichtenstein; see pages 78, 79).

On the Back Cover: From left to right:
"Panorama of the City of New York" (Courtesy of the Queens Museum; see page 92), 1964–1965 New York World's Fair site scale model (Courtesy of the Queens Museum; see page 92), "Miniature Trip through New York" model (Courtesy of Robinson-Capsis-Stern Associates; see page 25).

IMAGES
of Modern America

NEW YORK STATE PAVILION

Christian Kellberg

ARCADIA PUBLISHING

ISBN 978-1-4671-2243-6

Published by Arcadia Publishing
Charleston, South Carolina

Printed in the United States of America

Library of Congress Control Number: 2014934914

For all general information, please contact Arcadia Publishing:
Telephone 843-853-2070
Fax 843-853-0044
E-mail sales@arcadiapublishing.com
For customer service and orders:
Toll-Free 1-888-313-2665

Visit us on the Internet at www.arcadiapublishing.com

To George Capsis, who provided help and inspiration for this book as a designer of the New York State pavilion's "Miniature Trip through New York"

Contents

Acknowledgments

Sincere thanks go to the following people and organizations: Rich Lando for his touching commentary and the photographs of his band playing at the New York State pavilion; Bill Cotter for contributing photographs from his personal world's fair collection and publishing advice; Denise Kelly for her photograph and story behind Led Zeppelin's concert at the New York State pavilion; Christine Rafalke for her photographs of the roller rink and its history; my junior high friend Karl Baker for his father's construction photographs; Larissa Harris, curator of the Queens Museum, for her help going through its archives; Ryan Ritchey and Mike Kraus for their rare photographs of Pop Art; Ryan Ritchey, again, for his worldsfairmovie.com effort; David Troup, the communications director of the Farnsworth Museum in Rockland, Maine, for his photograph of Robert Indiana's *EAT* sculpture mounted on the museum's roof; and Vince Marchese for providing my favorite world's fair photograph of all time. I am also thankful for the websites worldsfaircommunity.org and nywf64.com for the enormous amount of world's fair information they provided.

Special thanks go to John Piro for getting the New York State pavilion paint project started.

Unless otherwise noted, all photographs that appear in this book were taken by the author or are from author's family albums.

INTRODUCTION

The New York State pavilion, a legacy building from the 1964–1965 New York World's Fair, is located in the southwest corner of Flushing Meadow Corona Park, close to where the Long Island Expressway crosses over the Grand Central Parkway. From these freeways alone, the pavilion is seen by 390,000 motorists per day and is a symbol of the Empire State, the "Eiffel Tower of Queens." At 252 feet to the top of its aviation light, the pavilion is by far the tallest structure for miles; it is an exception to the height limits imposed by La Guardia Airport on its neighbors.

The pavilion has three parts, unified by a common circular theme: (1) The observation towers offer spectacular views across the borough of Queens, from the Whitestone and Throgs Neck Bridges to the Manhattan skyline. The four 60-foot-diameter observation decks, arranged atop a group of three slender towers, have a flying saucer–like appearance. (2) The Tent of Tomorrow is a football field–sized event plaza and is surrounded by sixteen 115-foot-tall columns, which support the world's largest prestressed cable roof. Covering the cable roof was a 305-by-225-foot oval expanse of translucent fiberglass panels, arranged in a four-color pattern. A street-level circular plaza, under the tent (roof), contains the world's largest map, a terrazzo-tiled, 130-by-166-foot scaled reproduction of the 1964 New York State Texaco road map. (3) Theaterama was a 100-foot-diameter, 44-foot-tall building that showed a film tour of New York State using the interior wall as a 360-degree screen. During the fair, 10 large Pop Art displays, some up to 20 feet across, by emerging Pop artists, were spaced along the outside wall of the Theaterama.

By the time planning for the world's fair was under way, the pavilion's architect Philip Johnson was already well established. His portfolio included private residences, galleries, university buildings, and a connection to then New York governor Nelson Rockefeller by way of commissions for the guesthouse of Blanchette Rockefeller, wife of John D. Rockefeller III, on East Fifty-second Street (1950), the Museum of Modern Art's Abby Aldrich Rockefeller Sculpture Garden (1953), and the Nelson Rockefeller Art Gallery in Seal Harbor, Maine (1957). Philip Johnson's designs for the New York State pavilion and the New York State Theater, in Lincoln Center, were selected in February 1962 to showcase the state's prowess in art and architecture for the world's fair. Both the pavilion and theater were completed with state funds, and ownership for both buildings was transferred to the City of New York at the conclusion of the fair. From October 18, 1965, through June 2, 1967, the world's fair site was closed to the public and returned to its configuration as Flushing Meadow Corona Park. During this period, 170 pavilions were demolished or disassembled; only the paved walkways and stand-alone sculptures were left behind. The park's 646 acres were landscaped to cover any foundation remnants below the required three-foot removal depth. Only the following five pavilions from the 1964–1965 New York World's Fair were kept as permanent structures: the New York State pavilion, the Hall of Science, the Port Authority Heliport, the United States pavilion, and the Singer Bowl. After the June 2, 1967, reopening, the New York State pavilion saw only limited use for events and was essentially abandoned until the Tent of Tomorrow rotunda was leased as a roller skate rink, opening on St. Patrick's Day 1970. The successful venture helped to attract up to 100,000 visitors per year to the pavilion, but the rink was shut down in July 1974 amid concerns that some of the 1,488 colorful translucent roof panels had become loose. The novel fiberglass panels were eventually removed, but the skating rink never returned. This was the last adaptive reuse of the largest part of the New York State pavilion.

What has found a reuse for most of its post-fair years has been the Theaterama part of the pavilion, which has operated as a playhouse since 1972. Taking the name Queens Theatre in the Park, after a 1993 $4 million remodel, it grew to 464-seat theater putting on 300 performances for 100,000 visitors per year. A second expansion in 2008 added a glass-walled, 3,000-square-foot lobby, and a 75-seat cabaret performance stage.

The New York State pavilion has also provided the setting for a number of films and television shows. In 1972, an episode of the detective television series *McCloud*, with Dennis Weaver in the title role, was shot at the pavilion; on site, McCloud rappelled down the towers. Titled "Showdown at the End of the World," the episode aired on January 7, 1973. The pavilion again found use for filming as the set of *The Wiz*, a remake of the *Wizard of Oz*, starring Diana Ross as Dorothy, in early October 1977. In 1997, a scaled-down mock-up of the towers, now at the Theme Parks at Universal Orlando Resort, was featured in the *Men in Black*. More recently the pavilion appeared in two episodes of *Crime Scene Investigation: New York*, which aired on November 17 and 25, 2009, and a virtual pavilion, along with a revitalized world's fair park, was prominently featured in the May 7, 2010, release of *Iron Man 2*.

After three years of lobbying, in 2004, the CREATE Architecture Planning & Design Firm proposed the Air & Space Museum at the New York State pavilion, which would have initiated repairs on the towers and rotunda. The proposal accomplished the remarkable task of enlisting the participation of every major contractor involved in the original 1964 construction of the pavilion, including the endorsement of Philip Johnson himself; however, it was never accepted. The towers and rotunda of the New York State pavilion have awaited repurposing ever since. One exception was a 2008 National Academy of Arts–funded restoration of 4 of the 576 terrazzo panels that form the floor map of New York State.

A 2009 study by Robert Silman Associates, using information extrapolated from two earlier studies commissioned by the park's department (the Geiger report from November 17, 1992, and the Ciardullo study from October 2, 1996), estimated that stabilizing the pavilion would cost from $20.3 million to $29 million and that demolition of just the Tent of Tomorrow portion would cost $9 million. The debate over adaptive reuse has gone on since then, with uncertainty over the condition of the foundation becoming one of the main sticking points. In a 2013 study by Perkins & Will, the cost had grown to over $14 million for demolition and $73 million for restoration.

On September 15, 2009, the New York State pavilion was approved to become a state landmark and added to the State Register of Historic Places.

With regard to New York City landmarks, there is an interesting circle of history involving Madison Square Garden, Pennsylvania Station, and New York State pavilion. For starters, Madison Square Garden's cable-suspension roof, the world's largest cable-suspension roof, used Lev Zetlin's concept from the 1959 Utica Auditorium, and it was Lev Zetlin who designed the New York State pavilion's Tent of Tomorrow, which was also based on his Utica Auditorium. On July 27, 1961, the fight to save the Pennsylvania Station started with the announcement that the station would be demolished and a new Madison Square Garden, to be completed in time for the 1964–1965 New York World's Fair, would rise at its site. (The new Madison Square Garden, however, was not completed until February 1968.) On February 20, 1962, the then New York City parks commissioner, Newbold Morris, advanced the idea that Pennsylvania Station's 84 Doric columns could be moved to Flushing Meadow Corona Park for use at the world's fair, but they would end up as landfill in the New Jersey Meadowlands. The destruction of Pennsylvania Station led to the New York Landmarks Law on April 19, 1965. Who would have known at the time that the New York State pavilion's iconic columns would become the subject of another discussion on landmarks preservation?

One

Construction of the Tent of Tomorrow

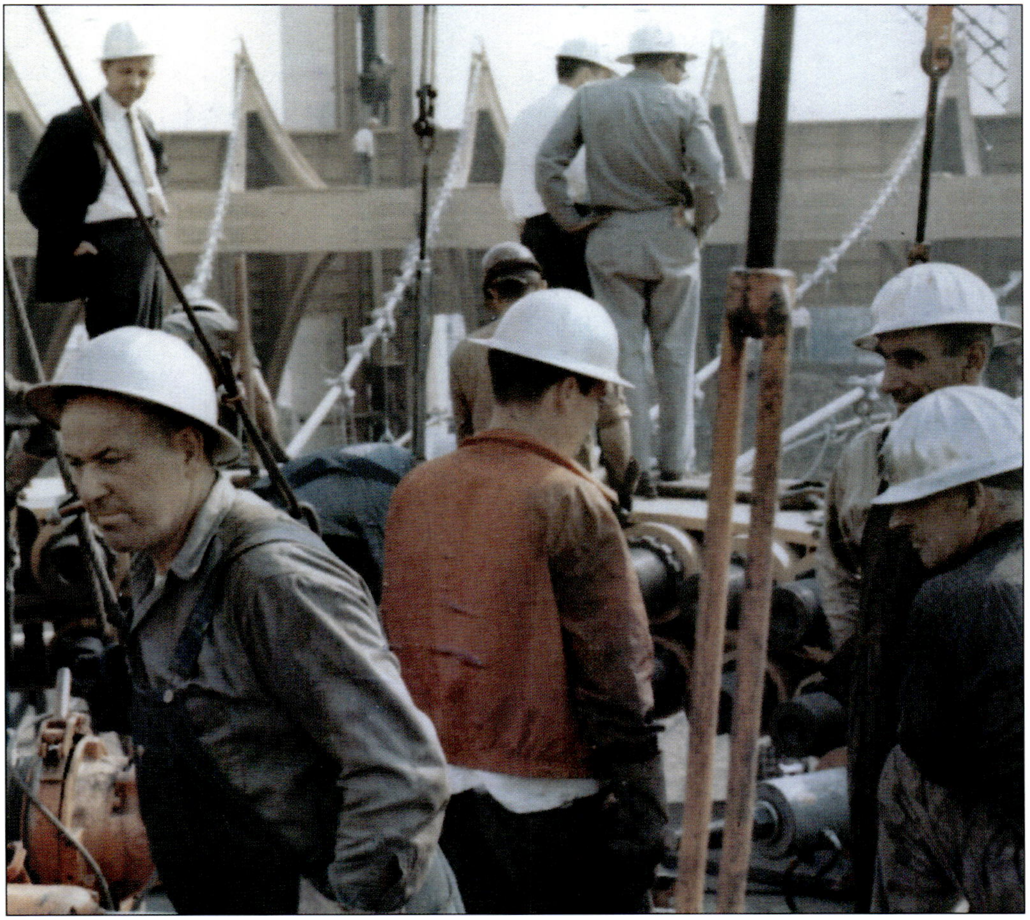

The New York State pavilion was constructed using a novel approach that has certainly withstood the test of time after 50 years. Designed by Lev Zetlin Associates, the 305-by-225-foot oval Tent of Tomorrow was the world's largest prestressed cable roof. Covered by 1,488 fiberglass panels at only nine pounds per square foot, it is considered the lightest permanent cable-suspension roof. (Courtesy of Joseph Seebacher and Karl Baker.)

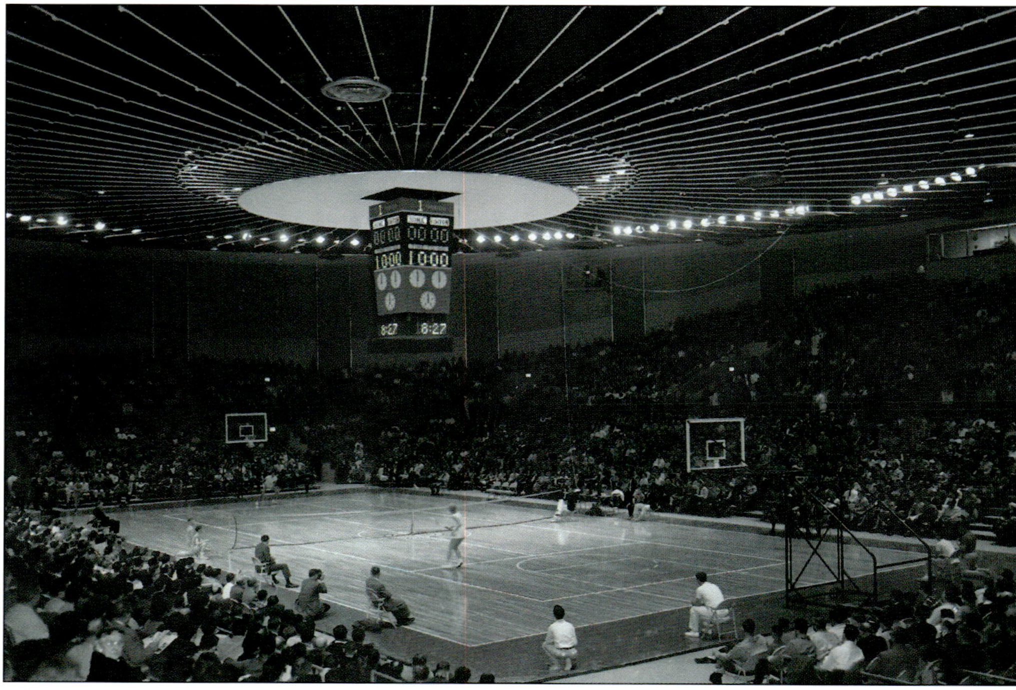

The predecessor to the New York State pavilion's Tent of Tomorrow was Lev Zetlin's double-layer "bicycle spoke" design for the Utica Auditorium, completed in 1959. This 250-foot-diameter roof formed the basis for the Tent of Tomorrow. In 1968, Madison Square Garden in New York City, by Charles Luckman, became the world's largest cable-suspension roof with a diameter of 404 feet; it was also modeled after the Utica Auditorium.

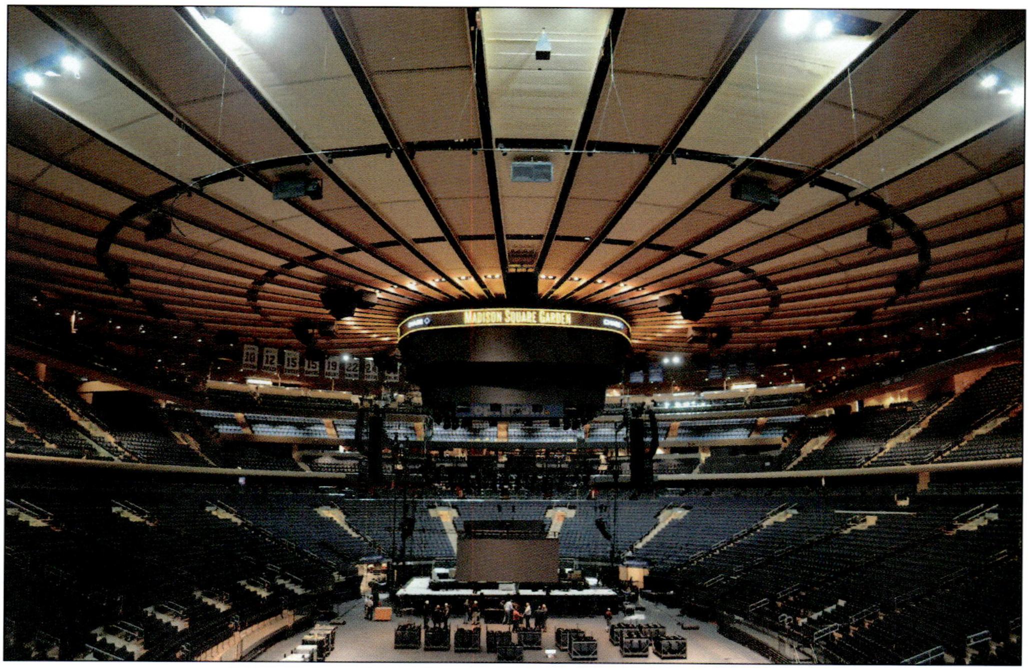

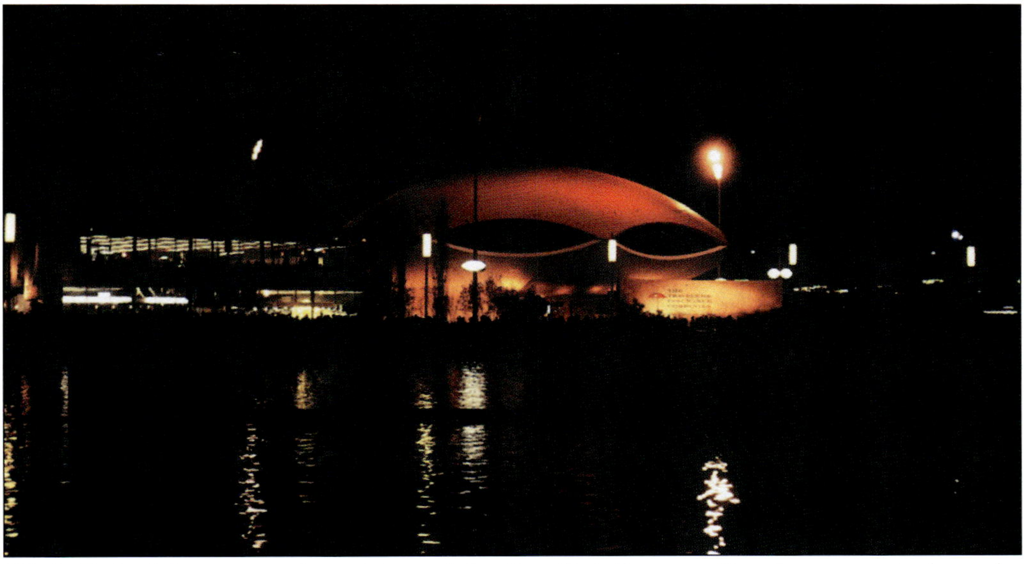

While Philip Johnson was the architect of the New York State pavilion, less recognized was the structural engineer, Dr. Lev Zetlin. It is not common knowledge that he also designed the Traveler's Insurance pavilion for the 1964–1965 New York World's Fair. The 160-foot-diameter roof was built to look like an umbrella (the Traveler's corporate symbol). The interior had no support columns to maximize space for 13 life-sized dioramas used in a walk-through history exhibit titled The Triumph of Man. The pavilion was made up of a circular arrangement of 18 boomerang-shaped beams tied together with tension cables, forming an 80-foot-diameter cap. A computer model of the structure is superimposed on an aerial photograph to show the relationship.

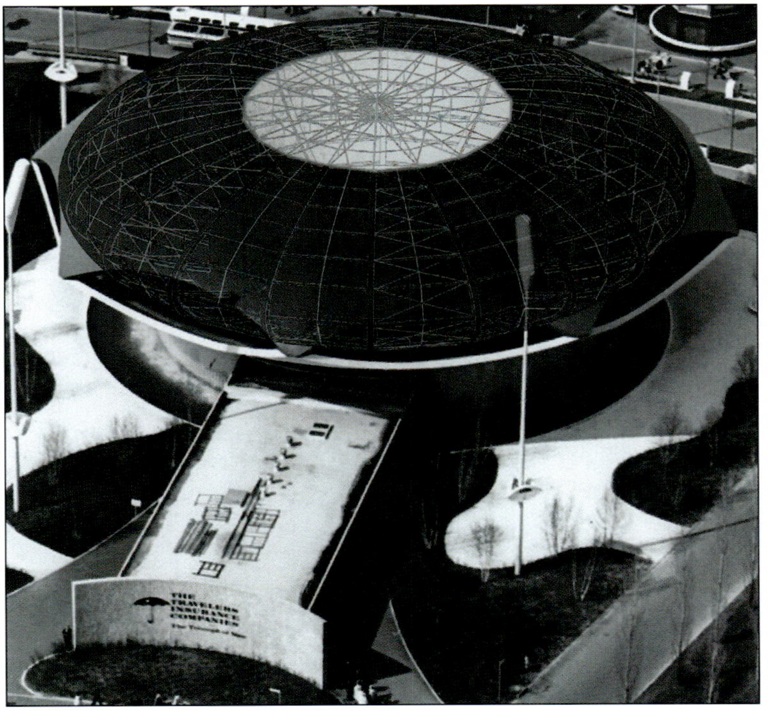

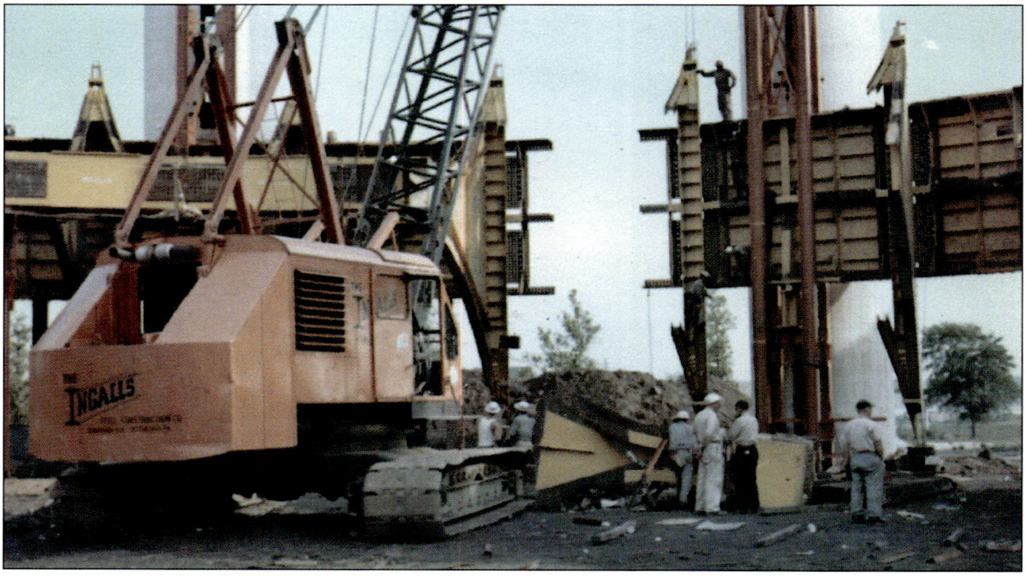

A crane lifts the last section of the "crown," a 2,000-ton steel compression ring for the cable roof, to be bolted in place. The Ingalls Construction Company, of Birmingham, Alabama, did the assembly. A construction worker is dwarfed standing near the top of one of the tall vertical needle beams that will hold the cable ends. The concrete columns seen bordering the crown were continuously poured, starting in December 1962, using a slip-form method, developed by the Nicholson Company. (As the concrete hardened, the forms were shifted up at a rate between 12 to 18 inches per hour.) Despite cold weather, the 16 massive 118-foot, 90-inch-tall columns were completed by January 1963. Although they are 1-foot-thick shells and 12 feet in diameter, they appear slender in relation to the open space of the amphitheater. (Both, courtesy of Joseph Seebacher and Karl Baker.)

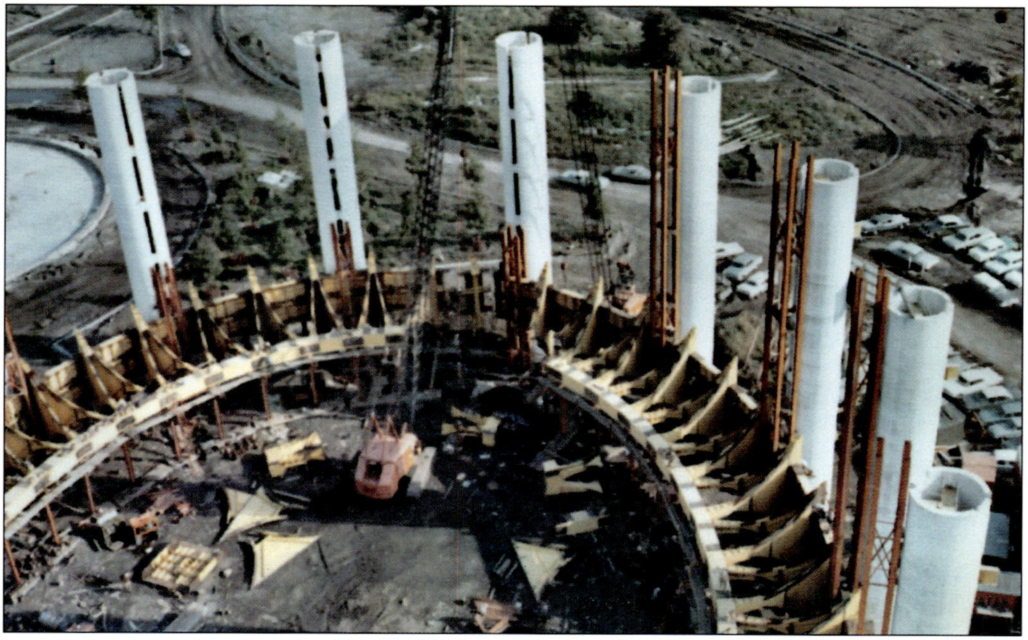

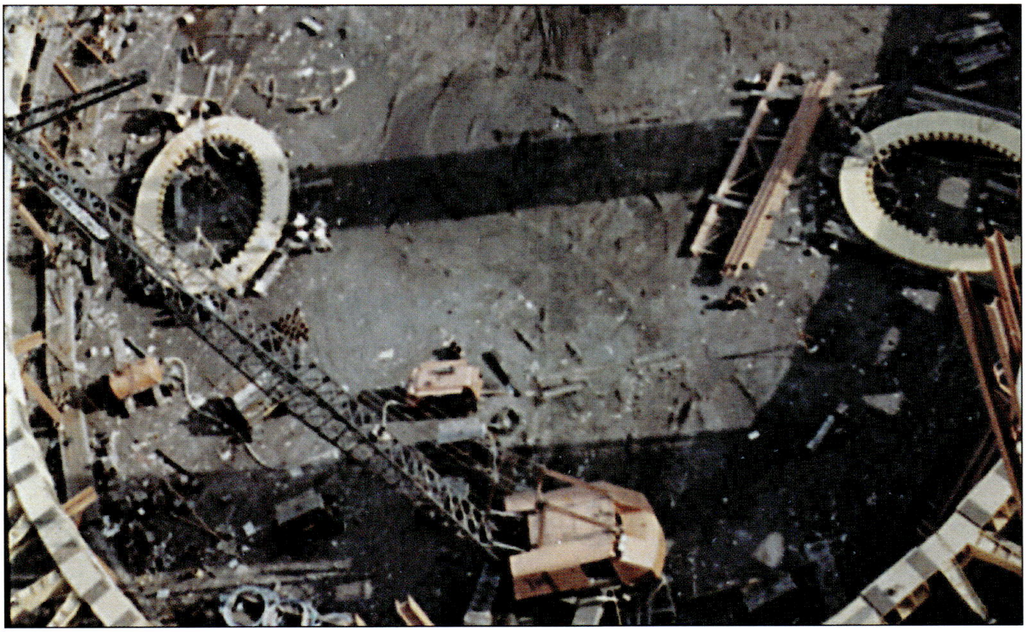

The top and bottom sections that will become the center tension ring are seen on the ground, waiting to be assembled. The two sections will each hold a layer of 48 Roebling cables. Sets of 4 steel columns go up in front of each of the 16 concrete perimeter columns to serve as guides on which the crown will be supported during the raising of the cable roof. Below, a construction worker has his foot on one of these steel columns, with predrilled holes along its length, to which the crown was be pinned after each 30-inch lift segment in a 100-foot ascent. (Both, courtesy of Joseph Seebacher and Karl Baker.)

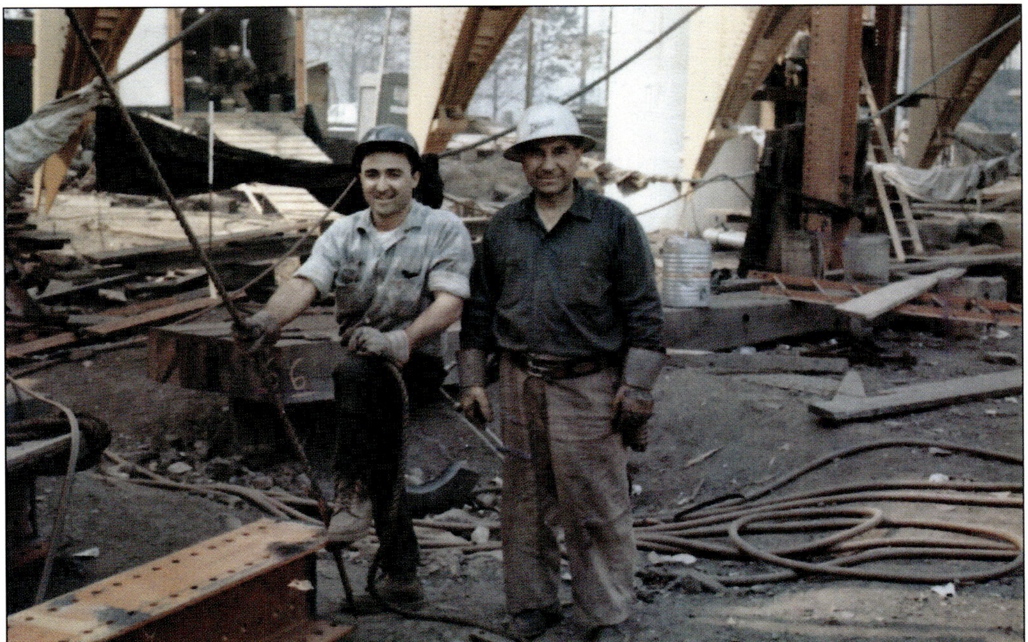

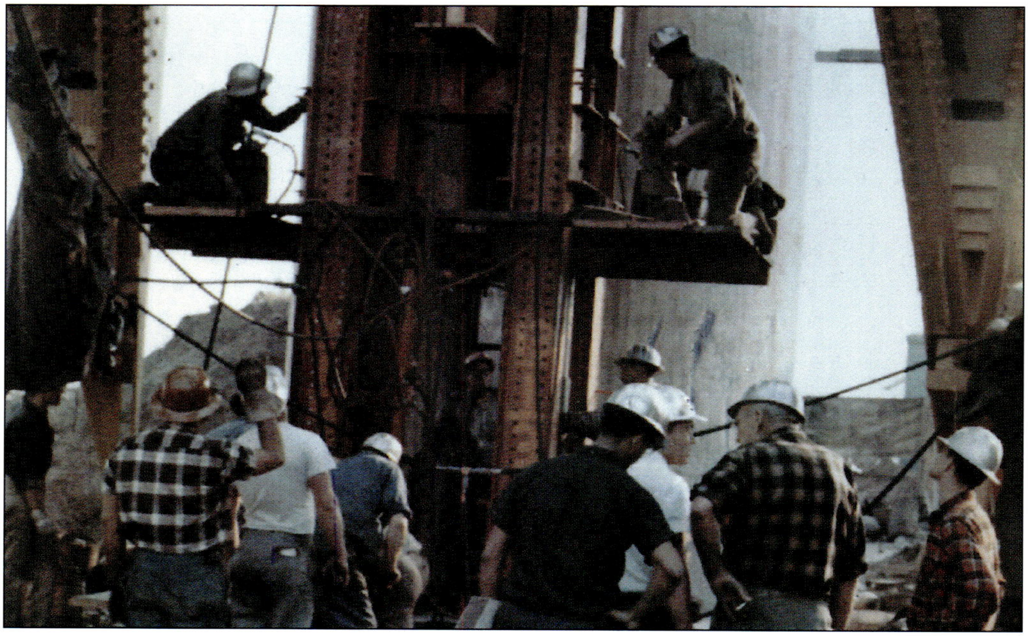

The lifting platform for the hydraulic jacks is put into place under the roof crown and pinned to the four steel columns. The cables were then strung from the top and bottom of the crown's vertical needle beams to the center tension ring. The crown itself rests on a stub of a 36-inch-wide flange beam positioned on the platform (the largest standard size, only manufactured at the Bethlehem Steel plant). When the roof crown reached its final height, the stub was clamped together with a matching beam at the top of the column and welded, a process repeated for each of the 16 columns. (Both, courtesy of Joseph Seebacher and Karl Baker.)

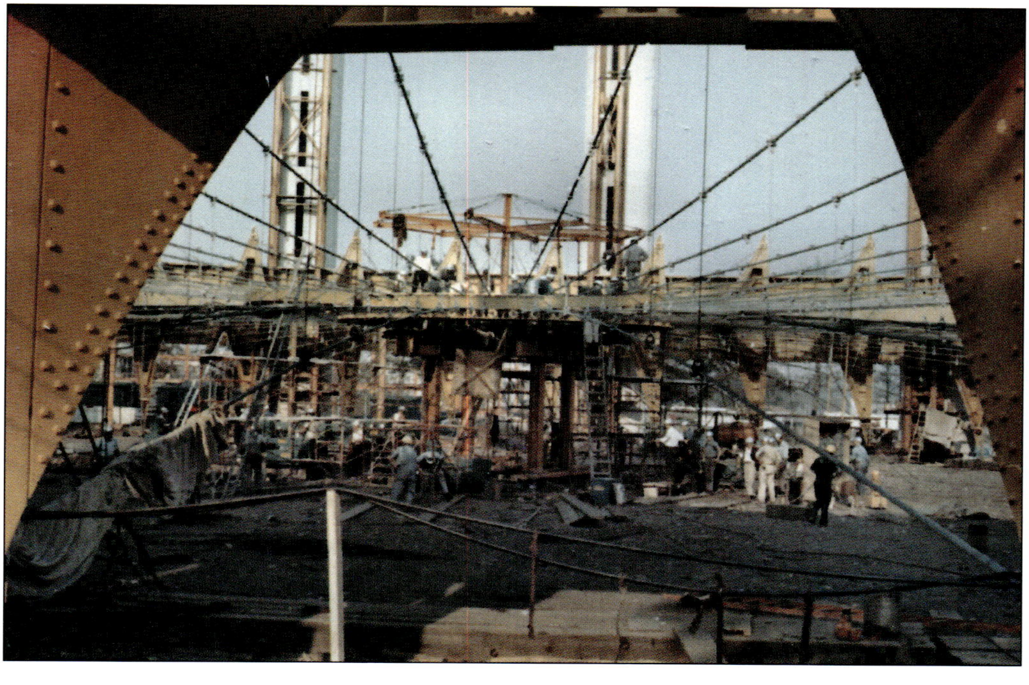

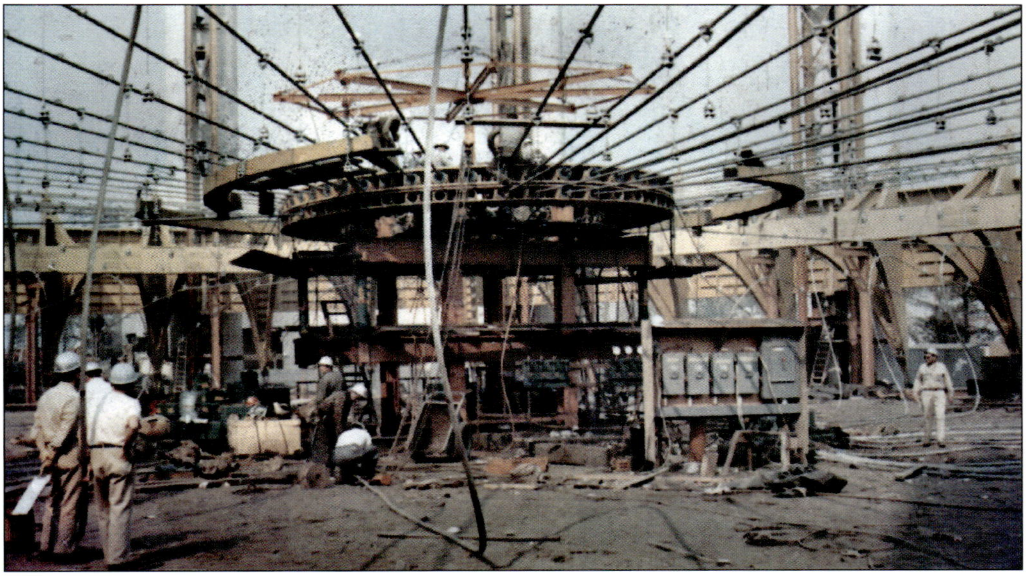

The two halves of a drainage troth were then assembled over the center tension ring, and four pipes were attached. (They still hang there to this day but are not connected.) They would divert runoff from the 55,000-square-foot roof down through pipes in four of the columns. Once all the hydraulic jacks and lifting rigs were in place, a master pumping station was set up in the center to electrically monitor that all 32 jacks would operate at exactly the same time for each 30-inch lift stage. The white structure with square openings in the background below is the 100-foot-diameter-by-44-foot-tall building that will become Theaterama, today's Queens Theatre in the Park, the third element of the New York State pavilion. (Both, courtesy of Joseph Seebacher and Karl Baker.)

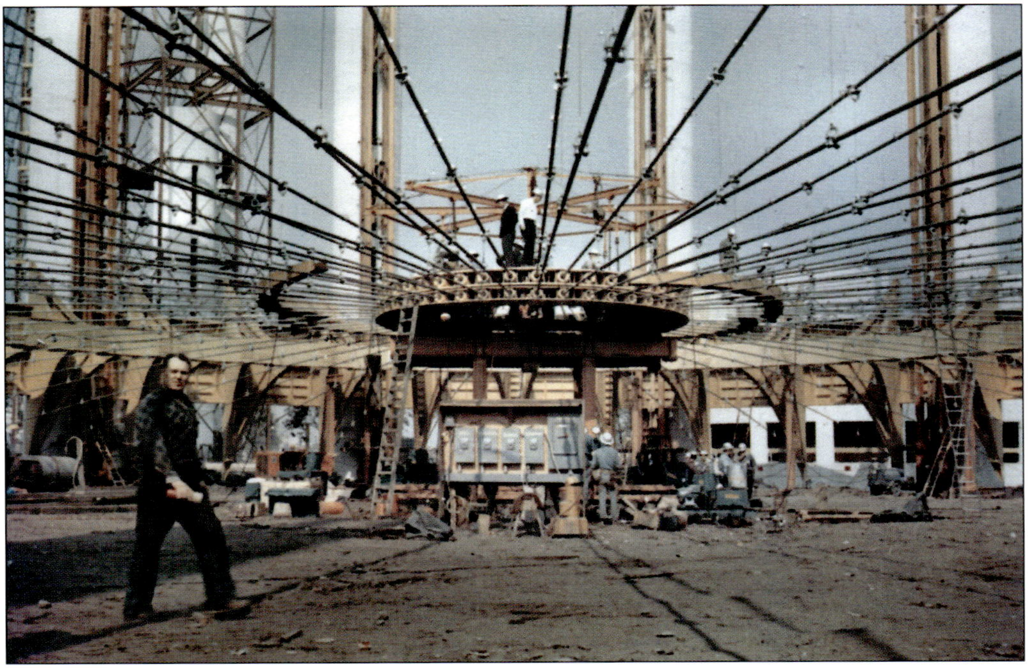

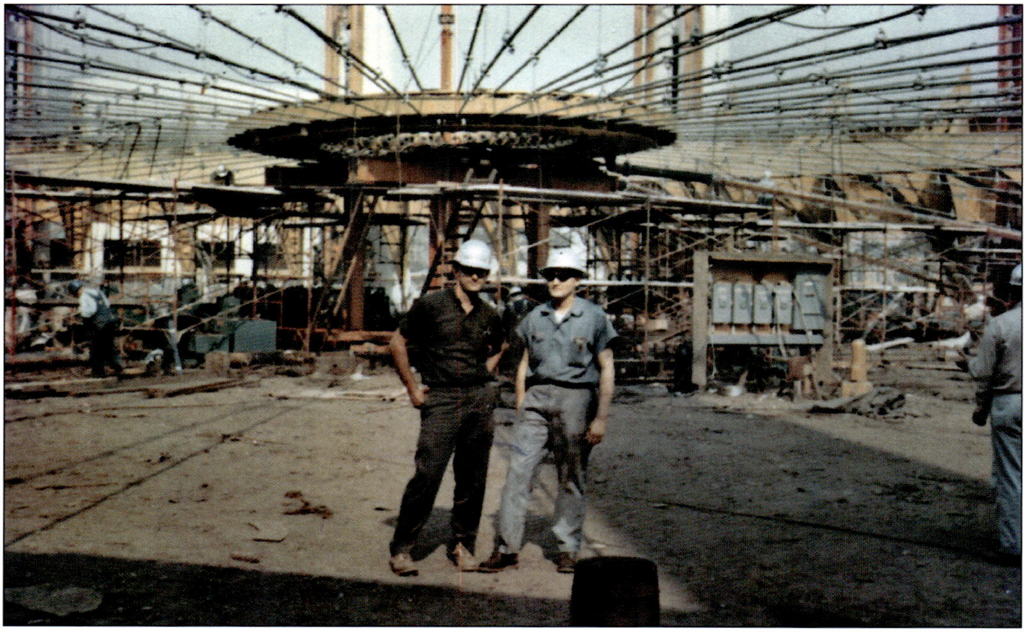

A nice 1960 four-door Chevrolet Bel Air is parked in front with a completed tension ring assembly in the background. In just one of the 48 outer faceplates of the crown, 428 bolts can be counted. The crown and center tension ring were then slightly lifted off the support bracing, and the cables were adjusted for equal tension. The top layer of 48 cables is 2.25 inches in diameter, and the bottom layer of 48 cables is 1.6875 inches; by way of comparison, the larger 405-foot-diameter roof of Madison Square Garden uses 48 1.75-inch-diameter cables. (Both, courtesy of Joseph Seebacher and Karl Baker.)

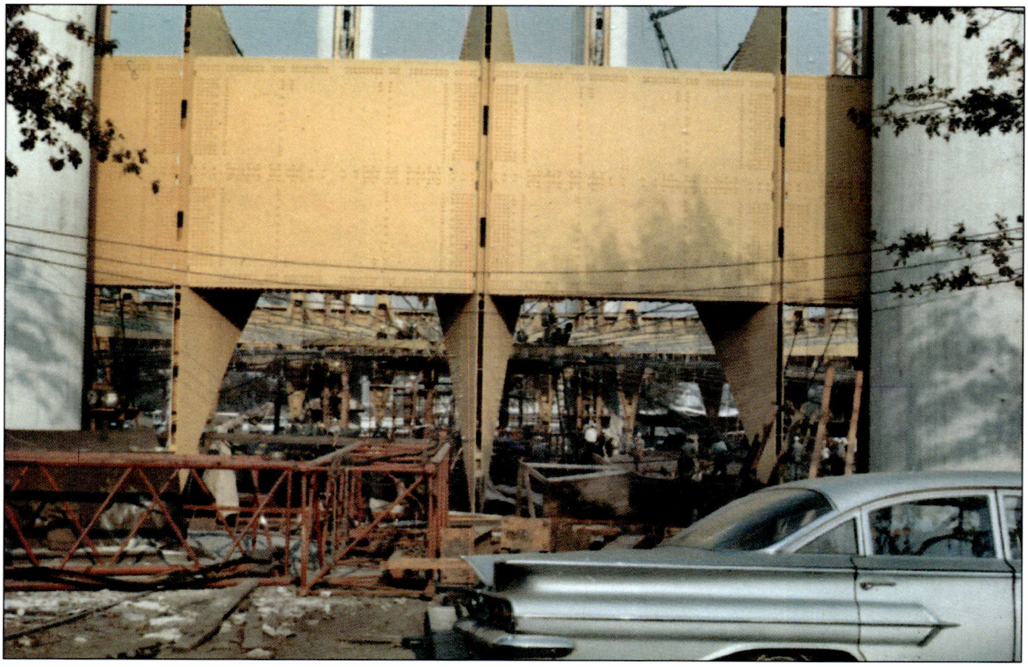

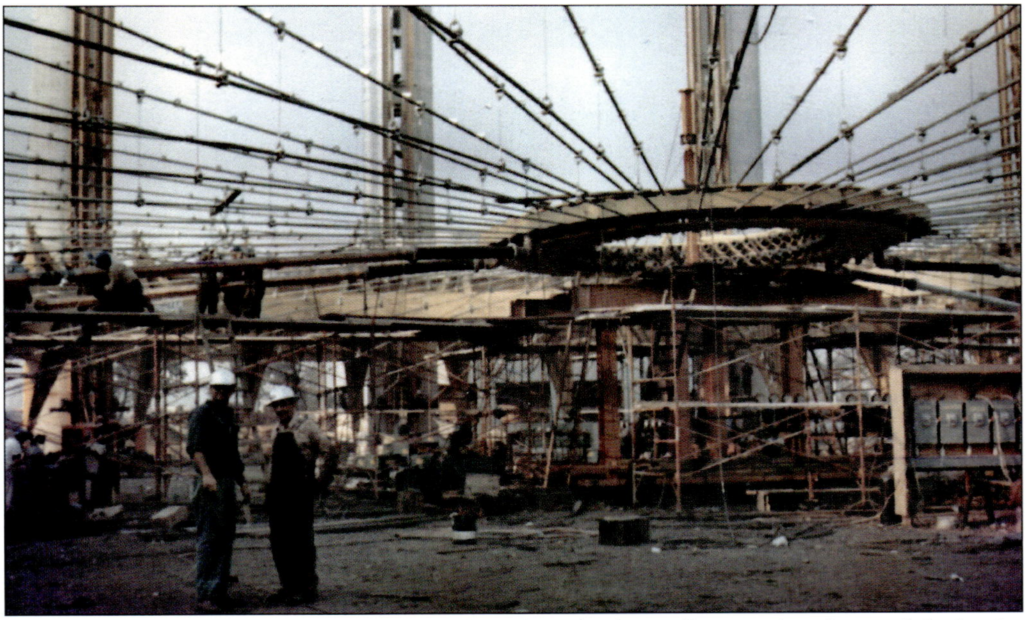

Before the raising of the roof began, a horseshoe-shaped safety collar was placed on each hydraulic jack piston to limit any backsliding to less than one inch. The hydraulic jacks were in actual operation for only two hours out of the entire two-week lifting operation. For most of that time, the hydraulic jacks were used to raise the lift rig platform and pin it to the temporary steel support columns for each subsequent 30-inch lift step. The four drainage pipes were also pulled up along with the roof while attached to the tension ring through a flexible section. (Both, courtesy of Joseph Seebacher and Karl Baker.)

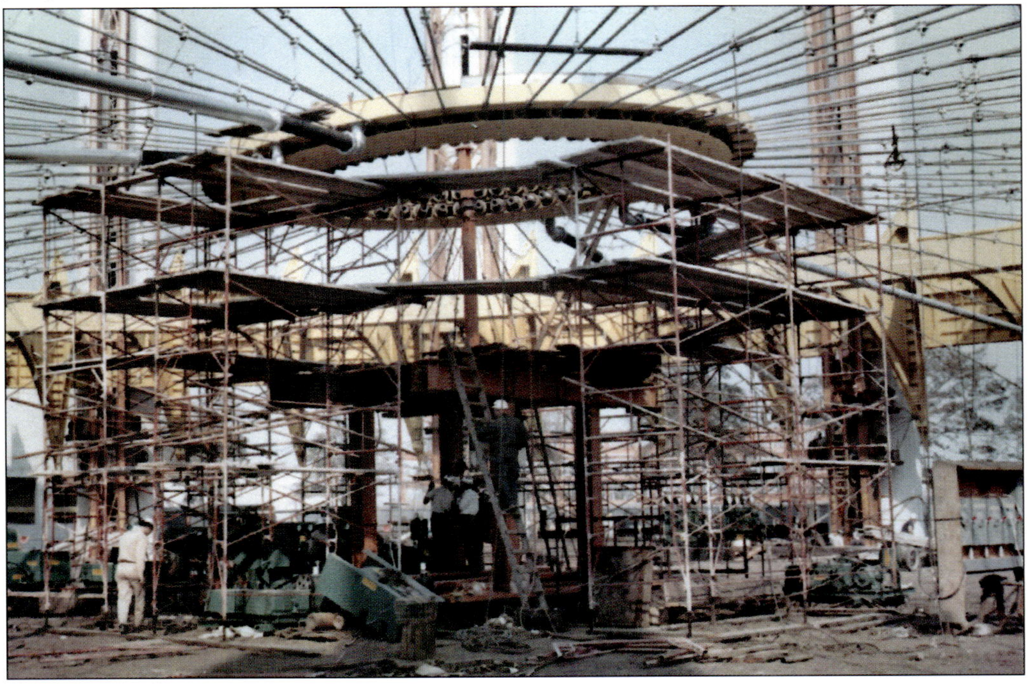

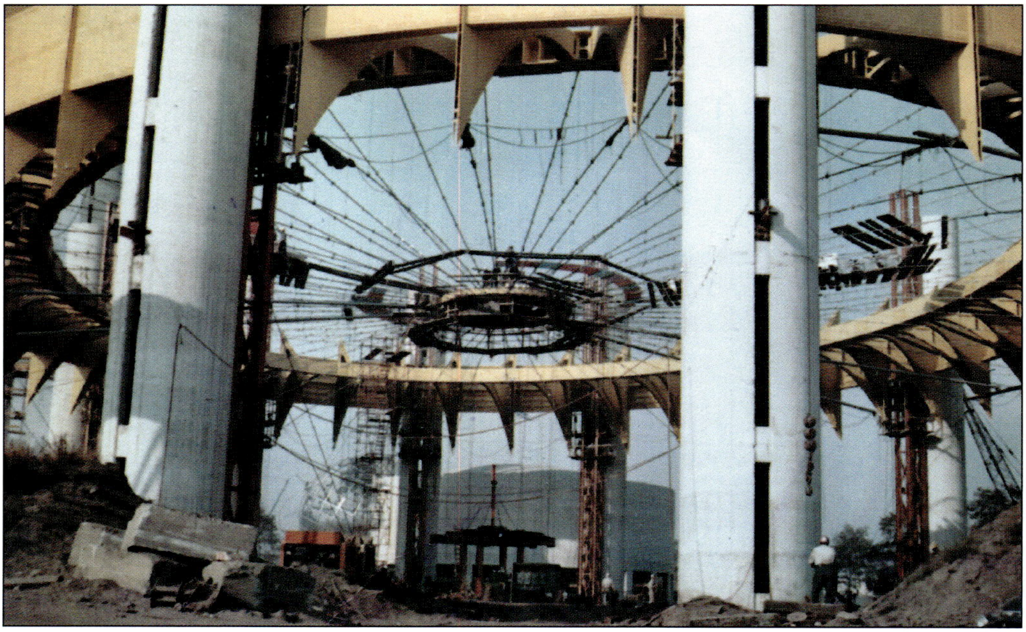

While the roof was still being raised, placement of the Kalwall translucent panels began, starting from the tension ring hub out. These 2.75-inch-thick panels were a lightweight sandwich construction of fiberglass face sheets bonded to an open lattice aluminum core. The panels came in four colors that were laid down with a pattern repeated for every fourth radial, between each pair of the 48 top layer cables, producing a subtle spiral pattern. The panels could easily support the weight of the workers who walked on them to seal the seams with Interchem Corporation's Presstite flexible elastic tape. (Both, courtesy of Joseph Seebacher and Karl Baker.)

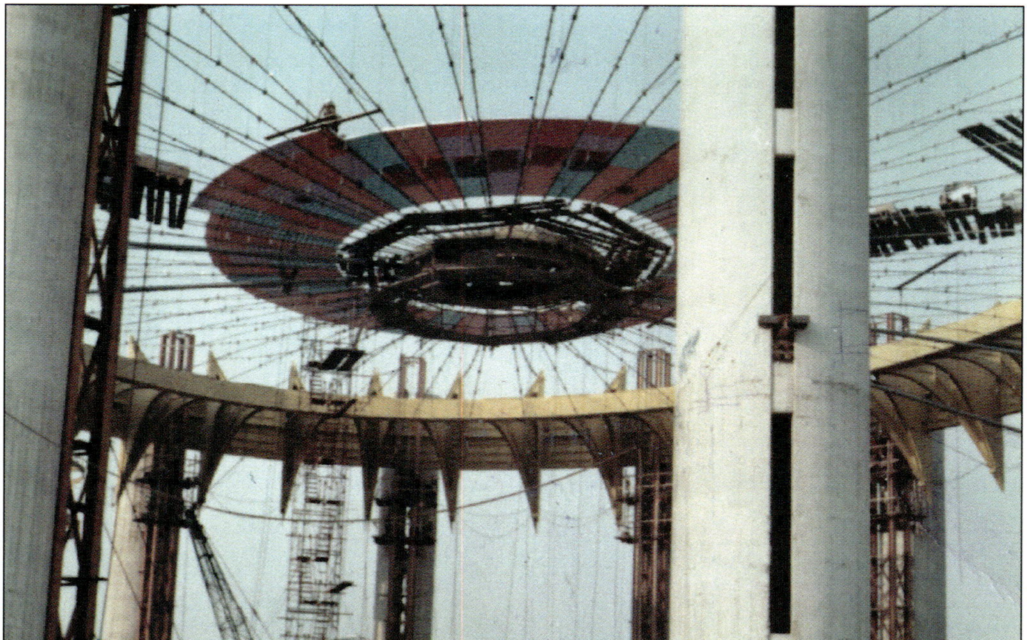

These construction photographs appear courtesy of an old junior high school friend whose father, Joseph Seebacher, was a welder who worked on the pavilion. He went about the job site with ease, not only taking key photographs of the build, but also capturing the construction workers in a very natural way, with the acceptance that would only have been given to a peer. His job was among the most important because when the roof was raised to its final position, the 36-inch-wide flange beams were welded to the matching stubs under the crown, mentioned earlier, 100 feet off the ground, supporting 2,000 tons of structural steel. Pictured at right is Joseph Seebacher at the site of the World Trade Center, and seen below is the point of support that those welds provide at for the Tent of Tomorrow's 16 columns. (Right, courtesy of Joseph Seebacher and Karl Baker.)

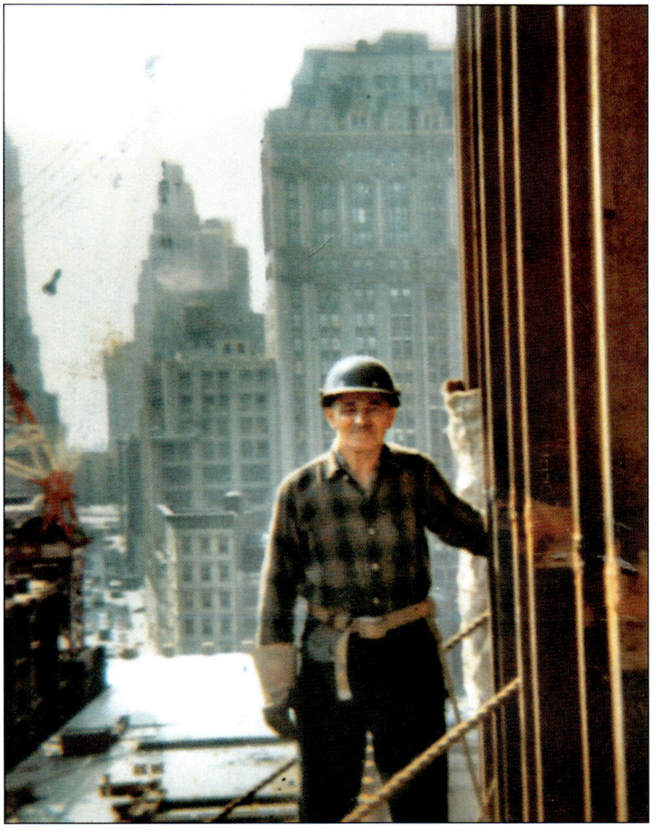

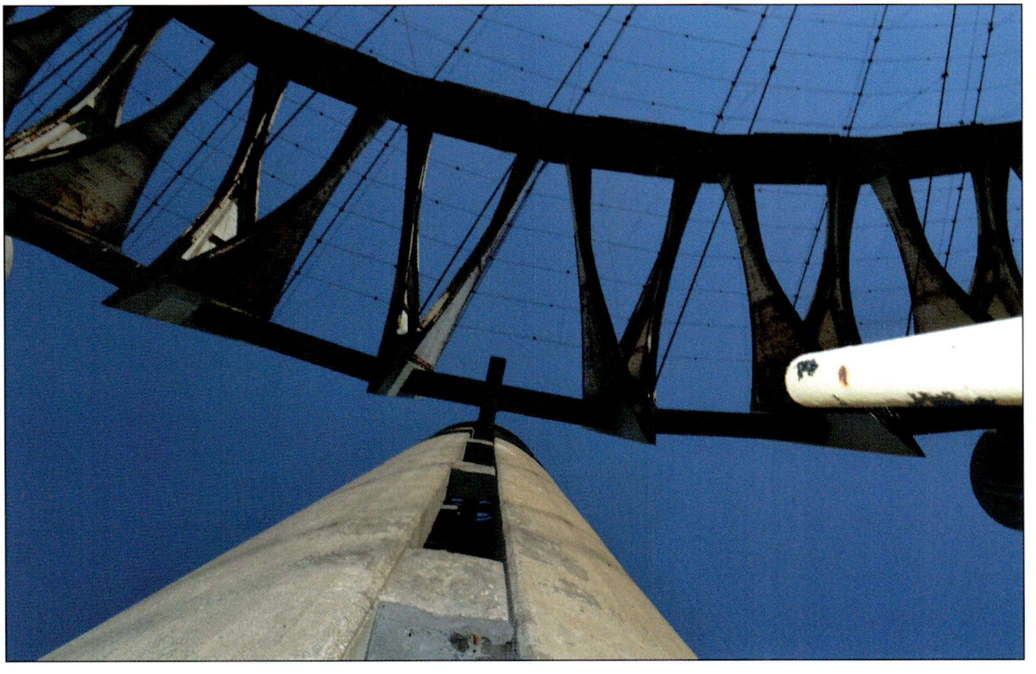

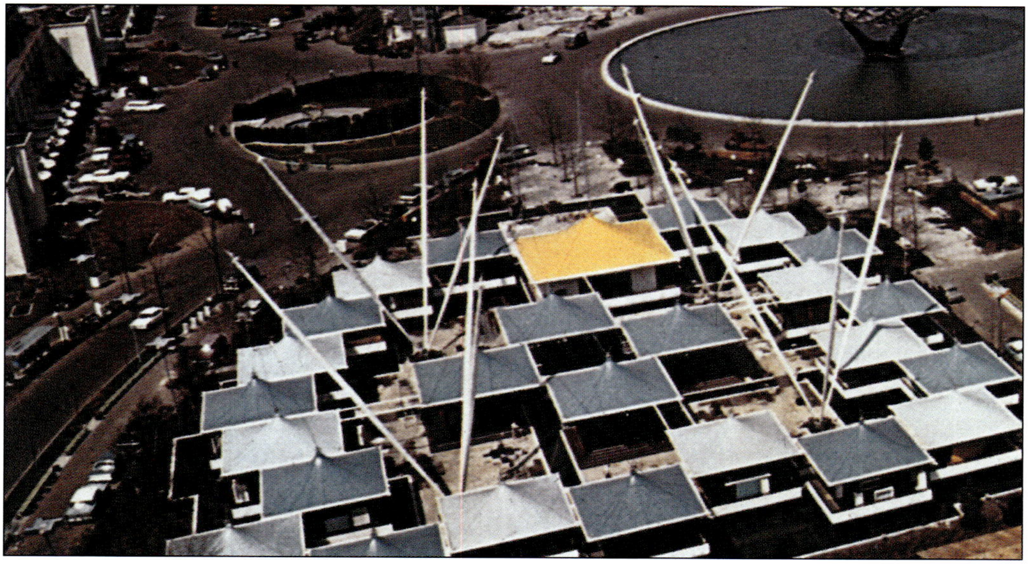

Here are two construction photographs of the world's fair nearing completion. One shot was taken from the observation platform of the New York State pavilion, looking over the 26 square canopies of the New Jersey pavilion and toward the base of the Unisphere, with the New York City pavilion just in view on the left. The other photograph was taken from a helicopter looking toward the Unisphere with the New York State pavilion on the right, with Pop Art already installed on the Theaterama building, and the tower platforms still wrapped in protective plastic to allow work to continue through the winter. The large number of cars parked around the pavilions belonged to the contractors and construction workers. (Both, courtesy of Robinson-Capsis-Stern Associates.)

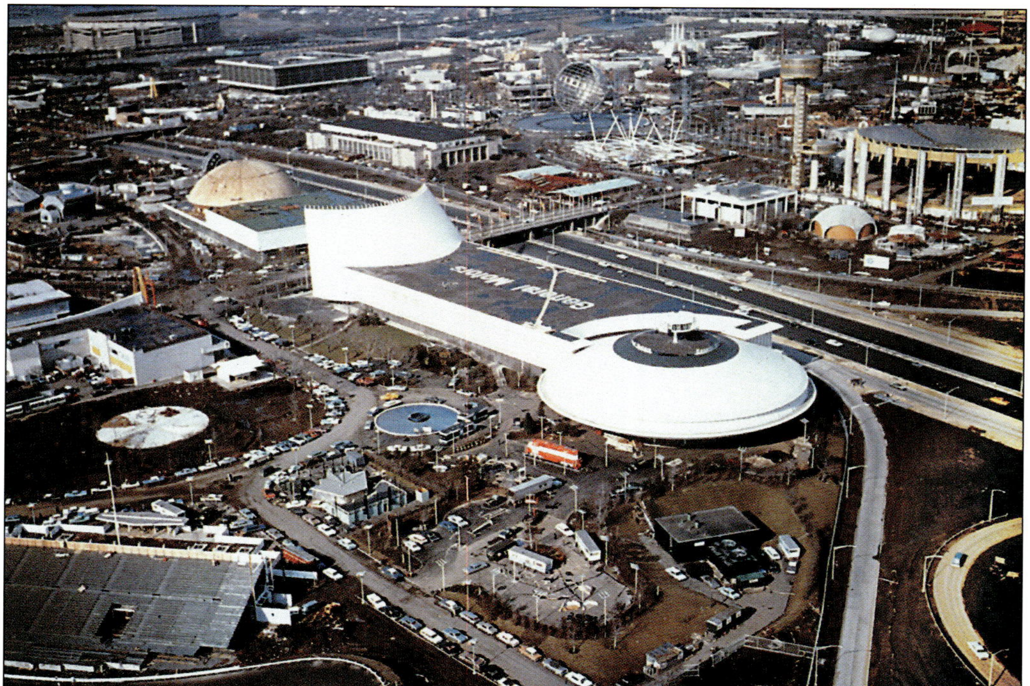

Two

A "MINIATURE TRIP THROUGH NEW YORK"

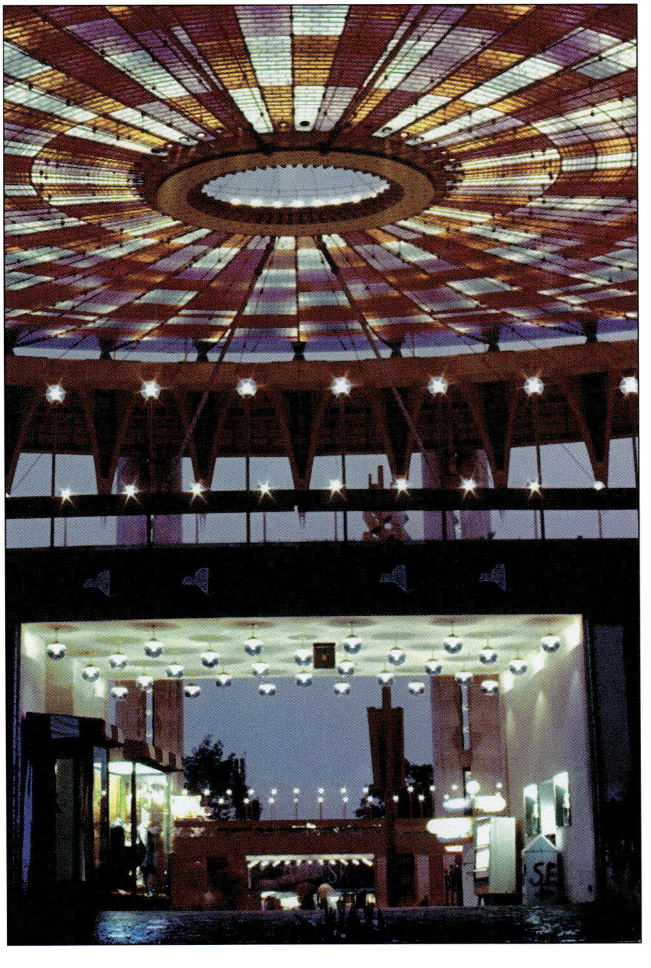

Robinson-Capsis-Stern Associates formed to bid on contracts for the 1962 Seattle World's Fair. Alfred Stern was a set designer for Radio City Music Hall and former assistant director of exhibitions at the 1939 New York World's Fair. Their 1964–1965 New York World's Fair exhibitions included the following: Central America, Borden, RCA, Clairol, Electric Power and Light, and the New York State pavilion. This photograph is of New York State pavilion before opening day. (Courtesy of Robinson-Capsis-Stern Associates.)

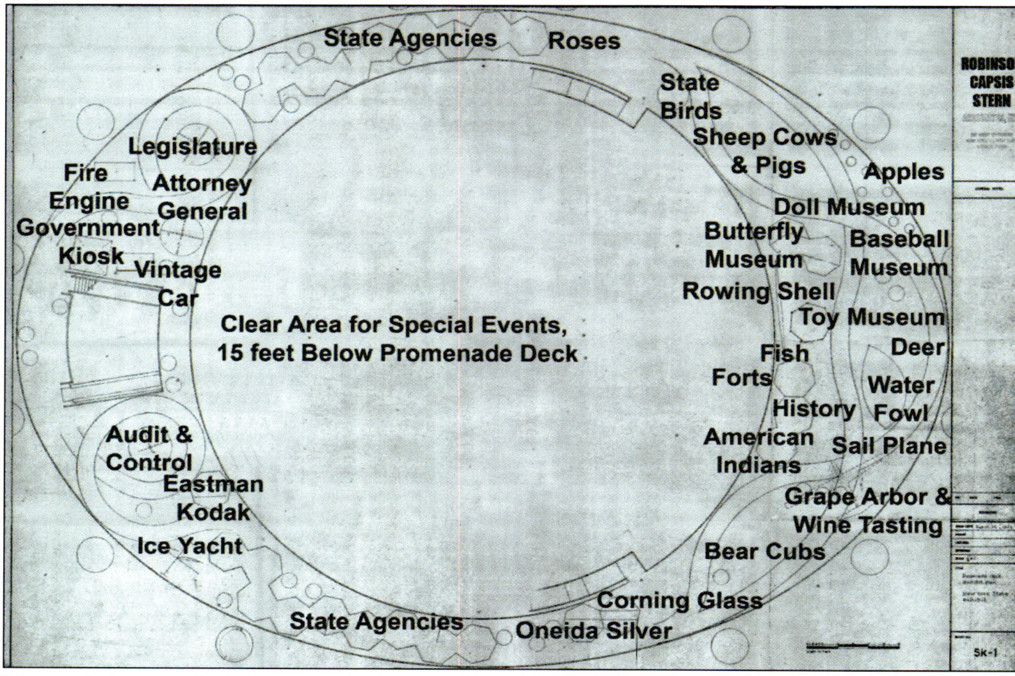

Pictured above is Jack Robinson's August 22, 1962, sketch of the mezzanine. It is interesting to note that 19 months before the world's fair opened, this layout was fairly close to what was actually built. Pictured below is the concept model of this layout by Robinson-Capsis-Stern Associates. The following is from a March 20, 1964, press release from the New York State Commission on the world's fair: "Reaching the mezzanine via escalator, visitors will embark on a trip through the state. The first 'stop' will be Albany at the 'Governor's Office,' where animated and still displays will set the pattern for the balance of the journey, and literature about the state will be available. Leaving Albany, the travelers will visit winter and summer recreational areas showing the hunting, fishing, hiking, camping, wildlife and myriad of outdoor activities available in the state." (Both, courtesy of Robinson-Capsis-Stern Associates.)

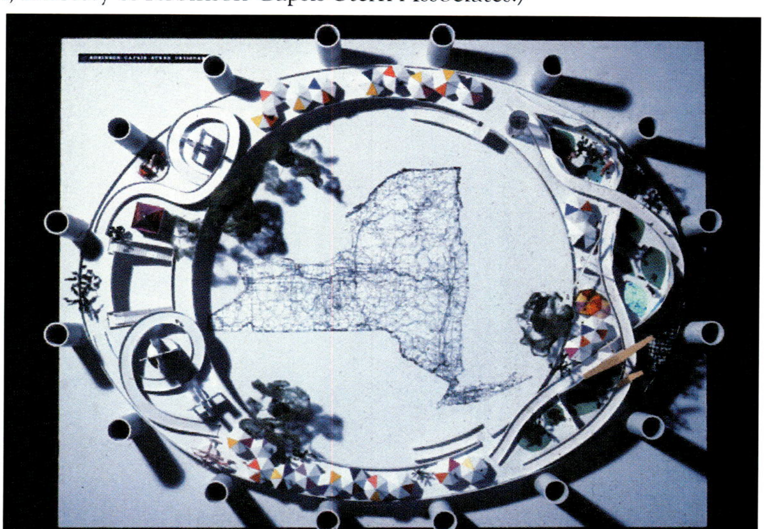

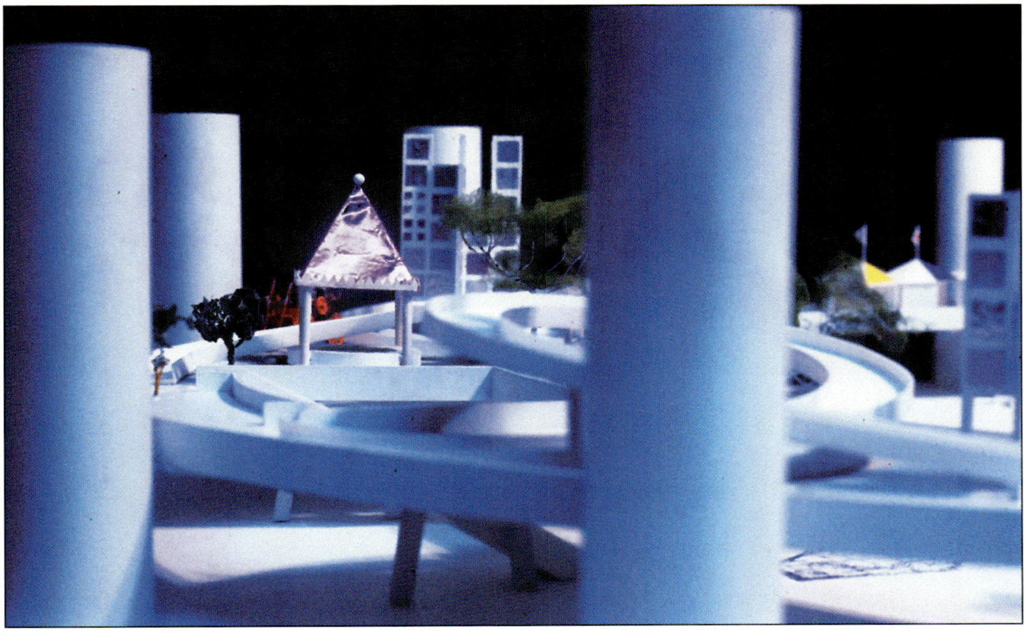

The mezzanine was originally conceived as a raised deck, open underneath, with a path for the "Miniature Trip through New York" that included crossover ramps and a series of covered displays. It is separate from the columns, supported by 24 steel bents on their own spread footings. While the outside of the mezzanine is an ellipse of 305 feet by 225 feet, the inside is a 190-foot circular opening down to the grade-level terrazzo floor 15 feet below. Later, the mezzanine concept had an enclosed area added underneath for more space, including an art gallery, restaurant, and exhibits. (Both, courtesy of Robinson-Capsis-Stern Associates.)

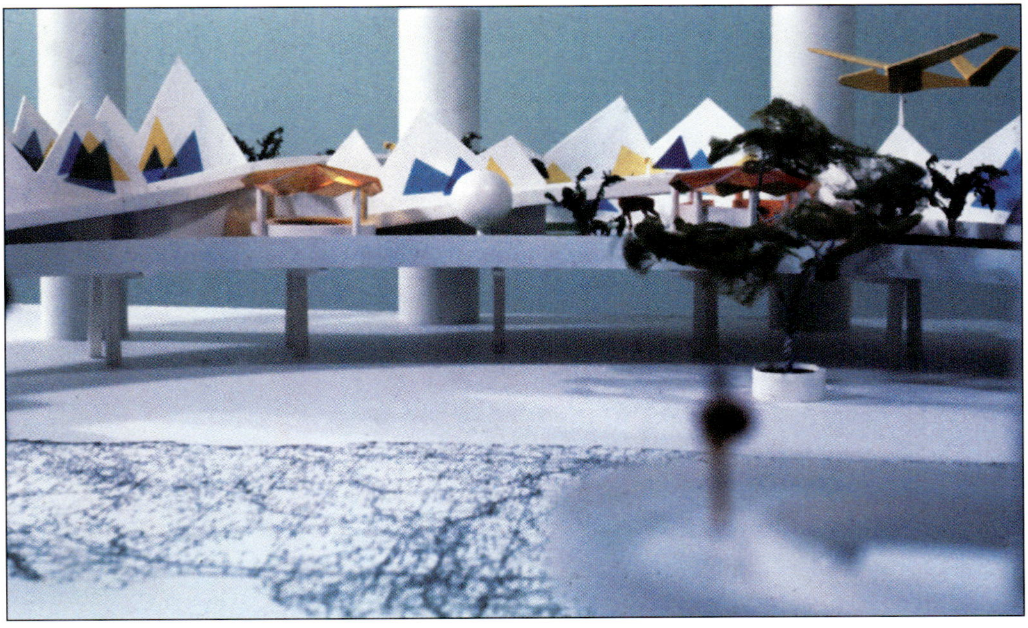

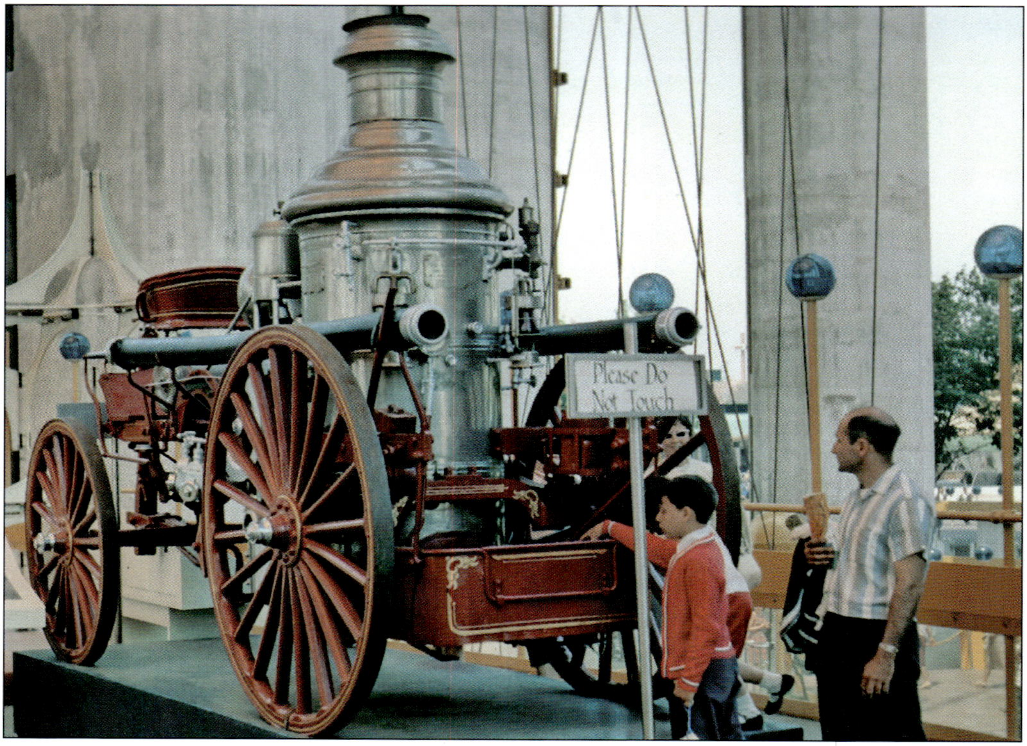

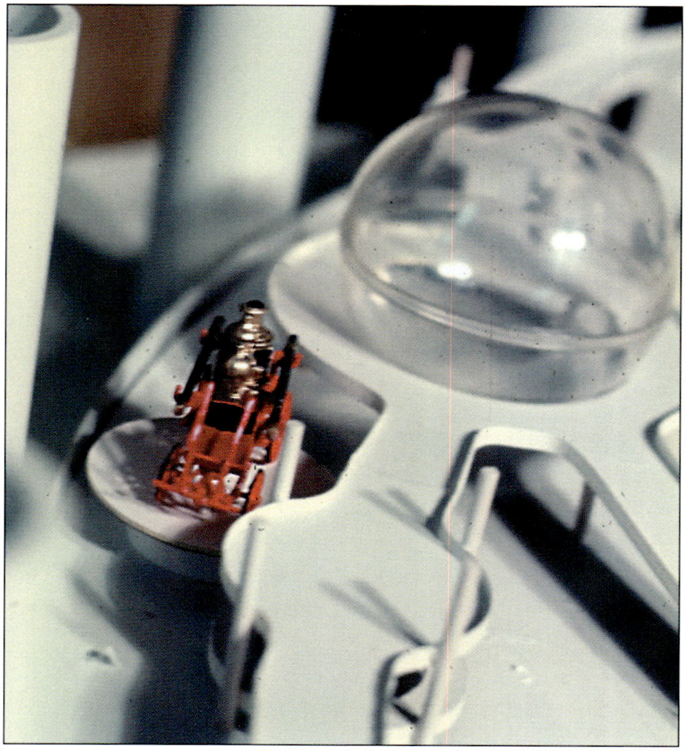

One close match between the concept model and the actual mezzanine exhibit was the Elmira New York La France steam-powered fire truck. American La France built hand-drawn, horse-drawn, and steam-powered fire engines in Elmira, New York, from 1873 to 1985 and later in the Elmira suburb of Southport. Elmira, the city, was once known as the "Fire Truck Capital of the World." On January 14, 2014, the American La France Manufacturing Company ceased operations. The 1890s-built, steam-powered fire truck seen above displays a "do not touch" sign to no avail. (Above, courtesy of the Bill Cotter collection; left, courtesy of Robinson-Capsis-Stern Associates.)

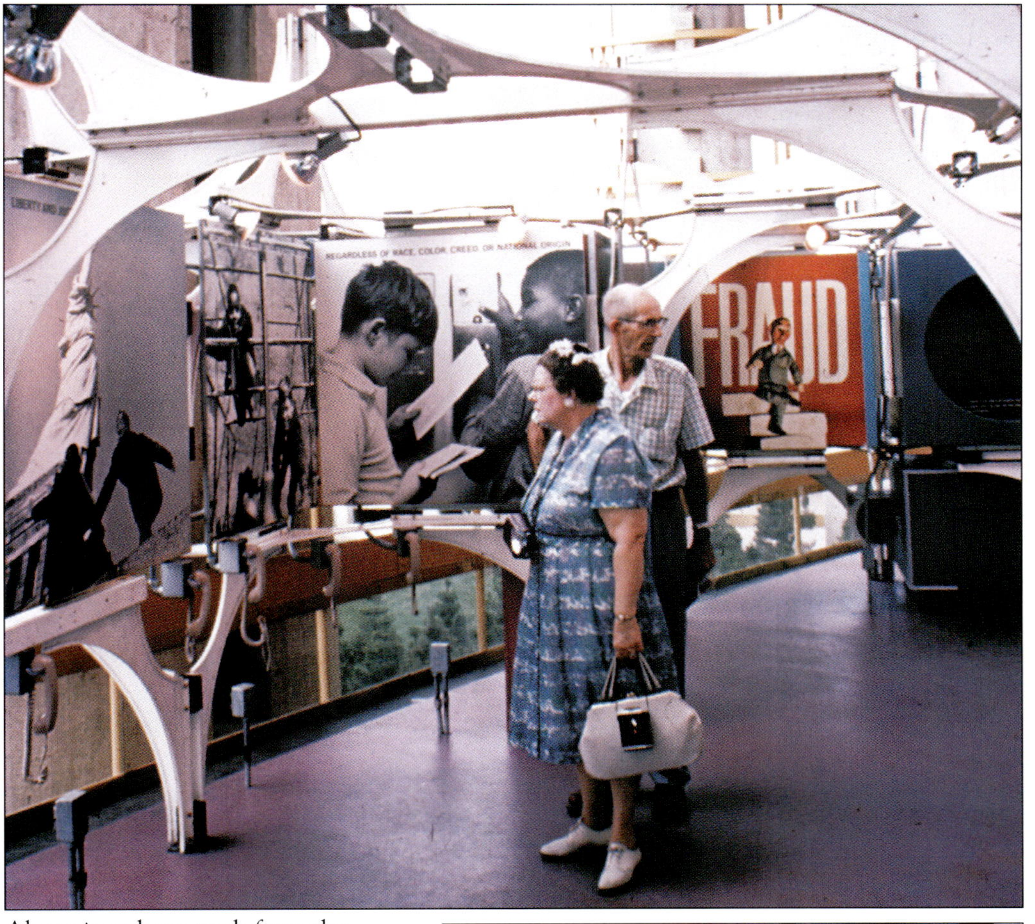

Above is a photograph from the exhibit for the New York State Attorney General's Office with displays showing how the office protects the individual citizen from fraud. The approach for separating the exhibits, shown in the concept model, evolved toward a simplified modular approach. Common frame elements were ultimately used for the mezzanine exhibits, a creative design that used the same scalloped angles for both the walls and overhead of each enclosure. They provided a lightweight, stackable, open-space solution to support the exhibits and also provided an interesting visual when seen from a distance. (Both, courtesy of Robinson-Capsis-Stern Associates.)

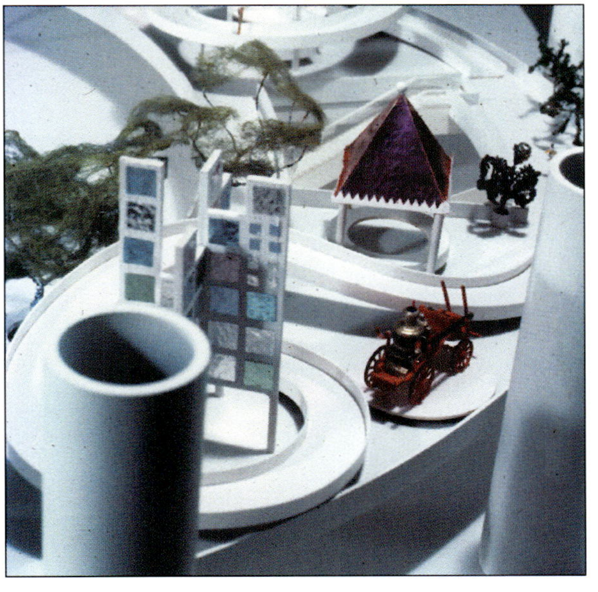

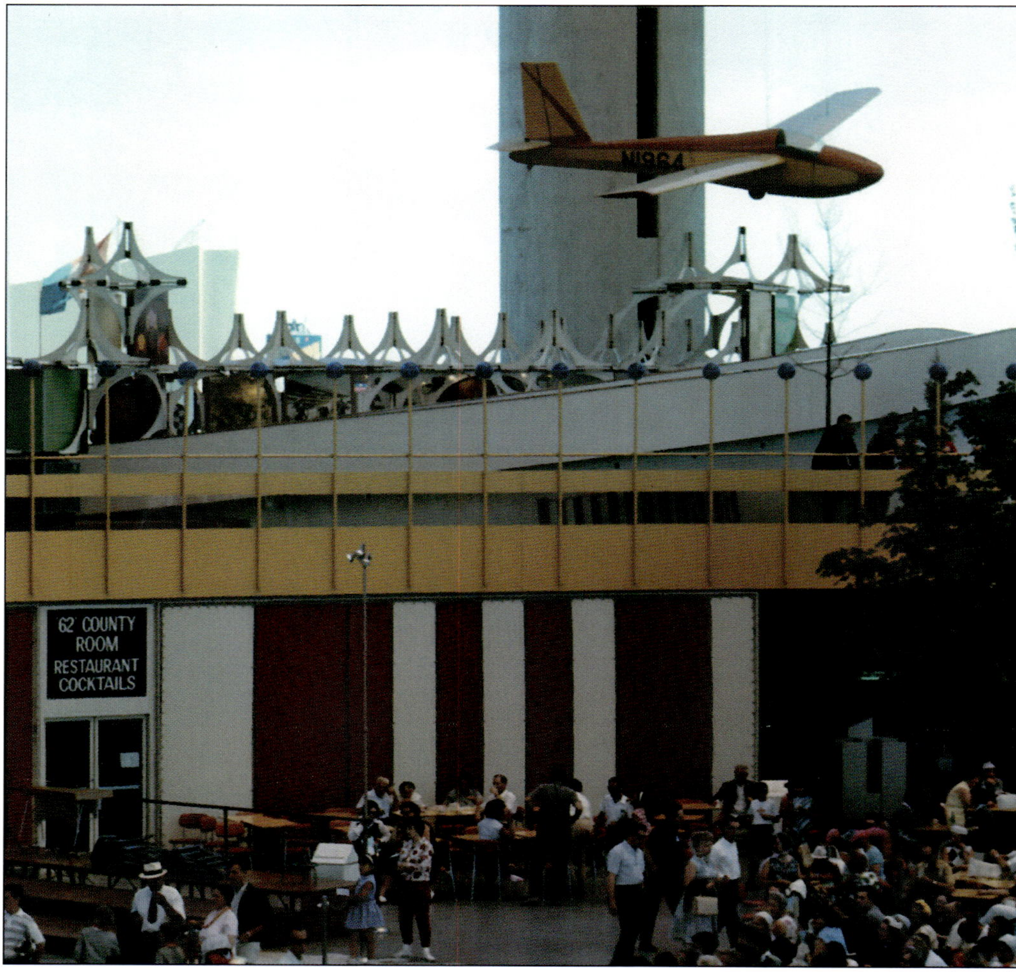

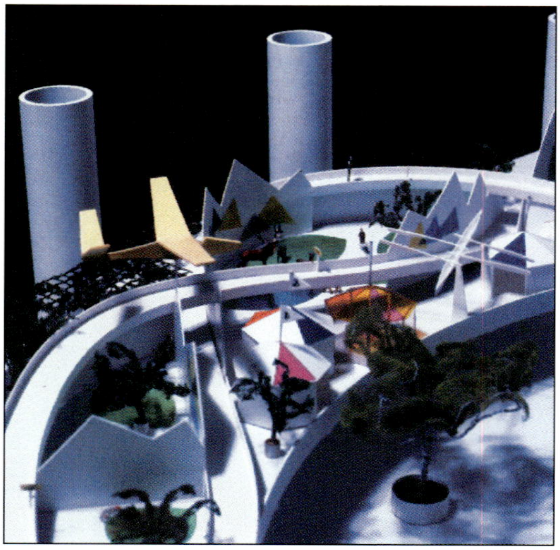

The Schweizer 2-32 sailplane, built in Elmira, New York, matches the concept model in position and relative size. The Schweizer SGS 2-32 was designed as a two-seat sailplane. Besides being a big high-performance sailplane, the SGS 2-32 has a wide fuselage, bubble canopy, and dorsal fin. Since 1962, a total of 87 were built. The sailplane lived up to its function, when on September 1, 1965, wind gusts of 60 miles per hour broke it free from its support cables and launched the 40-foot glider, injuring an 18-year-old Boy Scout who lost a tooth. The photograph at above is from October 1964. (Above, courtesy of the Bill Cotter collection; left, courtesy of Robinson-Capsis-Stern Associates.)

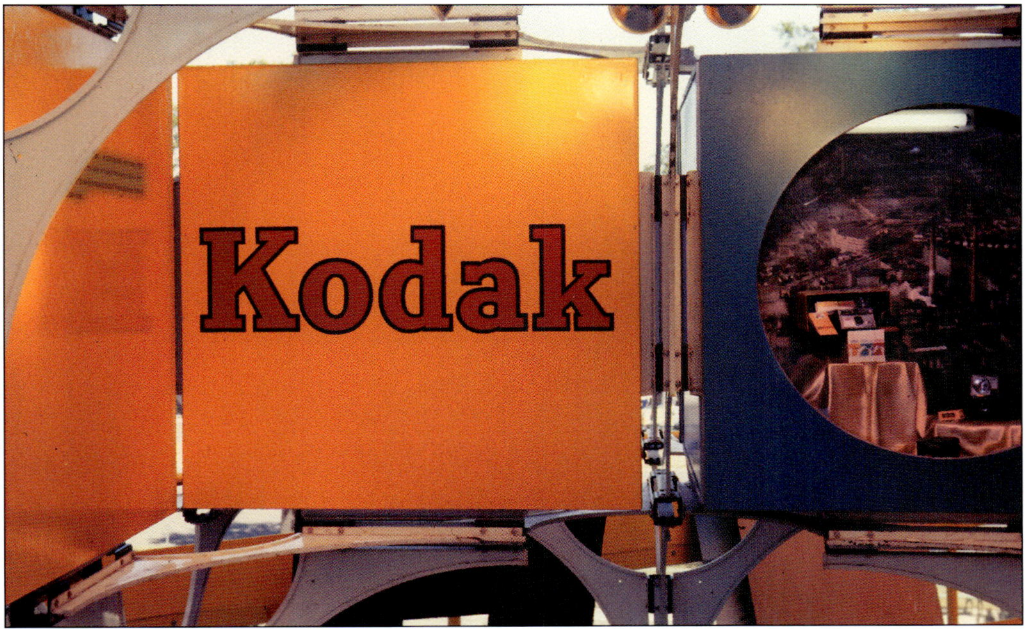

Pictured are the concept model and actual Kodak exhibit for the Eastman Kodak Company, founded in New York in 1892. Even though Kodak already had a prominent pavilion at the fair, this display was provided for the mezzanine's "Miniature Trip through New York State"; the display featured the world's largest outdoor photographic prints on a six-sided tower atop a lunar landscape-styled roof, which could be seen at a distance from almost anywhere in the fair. This exhibit mentions Kodak's business progress in Rochester, New York, and a "three-dimensional plotter to visualize new theories" display, well before the dawn of stereo lithography. (Below, courtesy of Robinson-Capsis-Stern Associates.)

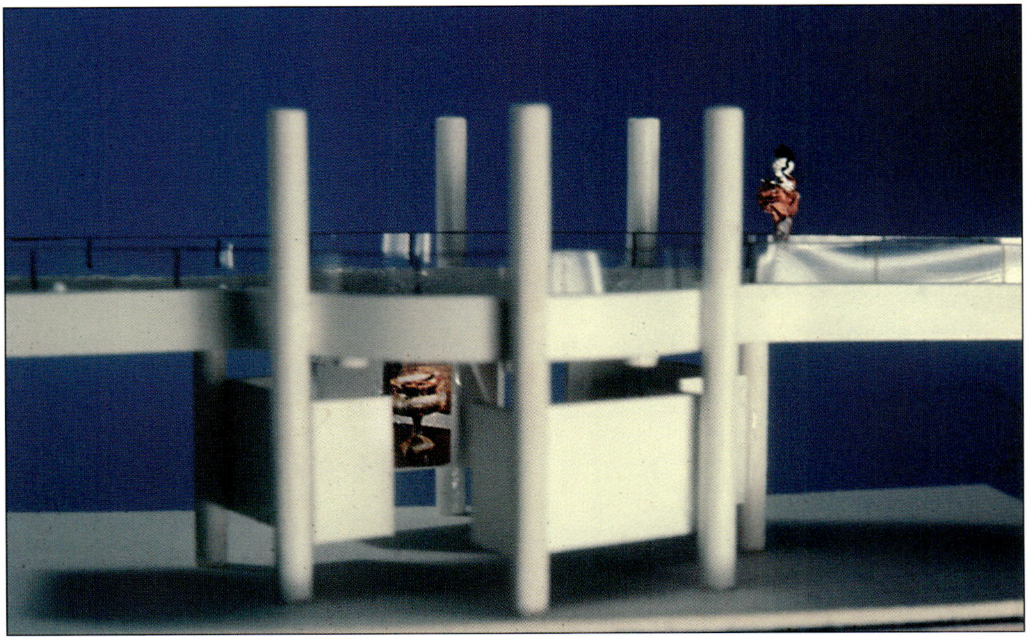

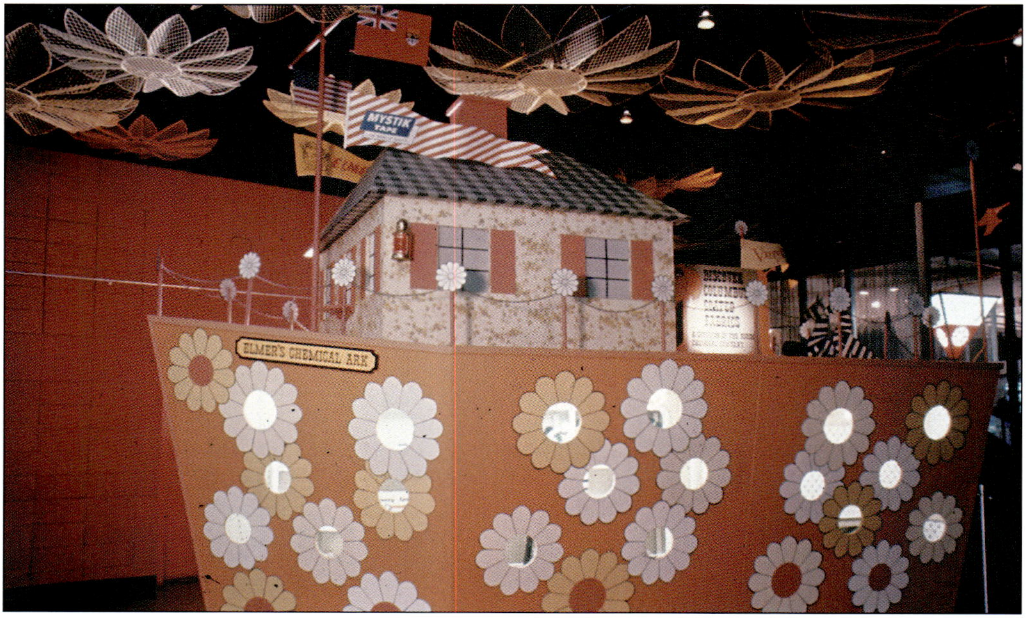

Among Robinson-Capsis-Stern Associate's exhibits was Borden's "All About Elsie Borden's Puppet Show" and Elmer's Chemical Ark in the Better Living pavilion. After making her first live appearance at the 1939 New York World's Fair, Elsie the Cow returned for the 1964 New York World's Fair. One of the top 10 advertising icons of all time, the "spokescow" for New York–based Borden Co. starred in her own musical revue with a score by the Broadway composer Kay Swift. The show featured Elsie presiding at a board of directors meeting, where an inventor tries to persuade her to market chocolate-covered onions. (Courtesy of Robinson-Capsis-Stern Associates.)

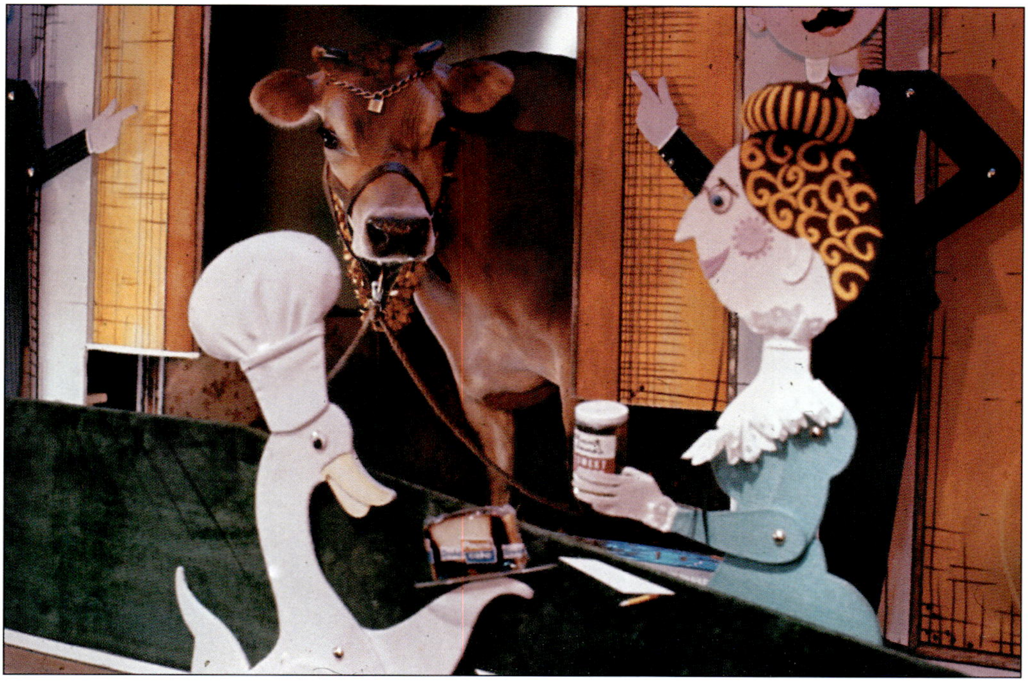

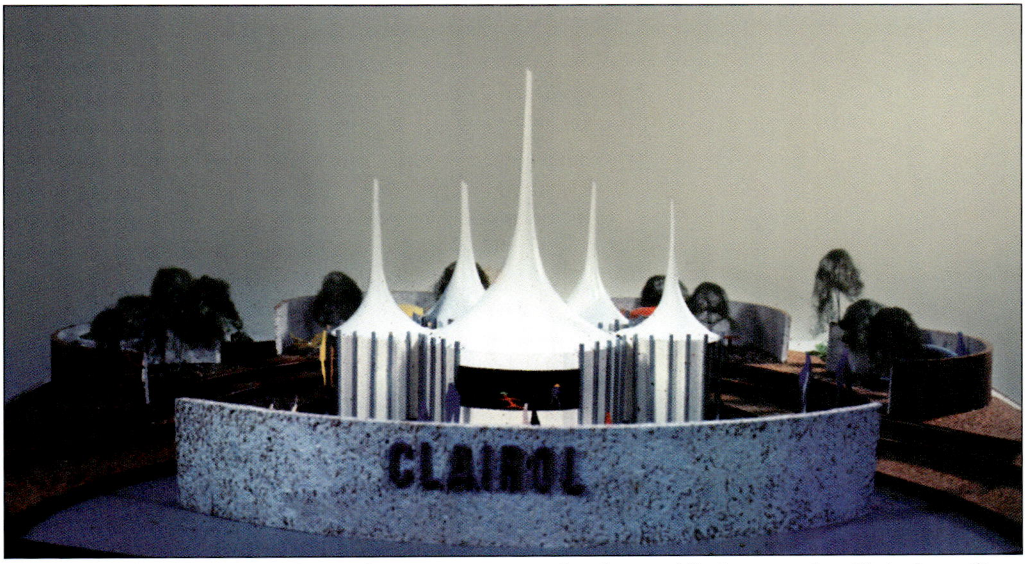

Another Robinson-Capsis-Stern Associates project for the world's fair was the Clairol pavilion, which had a rotating "color carousel" that used mirrors to show visitors what they would look like with different hair colors. Alfred Stern again commissioned Kay Swift, of Gershwin fame and a friend from his Radio City Music Hall days, to write the Clairol Color Carousel's theme song, "Nothing Is Too Lovely to Be True." (Courtesy of Robinson-Capsis-Stern Associates.)

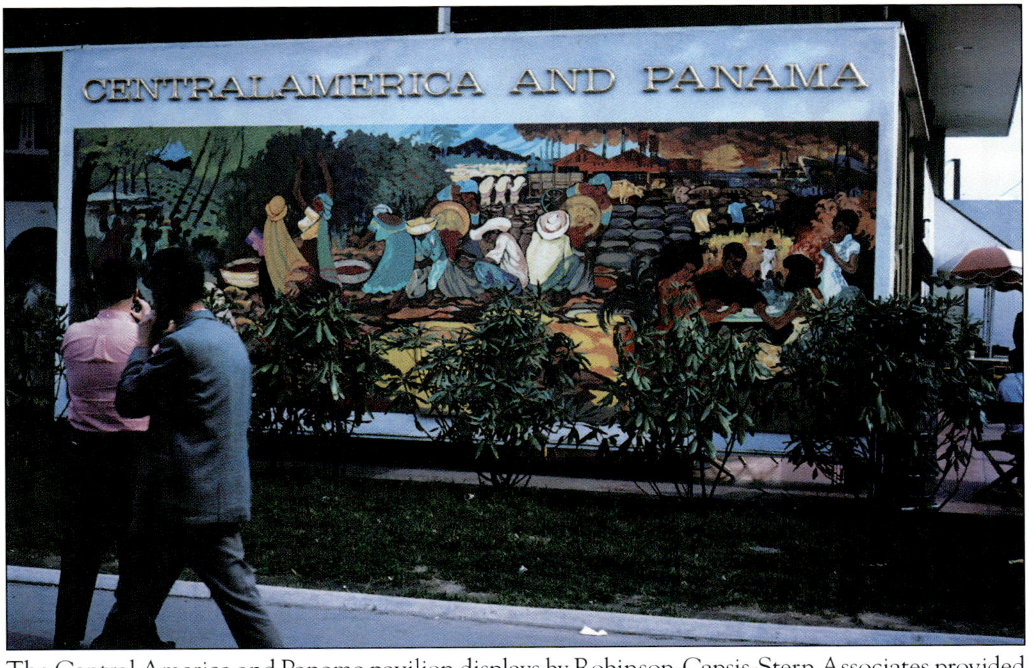

The Central America and Panama pavilion displays by Robinson-Capsis-Stern Associates provided another interesting story from George Capsis. He was sent to Guatemala to tour a new freeze-dried coffee processing plant that the firm wanted to feature in the pavilion. He told his host that what people really wanted to see was history and Mayan antiquities; they ended up having both with the addition of a coffee bar.

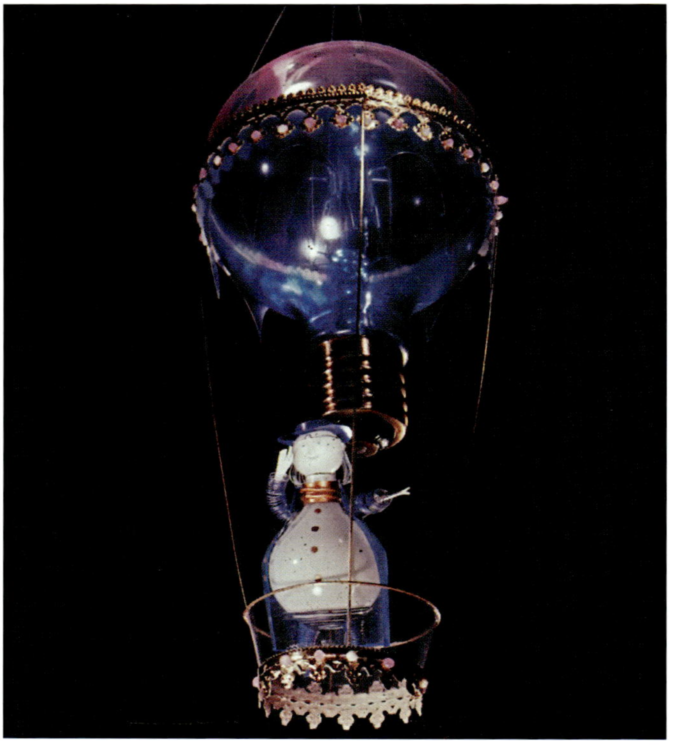

Most noted display was the Electric Power and Light pavilion's *The Brightest Show on Earth*, featuring "Uncle" Ben Franklin, star of Electric Power and Light pavilion's *Enjoyment of Electricity*. George Capsis's once said, "As a scriptwriter and producer, I felt that my prime mission was to create a show which would communicate successfully to and entertain those who are not intimately acquainted with the complex technology of America's electric utility industry. I have found this premise valid in the past as, while I have done three or four major productions for the U.S. automotive industry, I do not drive." Pictured are the concept sketch and the actual display. (Both, courtesy of Robinson-Capsis-Stern Associates.)

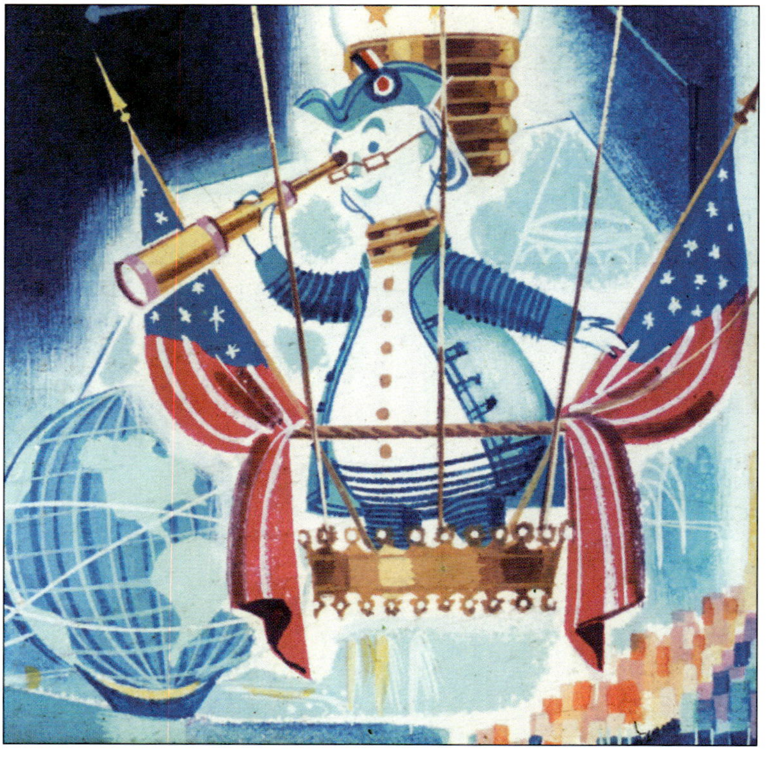

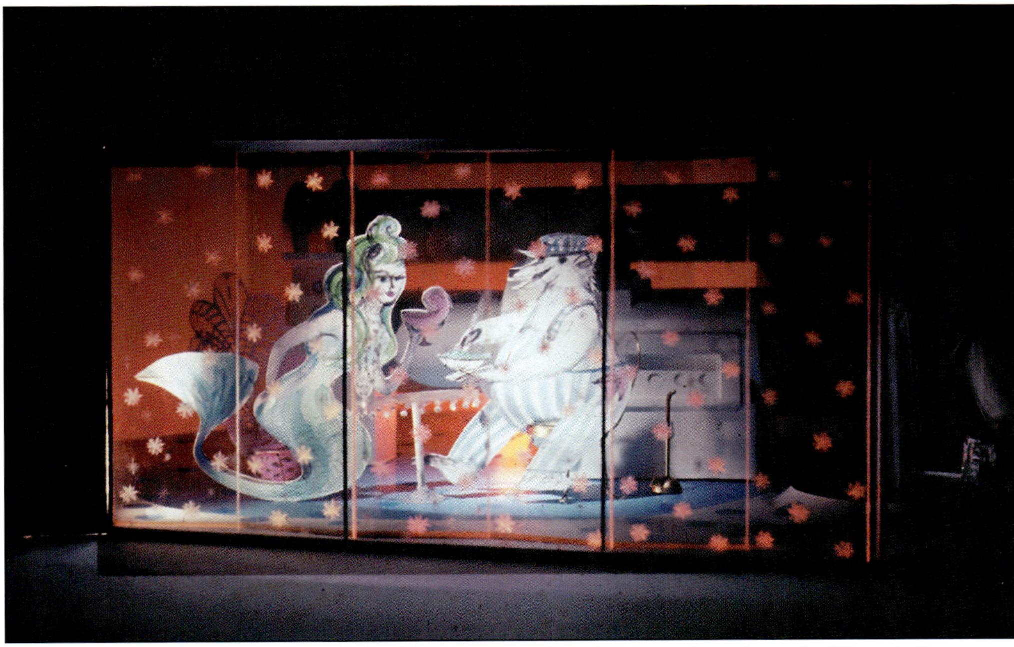

Robinson-Capsis-Stern Associates had been retained to design and produce the Electric Power and Light's exhibit, pavilion, and show for the New York World's Fair. Once a script began to evolve, new characters emerged, like a polar bear who understands that electric air-conditioning is ideal for hibernation and a mermaid who realizes that electric air-conditioning means one can control the temperature and achieve an ideal climate for, as she says, "Families spend more time together when they can control the weather." (Both, courtesy of Robinson-Capsis-Stern Associates.)

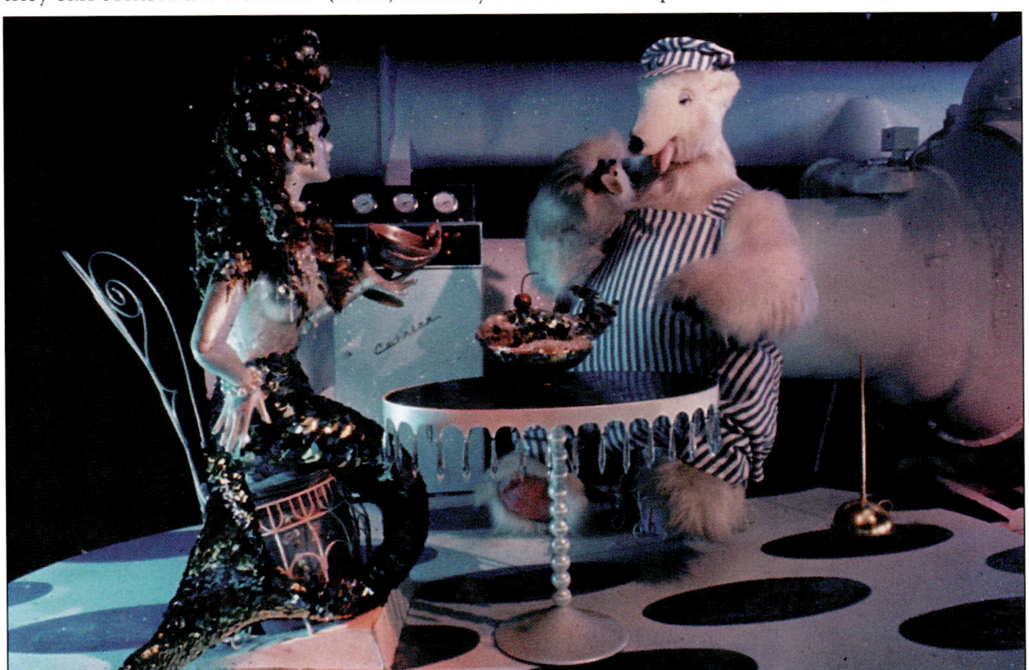

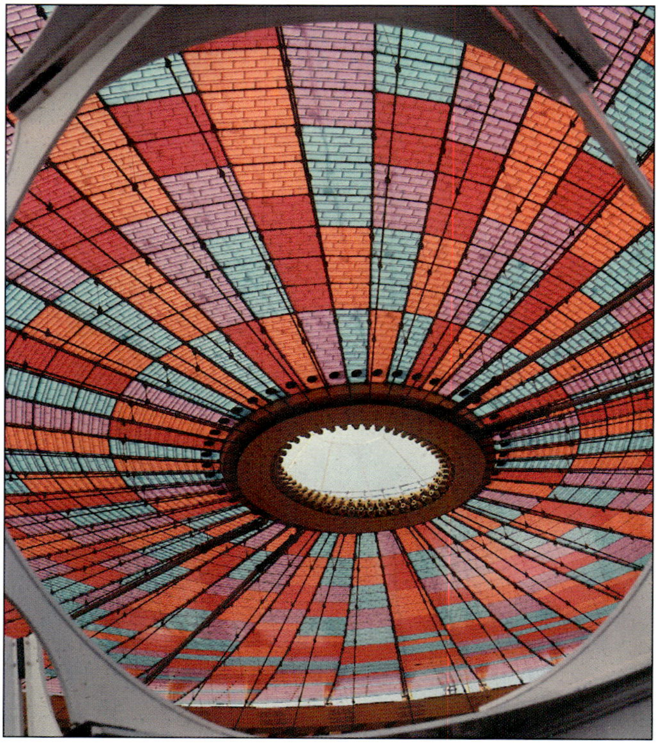

The following is from a March 20, 1964, press release from the New York State Commission on the world's fair: "There will be displays and demonstrations of the wine, glass, leather, photographic, glider, dairy, Apple and horticultural activities of New York spotlighted in bright 'snowflake' modules. Signs will direct tourists to symbolic displays of historic objects of the state's history and folklore, suggestive of New York's broad variety of museums." These lightweight display supports could be stacked and assembled in multiple ways to help separate the various exhibits while providing a place for mounting decorative accents, lighting, and signage. Van Williams took this photograph on April 26, 1964. (Courtesy of the Queens Museum.)

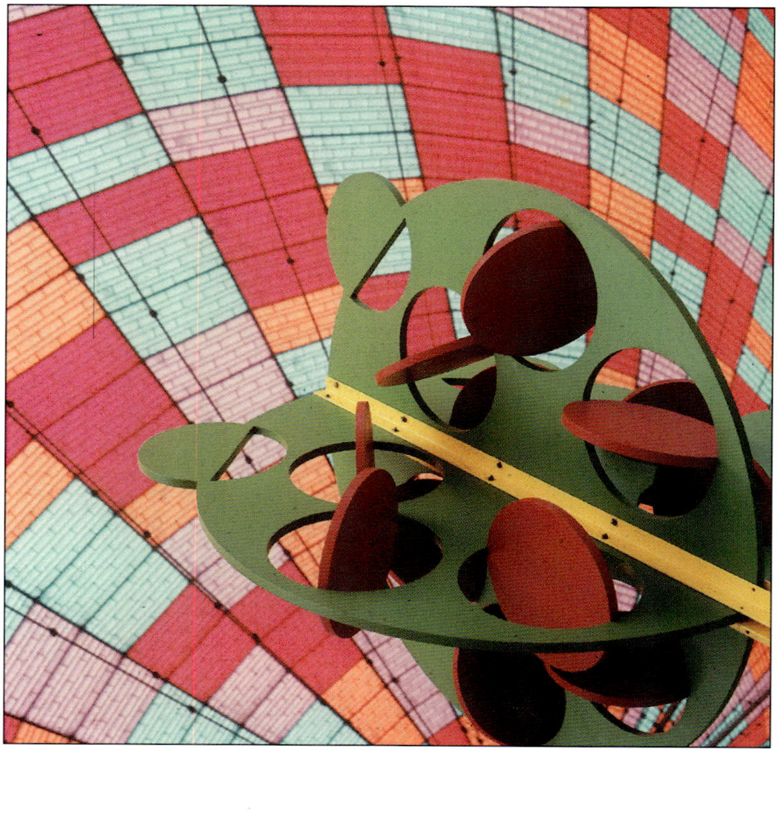

The "Miniature Trip through New York" modules nicely frame the four-color pattern of the Tent of Tomorrow in this April 26, 1964, photograph by Van Williams. (Courtesy of the Queens Museum.)

Three

THE TENT OF TOMORROW

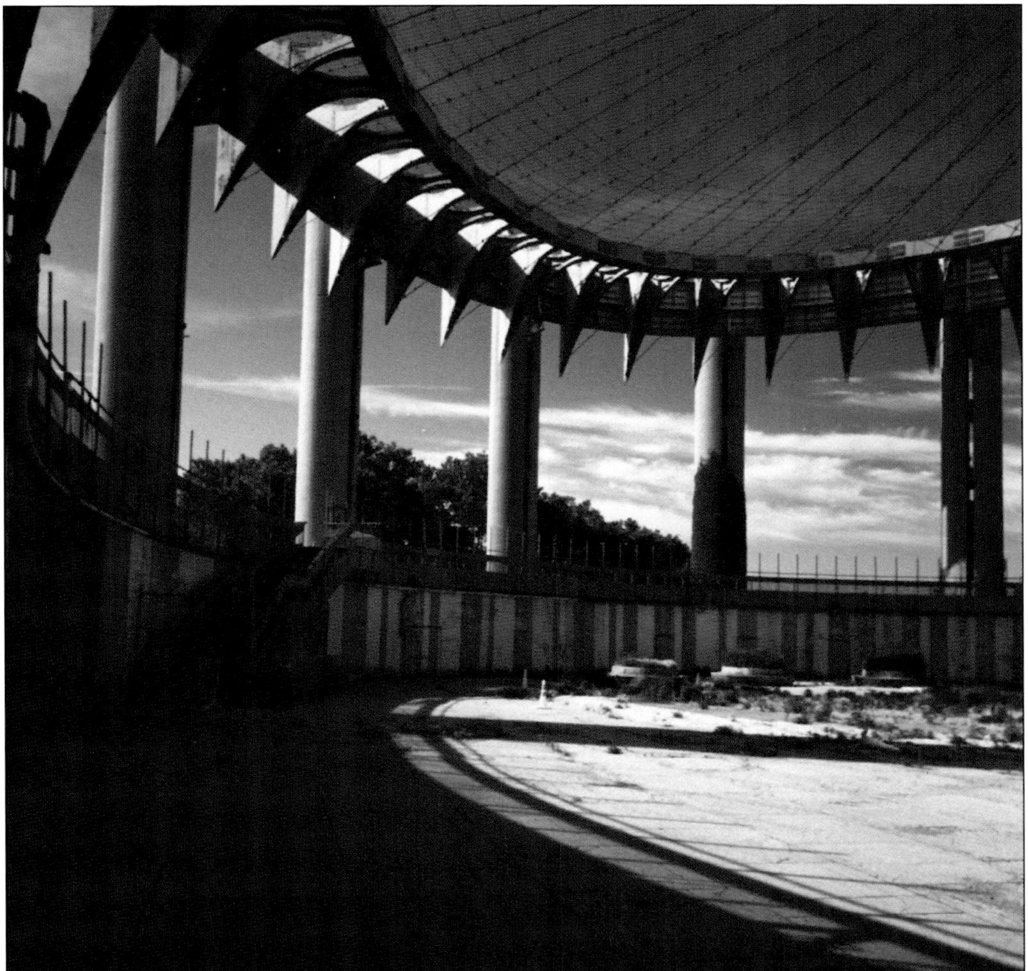

The June 2002 issue of *Journal of Structural Engineering* stated the following: "The history of civil engineering has repeatedly shown that new types of structures have been built before their behavior was fully understood. This is as true of modern shells as it was of the cathedrals of the Middle Ages; that a rational explanation for their success was found only after the persistence of their existence forced their recognition." This photograph was taken on June 29, 2007.

NEW YORK STATE EXHIBIT

NEW YORK WORLD'S FAIR 1964-1965

– Souvenir –

Special Events Program

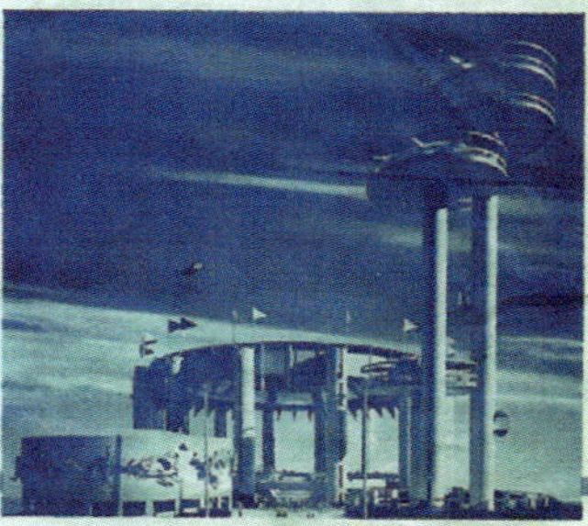

NEW YORK STATE-RENSSELAER COUNTY DAY Tuesday, July 13, 1965

10:45 & 2:30 THE ISLANDERS (Long Beach,N.Y.) This grup, founded in 1964, plays cha-cha, bossa nova and other Latin rhythms, jazz and folk music, some rock 'n' roll.

11:15 & 4:05 *THE NOVAS (Gloversville,N.Y.) This versatile vocal and instrumental combo plays all types of music, offering something for everyone's taste.

11:45 & 4:35 TOWN CRIERS (Westford, N.Y.) Dir: Steven Morris. A program of folk music by 3 boys and one girl who sing and accompany themselves on guitar and banjo.

12:05 & 4:55 & 7:00 *THE CEILI DANCERS (Troy,N.Y.) Teacher and Dir: Mrs. Roy Barnard. This is the only Irish Step Dance group in Rensselaer County and was formed about a year ago to keep Irish tradition alive in the Capital District.

12:40 & 5:30 THE RAY RUGGIERO TRIO (Carle Place,N.Y.) This is strictly a jazz trio. Some of the numbers in the program were written by Ray Ruggiero.

1:10 & 6:00 PARISIANS (Corona,N.Y.) Primarily a vocal and instrumental rock 'n' roll group, these boys also play old favorites - to please all.

1:40 & 7:35 HOSPITAL HELPING HANDS, INTERNATIONAL (Bronx,N.Y.) This volunteer, non-profit organization, founded in 1961 by Claire Manley, performs service in various city hospitals and state institutions. Program today: The Co-eds (singing group), magic clowning, harmonica player, magician, and others.

2:10 THE COLONIALS. The 5 members of this rock 'n' roll group come from various communities in Westchester County. Program: original songs, many of which are based on fairy tales and nursery rhymes.

3:00 CHRISTIAN CONCERT ORCHESTRA AND CHOIR (Seattle, Wash.) Dir: Marvin Honore. Choreog: David Lawrence. A group of outstanding young musicians and singers selected through competition from college and high school campuses of various states of the Pacific Northwest.

6:30 FRANKIE MARC (Brooklyn,N.Y.) Mus. Dir: Joe Pellegrino,Jr. Program: an impersonation of the late Al Jolson.

6:45 *JOE LAWRENCE (Flushing, N.Y.) A program of folk songs.

8:05 DOREEN PELLEGRINO AND THE HEARTACHES (Brooklyn) Vocal and pantomime group performing to the latest rock 'n' roll hits.

8:30 & 9:30 RENSSELAER COUNTY SQUARE DANCERS Caller: Al Aderente. A demonstration of legitimate square dancing for the fun of it, as contrasted with exhibition "tap" or "clog" type square dancing seen on TV or in nightclubs as part of a floor show.

9:00 THE MANIACS (Brooklyn) Dir: Joseph Pellegrino,Jr. A singing rock 'n' roll group with band accompaniment.

10:00 NEW YORK STATE "TENT OF TOMORROW" CLOSES

*Appeared on 1964 NEW YORK STATE SPECIAL EVENTS PROGRAM

(THIS PROGRAM IS SUBJECT TO CHANGE)

In the first season of the fair, 1,807 community groups performed at the pavilion. They included rock bands, orchestras, drill teams, glee clubs, acrobatic teams, roller skaters, baton twirlers, zither, banjo and recorder bands, 70 singing nuns, church choirs, fashion models, tennis demonstrations, and Gerry Marsden of Gerry and the Pacemakers. Special Honor Days were held as a tribute to the state's varied cultures, with folk dancers in their traditional costumes. Honor Days were set up with a daily schedule of performances, from 10:00 a.m. until 10:00 p.m., and printed on flyers, as shown on this example from Tuesday July 16, 1965, when the Parisians rock band would play. The members of the Parisians belonged to the St. Leo Sea Cadets of Corona, a local parish marching band, who also did a few engagements at the fair and in the pavilion. (Courtesy of Rich Lando.)

NEW YORK STATE COMMISSION ON THE WORLD'S FAIR
MRS. PAUL E. PEABODY, Vice Chairman

CHARLES J. BROWNE • WILLIAM T. CONKLIN • MRS. PRESTON DAVIE • IRA H. GENET
MORTIMOR S. GORDON • JOSEPH A. KAISER • OTTO KINZEL • HERMAN I. MERINOFF
JULIUS L. MINTZ • CLILAN B. POWELL • WILLIAM A. SHEA • JOSEPH T. P. SULLIVAN
CRAWFORD WETTLAUFFER • Ex-Officio: JOSEPH ZARETZKI • GEORGE L. INGALLS • ANTHONY J. TRAVIA
SAMUEL L. GREENBERG • EARL W. BRYDGES • JOHN T. SATRIALE • MOSES M. WEINSTEIN

NEW YORK STATE EXHIBIT

1964-65 WORLDS FAIR

Established by an act of the legislature of the State of New York in 1961, the New York State Commission on the World's Fair was given the responsibility for the planning, design, construction and operation of the state's exhibit at the 1964-65 World's Fair.

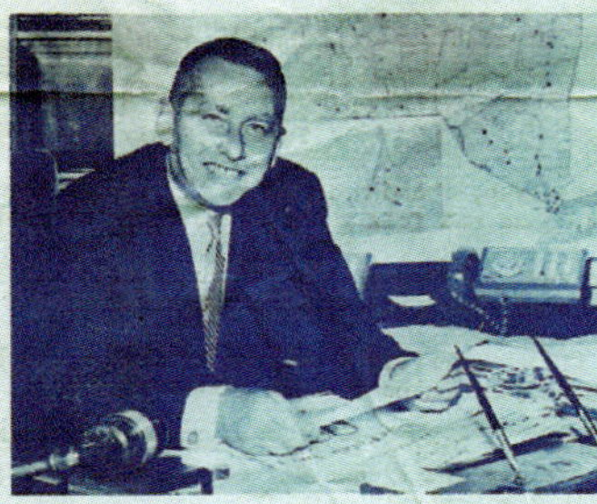

LIEUTENANT GOVERNOR
MALCOLM WILSON

was appointed chairman of the Commission by Governor Rockefeller. From the beginning, the exhibit has been considered a means of promoting the economic, social, educational and cultural interests and life of the state which is the repository of many of the nation's richest resources.

That the vision and work of the Commission, its staff, its architect and builders had borne fruit was realized on opening day in 1964 when one of the country's leading newspapers headlined the New York State Exhibit as "STAR OF THE FAIR" and on the closing day of the first season when figures revealed that 12 million 100 thousand people had passed thru its entrance, ranking it 3rd in popularity at the Fair.

WILLIAM J. DROHAN, Project Director of the State Exhibit, personally supervises the operation and is daily host to tens of thousands of visitors who are attracted by the dramatic architecture, air of festive gaiety in the huge Tent of Tomorrow, exciting trips to the High Spot of the Fair, thrilling 360° motion picture in the Theaterama and multitude of artistic, educational, industrial and recreational exhibits. Geared to the theme

"STATE FAIR OF THE FUTURE," THE EXHIBIT FEATURES:

THE TENT OF TOMORROW

The heart of the exhibit is a graceful open air structure, covered by the world's largest cable suspension roof. The 2,000 ton roof was assembled on the ground and the great, yellow, steel frame jacked 100 feet to its present position at the top of the sixteen 105 foot columns surrounding the floor. The entire design and operation represents an engineering breakthrough of the first magnitude. The huge map of the State of New York on the floor of the Tent of Tomorrow is the largest map in the world – 4000 times the size of the standard Texaco touring maps on which it is modeled.

THE TOWERS — "HIGH SPOT OF THE FAIR" (26 stories high)

The towers are 226 feet, 181 feet and 85 feet. The double deck top tower, which is the highest point of the fair, is for observation only. The middle tower is also an observation point where refreshments are available. The lowest tower is an enclosed room where members of the state legislature meet with their constituents. All are serviced by "outdoor" elevators providing a swift and safe ascent and descent. In 1964 1 million, 900 thousand fairgoers shared in the thrilling ride and view.

SPECIAL EVENTS PROGRAM

A constant round of daily activity takes place in this area. Representative non-professional performing groups from every community in New York State, as well as from other states, perform from 10:00 a.m. to 10:00 p.m., making the exhibit truly a "Fair within a Fair." The Special Events program (such as that listed on the reverse of this program) is under the direction of the Director of Special Events, FREDERIC B. VOGEL, assisted by JOHN H. WILSON, Production Coordinator. In 1964, 1,800 groups comprising 67,900 performers were featured in the mammoth program.

Also on the main floor of the Pavilion, one can visit the magnificent State Power Authority exhibit and a museum sponsored by the New York State Council on the Arts—where a stirring exhibit of New York Art created in this century may be seen. Attractive restaurant facilities are also located here. An outdoor café, under leafy trees, serves low-cost hot and cold meals and a comfortable air conditioned restaurant is available for more leisurely and complete dining, at extremely moderate prices.

THEATERAMA

A circular theater, 100 feet in diameter, 44 feet high. In it is shown the only 360° picture projected at 35 mm., entitled "A 'Round New York." It is a thrilling experience in an unusual medium of the motion picture. Last year's 490,000 viewers were enthusiastic in their praise.

For Further Information, Contact: JOHN J. O'CONNOR, Public Relations Counsel. Tel. 888-4553, 4554. or Ruth Kling, Publicity Director.

Pavilion hostesses outfitted by Russ Togs of New York
Organ – Courtesy of Magnavox

Raincoats – provided by 'Storm-Play' Fashions
Tympani – Courtesy of Ludwig Drum Co.

The back of the Honor Days schedule is a wealth of facts and highlights about the New York State pavilion and its relation to the world's fair; however, the following is a more-personal description given by Rich Lando, whose band performed at the New York State pavilion: "I lived 3 blocks away from the Park, on 43rd Ave and 108th St. I was fascinated by the idea of having all these buildings and amusements so close to my house. My Parents and Grandparents filled me with stories about the '39 Fair, I couldn't wait to see what was in store. I was 14 years old when the Fair opened, but even during construction, my friends and I would sneak in near the Ford Pavilion and wander around to have a peek." (Courtesy of Rich Lando.)

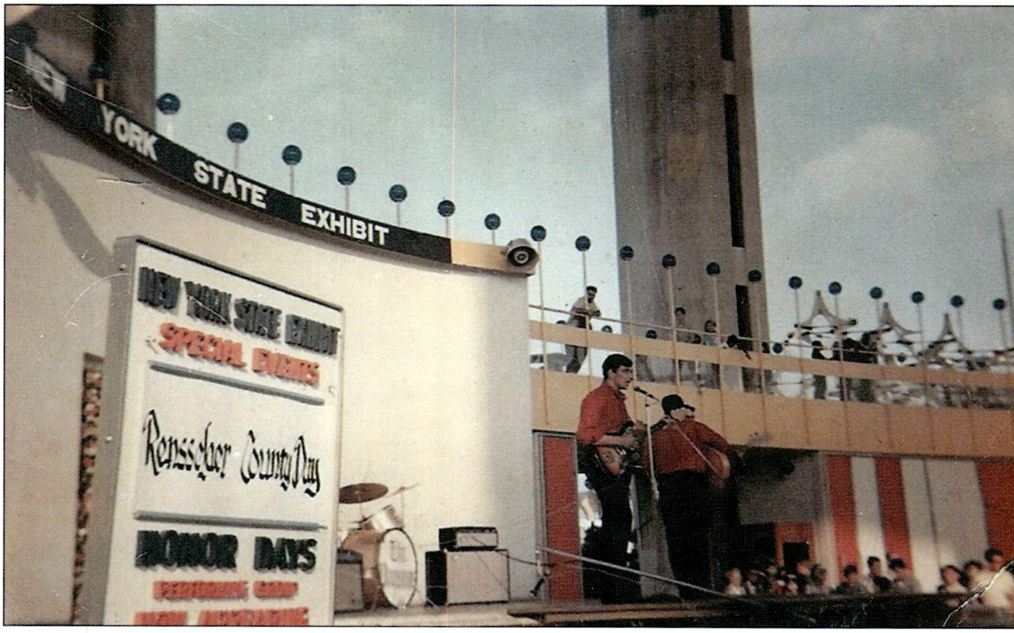

The Parisians included Rich Lando (bass guitar), Joe DeLorenzo (drums), Frank Nicoletti (lead guitar), and Anthony Bagnoli (rhythm guitar), performing on an Honor Day. Rich Lando said, "Like many others, I have a special place in my heart for the Park and all its buildings, having lived in Corona for 56 years. I brought my kids there to ride bikes or play sports and the New York State Pavilion, and other after Fair remains like the NYC Pavilion, Unisphere, Vatican Pavilion Memorial, statues, time capsules, carousel and zoo are woven into the fabric of our lives." (Both, courtesy of Rich Lando.)

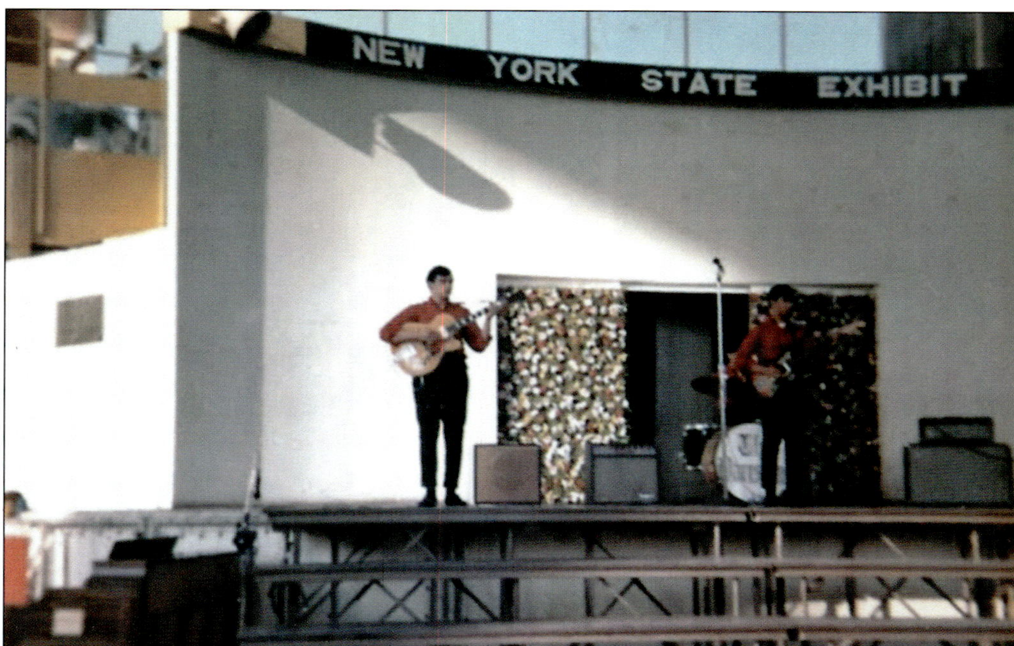

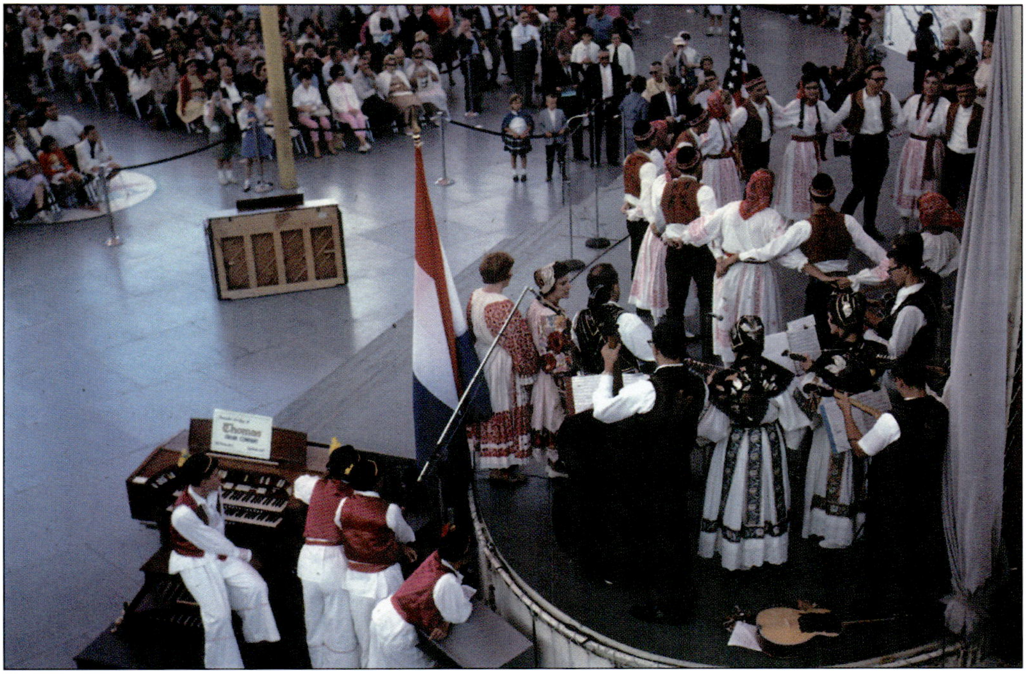

Among the many ethnic groups to appear during Honor Days were these dancers performing a Croatian kolo. The kolo, also known as the circle dance, is one the oldest forms of folk dance throughout the Slavic countries. A movable oval stage, mimicking the shape of the Tent of Tomorrow, was used for most performances. In the photograph below, a group of girls with lap harps from Belarus is practicing in front of the stage with the same Thomas organ seen in both photographs. Over 67,900 people performed at the New York State pavilion in the first season alone.

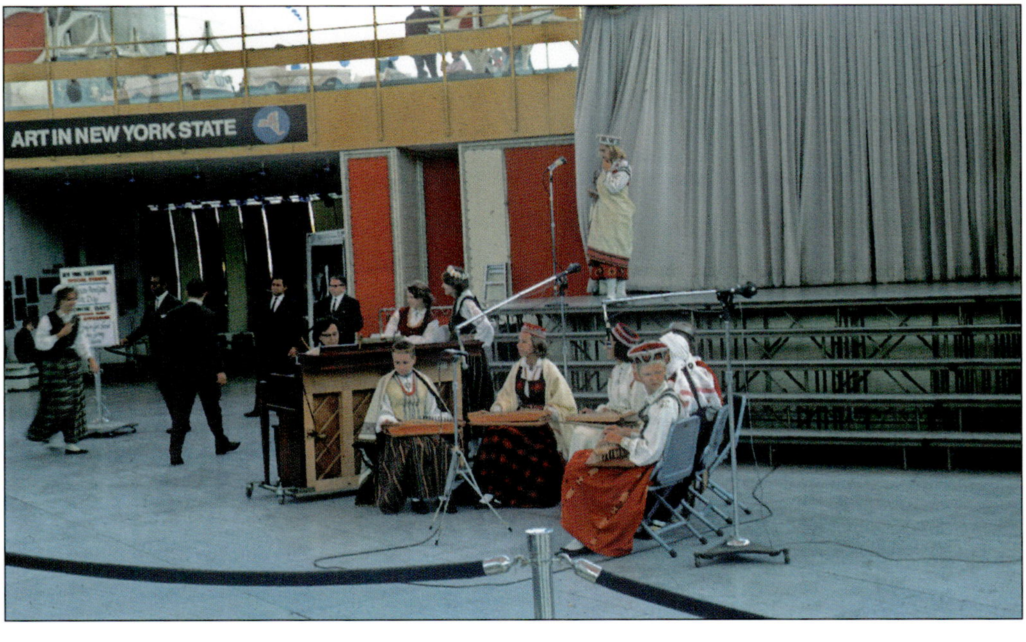

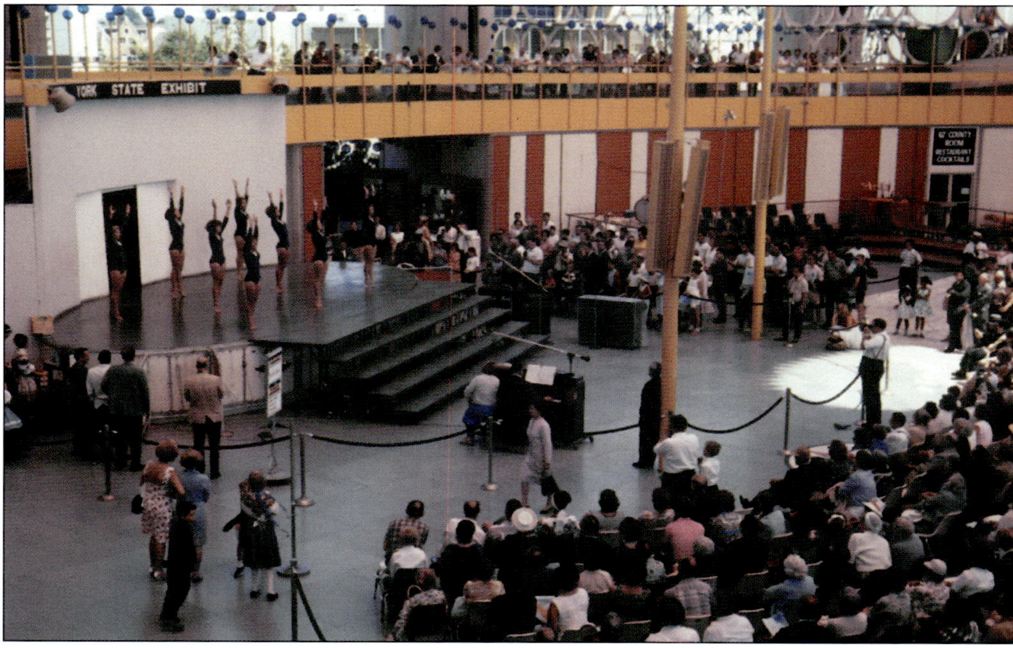

A girls' gymnastics team on the stage shows that Honor Days were not just limited to music and dance. In the background is a glimpse of the 62 County Room Restaurant Cocktails that occupied one of the spaces under the enclosed mezzanine. The Theaterama building was originally planned as a fashion theater called Circarama. The Fashion Industries of New York group was to use this building to showcase the state's role as a fashion center. The display cases in the background below are a scaled back version as Theaterama was used for projecting a film of New York State travel destinations.

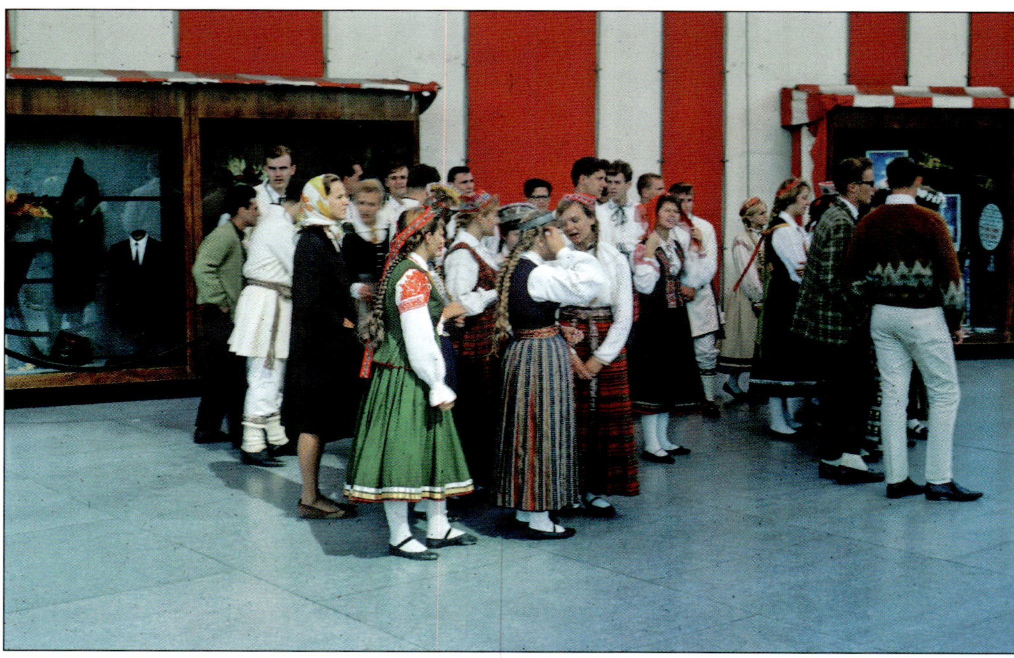

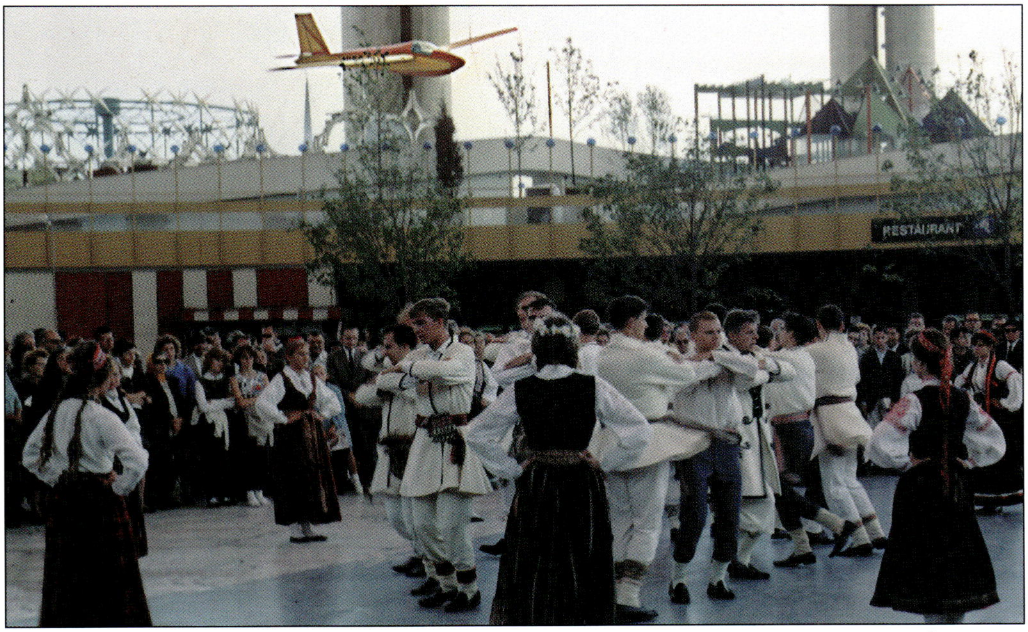

Honor Day events were also held directly on the terrazzo map, using it as an open performance space. In this case, another event was getting under way on the movable stage while people performed on the terrazzo map. In the photographs is a group Latvian folk dancers. One of the big cultural events known to many American Latvians is the Latvian Song and Dance Festival, celebrated at the summer solstice. Americans have been putting on these festivals around the country for over 50 years; they are performed with a partner in four or more couple formations. Steps are based on variations of the polka and gallop.

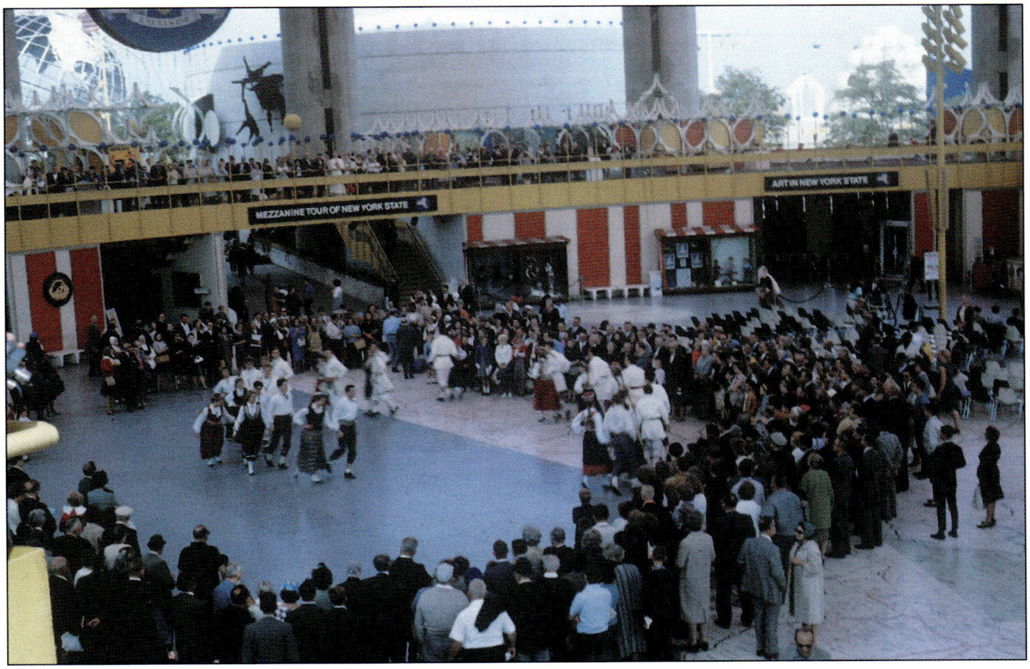

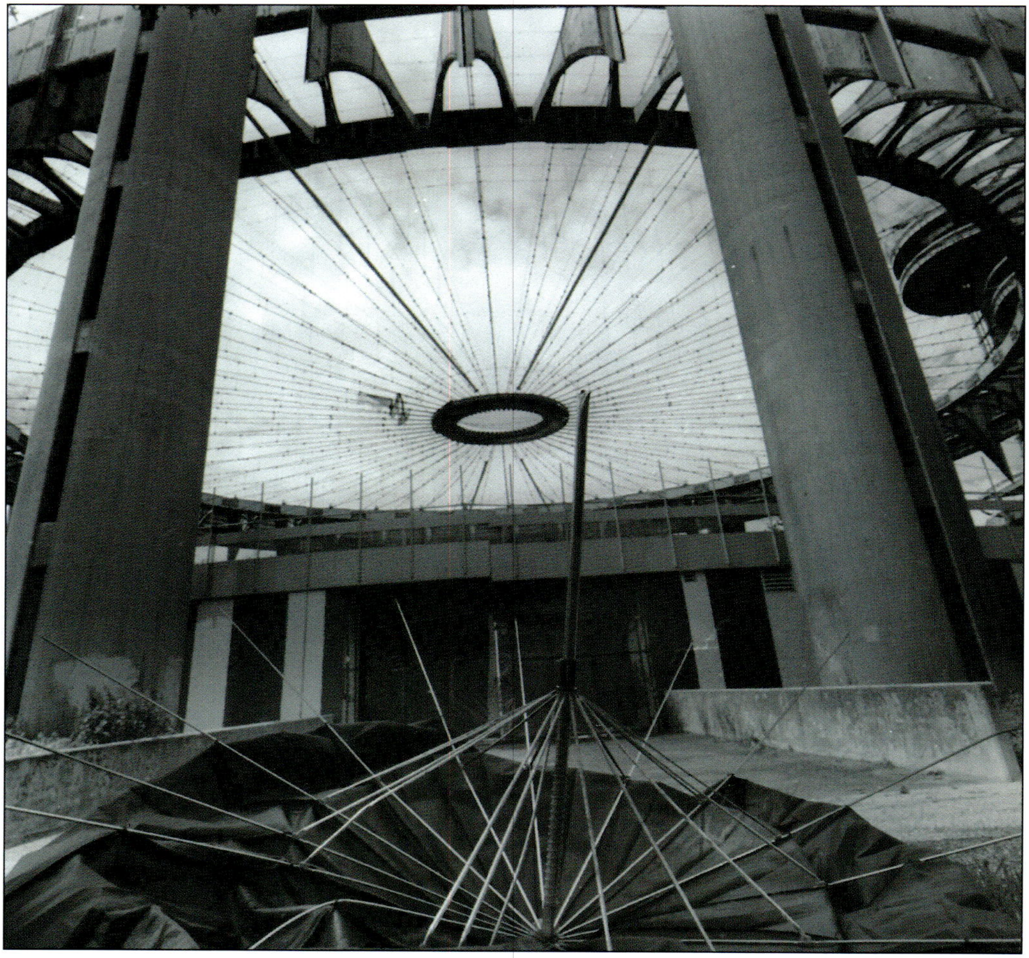

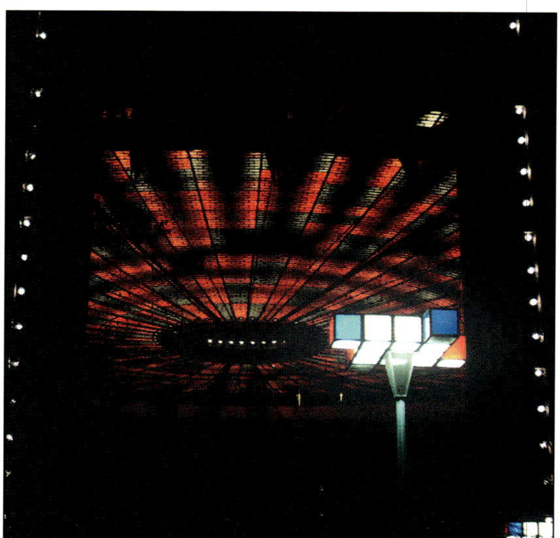

Pictured is the mighty Tent of Tomorrow on a windy, rainy day in 2013; note its colorful roof panels are long gone. During the world's fair, the New York State pavilion was a feast of lights in the evening. Vertical lights highlighted each column, and 500-watt lights illuminated the roof panels from behind. Street luminaires, in the foreground at left, added to the festive atmosphere. These lamps were arrangements of cubes color coded for the different areas of the fair and configured in many ways. They bring to mind the Rubik's Cube, introduced at the 1982 world's fair in Knoxville, Tennessee.

The translucent fiberglass Tent of Tomorrow roof is pictured from the Court of the Stars leading to the Astral Fountain. The staggered four-color panels were arranged such that the same pattern repeats for every fourth radial. A clear dome covering the tension ring is visible in the center. The Astral Fountain, which was long in disrepair, was replaced by the 16,000-square-foot Maloof competition skateboard park in 2010. The "Miniature Trip through New York," with its exhibit supports that were often referred to as snowflake modules, can be seen up on the 15-foot-tall mezzanine outer wall.

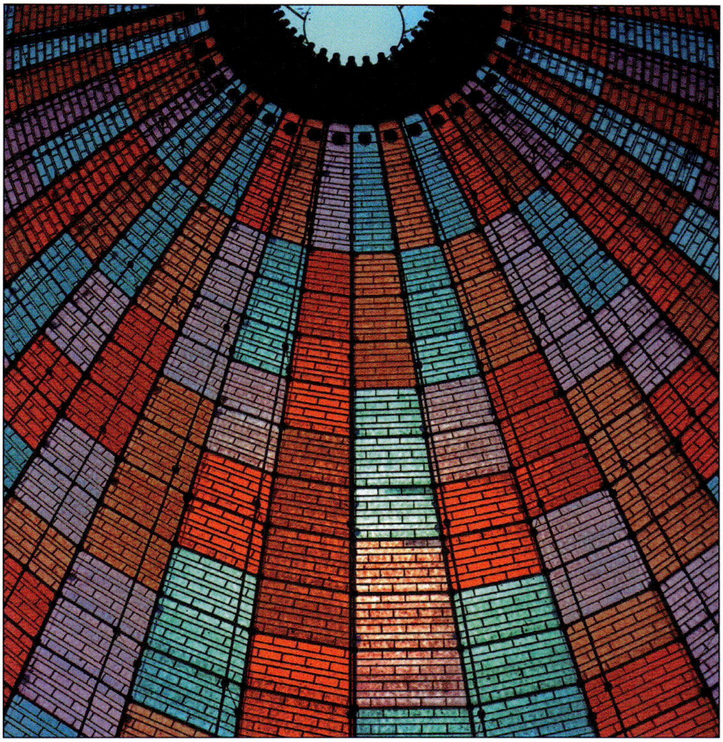

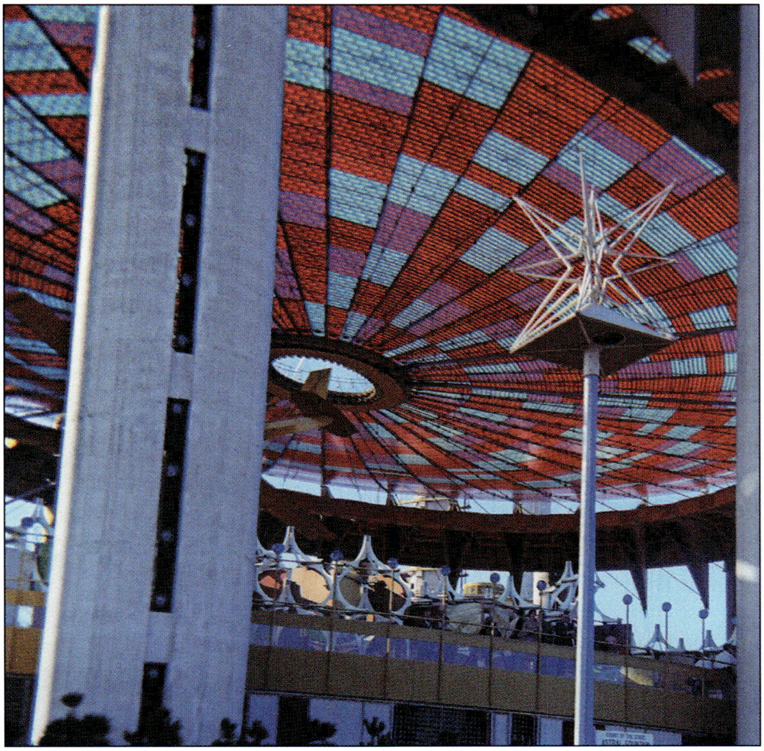

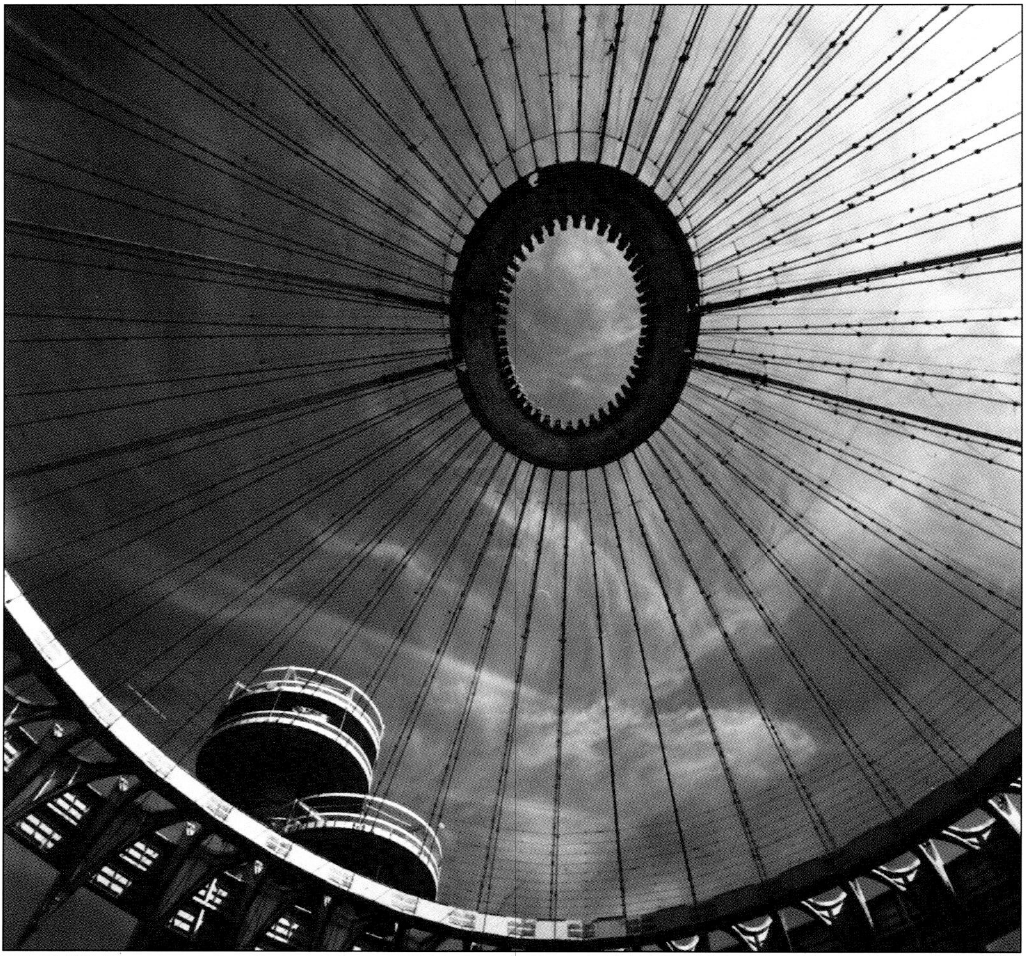

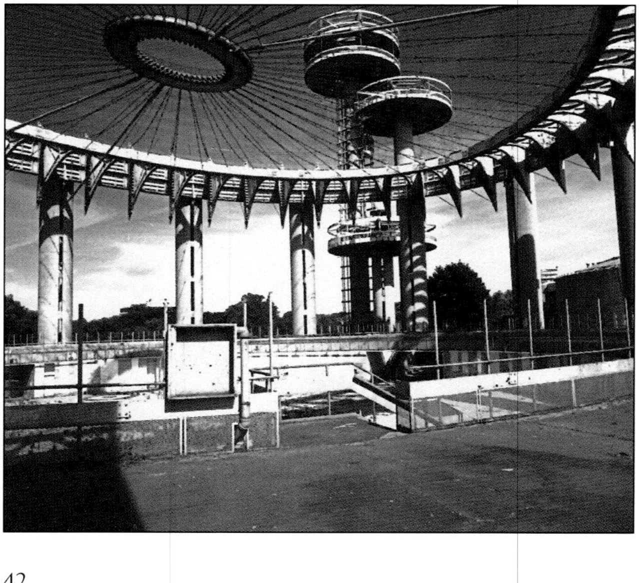

This is a 2009 view of the mezzanine when the Queens Theatre in the Park was still undergoing its transformation with the addition of a glass 3,000-square-foot lobby, turning the old Theaterama building into the stunning venue that it is today. With all the crowds gone and the "Miniature Trip through New York" exhibits removed after the end of the fair, the mezzanine conjures up images of a stark and barren trip through New York State. The empty fire hose cabinet in the foreground below was a 1967 fire-code addition to accommodate food concessions on the mezzanine.

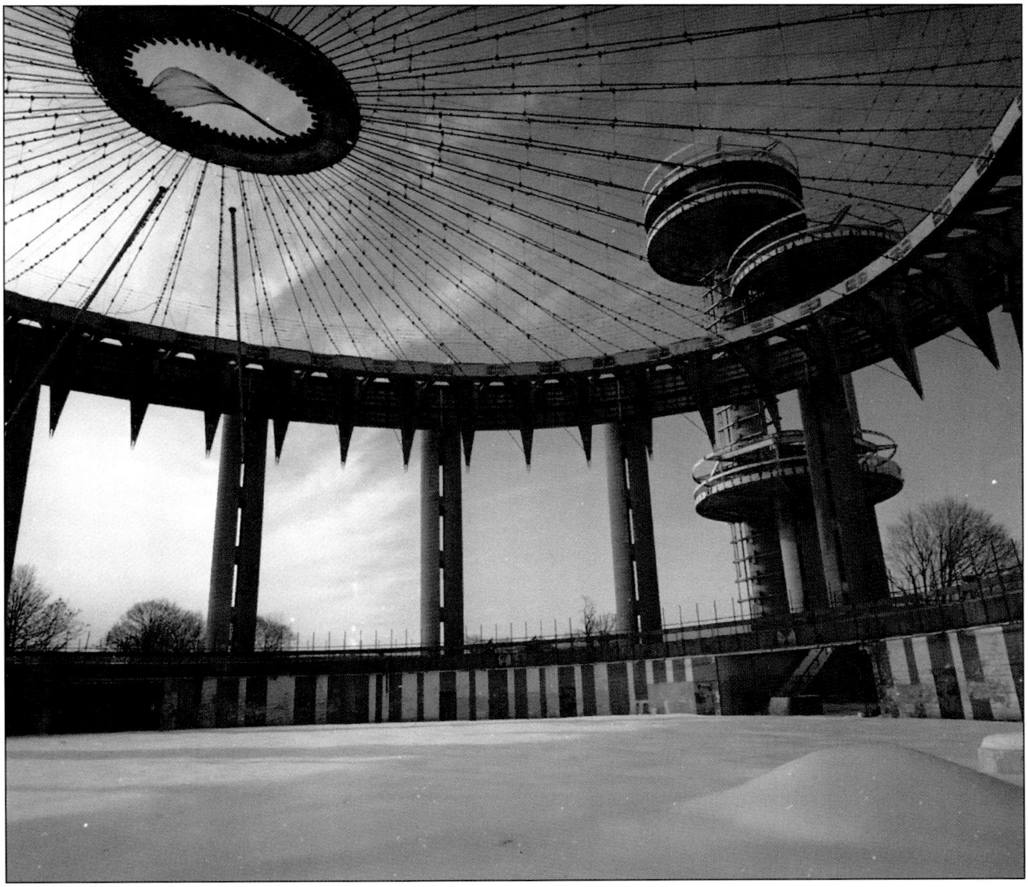

In 2009, the map was covered with a tarp, held down by bricks placed around its perimeter, and a layer of sand and gravel was added on top to inhibit weed growth. The remaining pieces of the largely broken-up map still lay underneath. Ten of the four-by-four-foot terrazzo panels and assorted loose letters and symbols from the map were removed for safe storage and eventual restoration. The 28,000-square-foot, 190-foot-diameter terrazzo floor with its giant 576 piece map of New York State lays under a shroud of snow in 2011 (above).

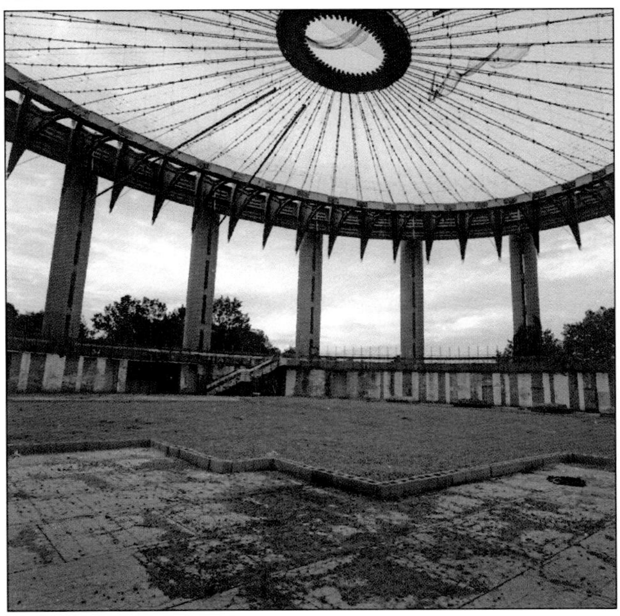

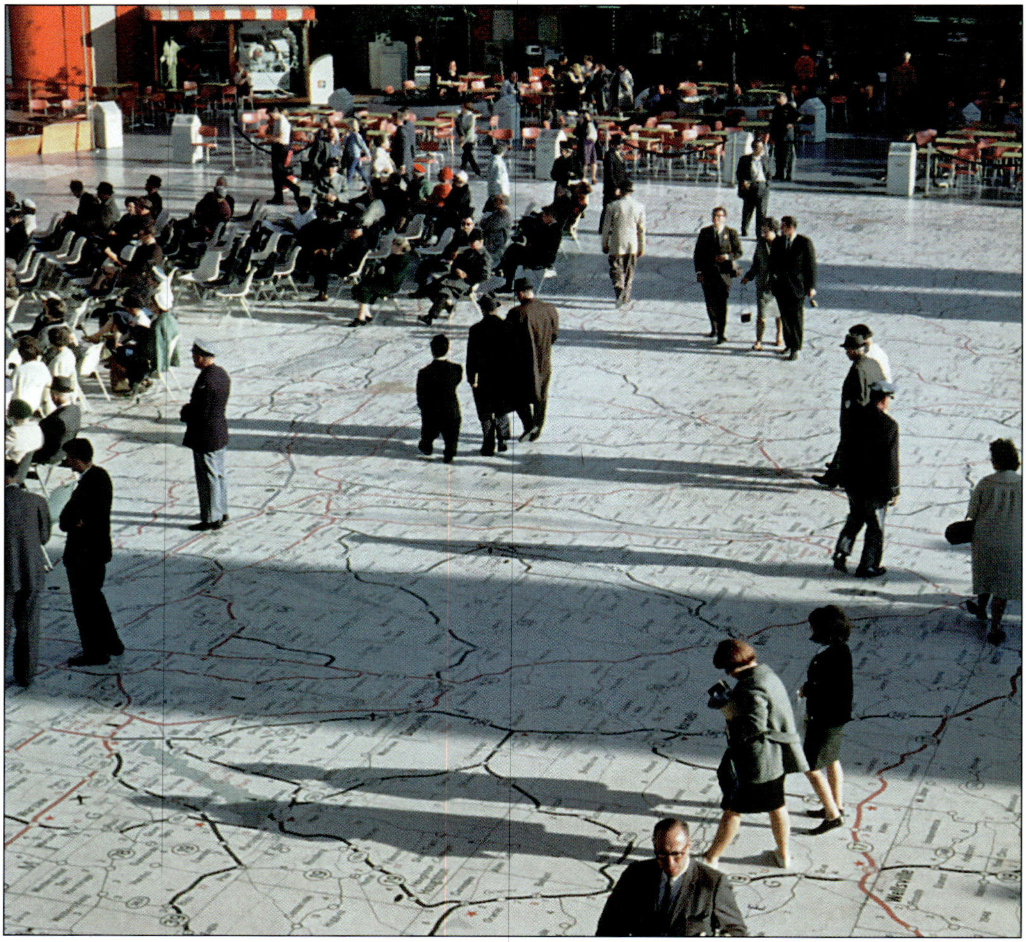

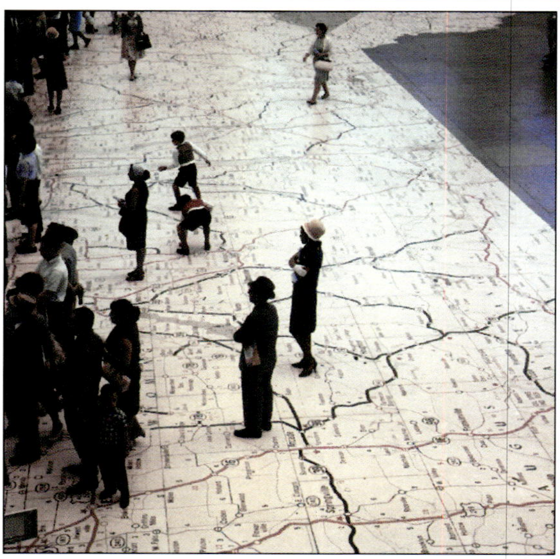

Each of the 400-pound terrazzo tiles that form the map was created in a unique way. First a group of Yale University art students used the projected image of a Texaco road map to make a set of tracings, scaled up by a factor of 64. The tracings were then used to create molds with aluminum borders, adding plastic letters, numerals, and other map symbols, at the Manhattan Tile and Terrazzo Company. The final step of pouring the various colors of terrazzo mix into the molds was done at the Port Morris Tile and Marble Corp. in the Bronx. (Above, courtesy of the Bill Cotter collection.)

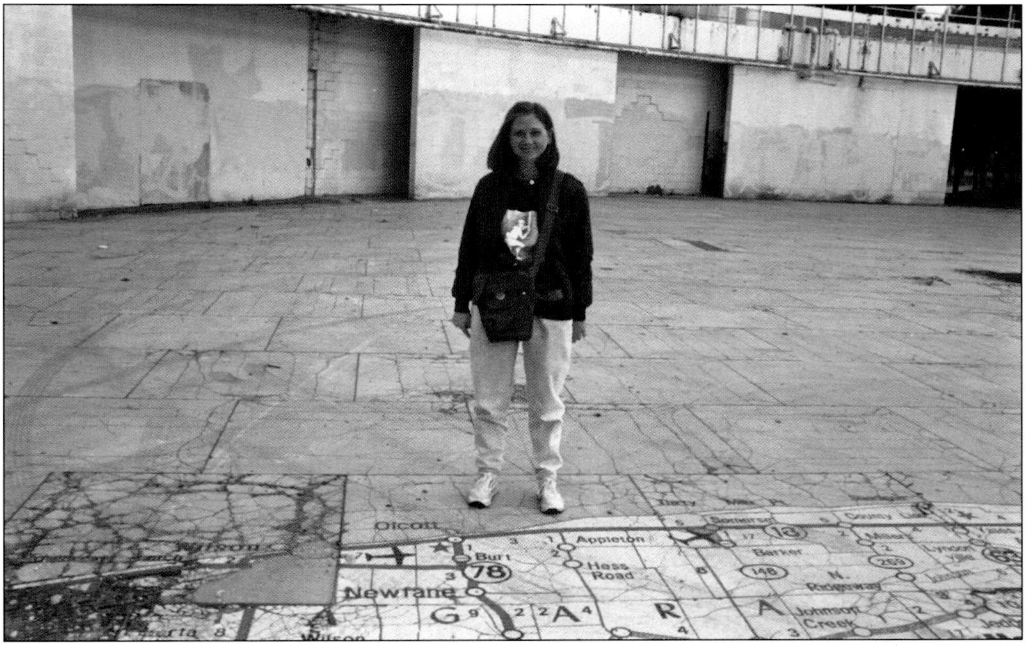

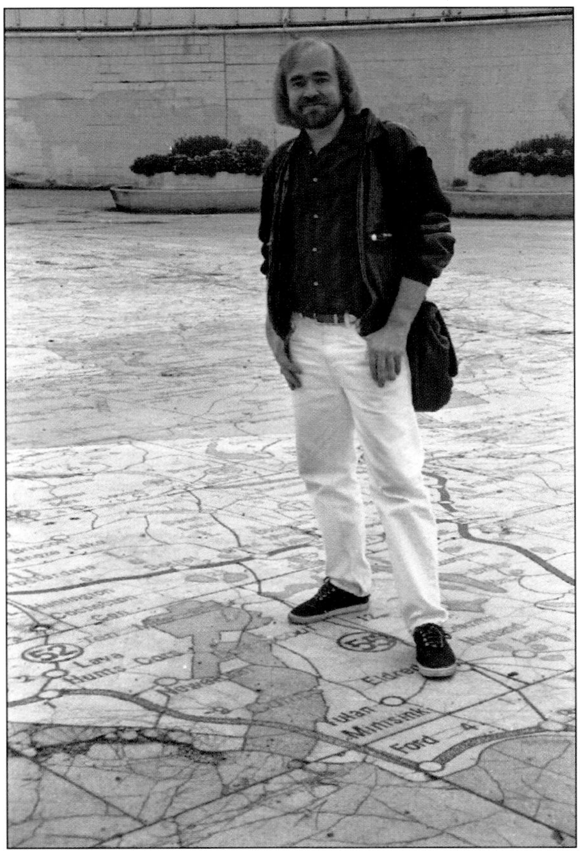

The author and his wife are seen on the map during a day when all the gates were open in October 1989. Like many who have posed for photographs during the fair, Patricia stands by her hometown of Newfane. Although the map was still mostly intact, the freeze-and-thaw cycle had started to take its toll. Gates were installed in 1986, and since 1989, they have been closed to keep souvenir hunters out. In a rare exception, the public was allowed in for a three-hour photo opportunity on April 22, 2014, to commemorate the 50th anniversary of the world's fair.

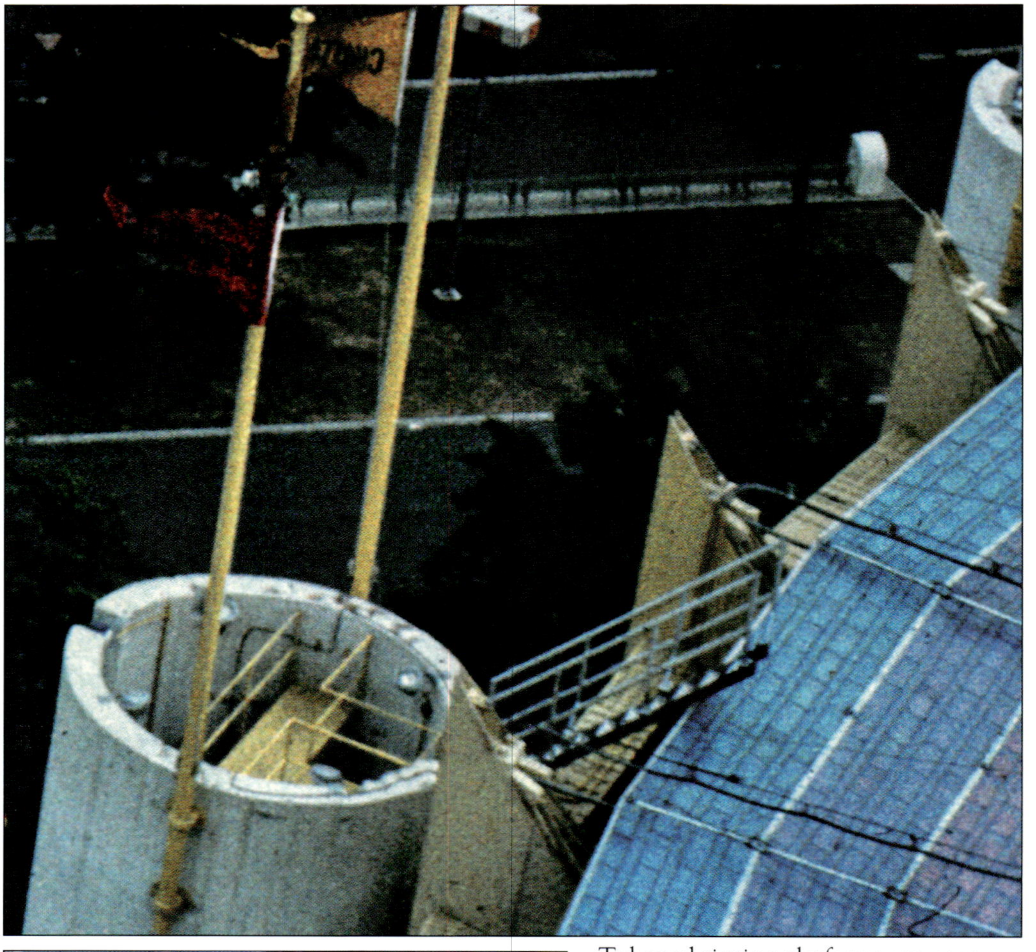

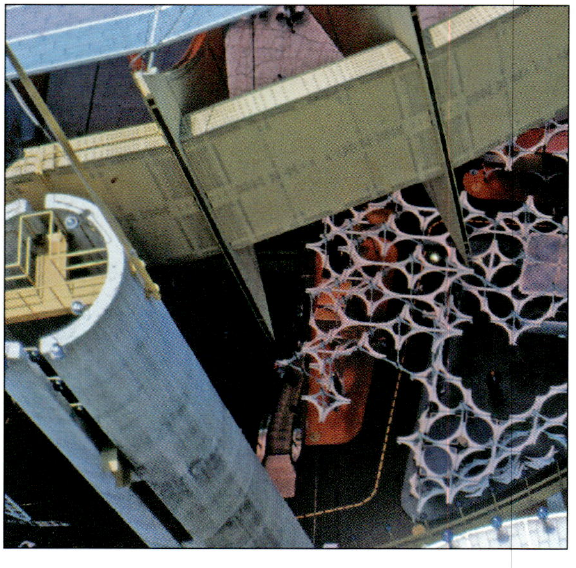

T-shaped rigging platforms are near the top of the Tent of Tomorrow's 16 columns. At an elevation of 115 feet, 9 inches, they provided access to change the flags and four spotlights that were mounted on each. The columns were lettered A through P, but only one had an access ladder reaching up to the roof panels, which was column I, near the Theaterama building. Maintenance people would need to walk on the roof to service the strings of 500-watt spotlights, 15 spaced on each of the 48 radial strings that gave the roof its multicolored glow at night. (Left, courtesy of Vincent P. Marchese.)

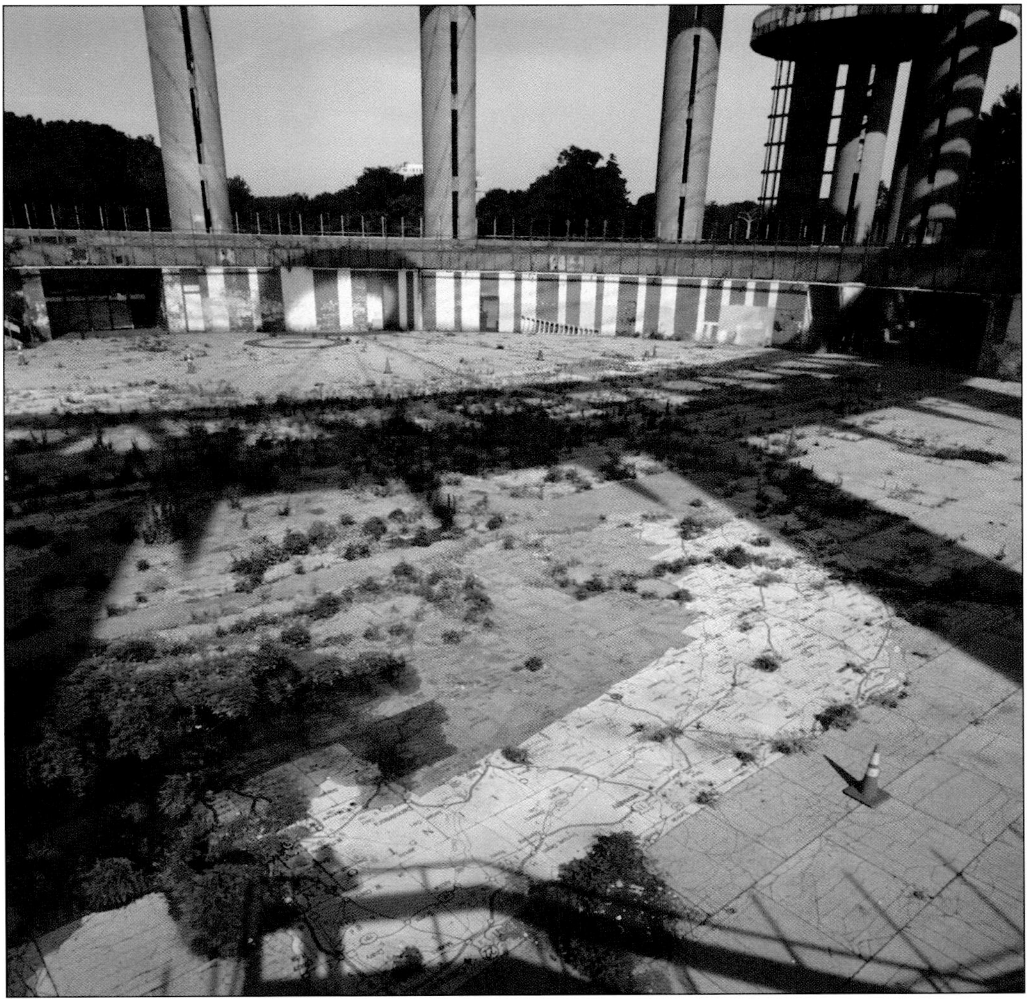

From January 27 to May 4, 2008, an exhibition titled Back on the Map appeared at the Queens Museum of Art. The University of Pennsylvania's School of Design Graduate Program in Historic Preservation, with a $40,000 grant from the National Endowment for the Arts, removed 10 tiles, completely restoring four that were the centerpiece of this exhibition. University of Pennsylvania's Prof. Frank Matero estimated it would cost about $1,100 to restore a panel, using epoxy resin and replacement terrazzo. The world's largest map is the 130-by-166-foot reproduction of a 1964 New York State Texaco road map.

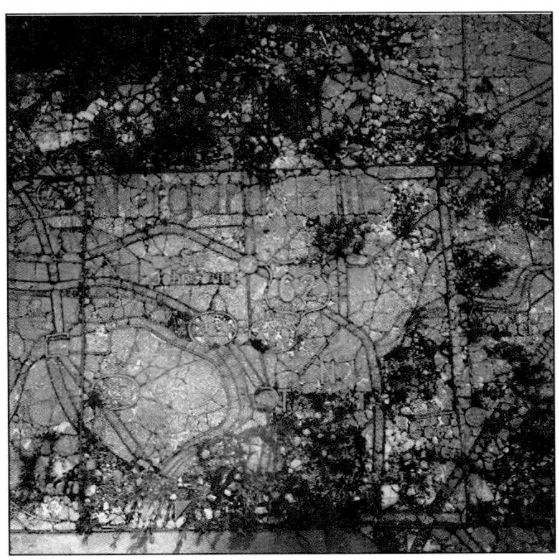

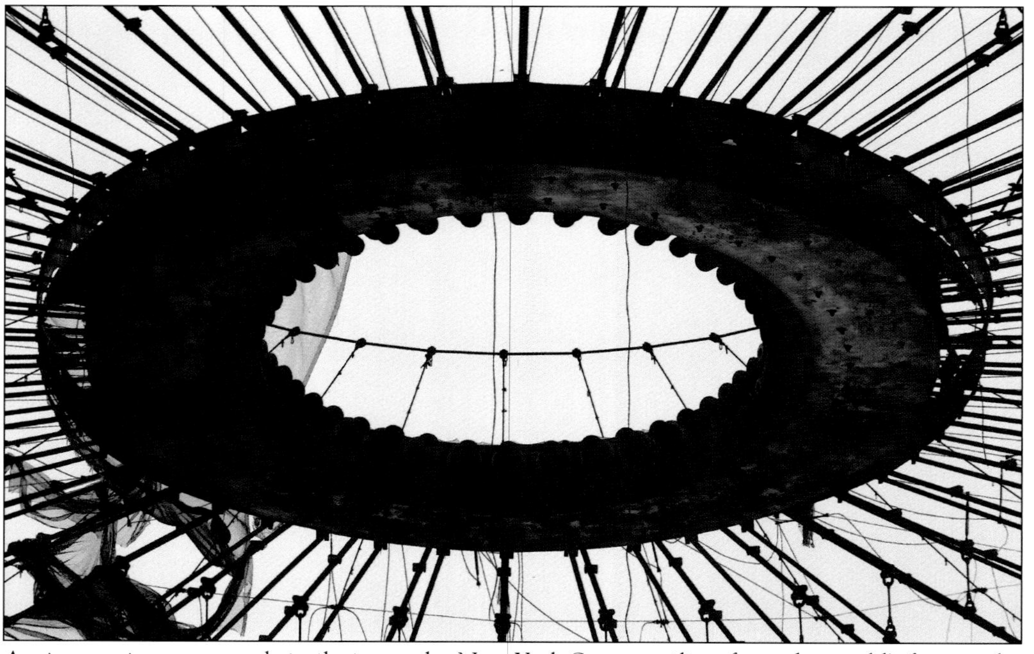

An interesting structural similarity to the New York State pavilion from the world's fair can be found in Flushing Meadow Corona Park today in the amazing 120-foot-diameter, 700,000-pound Unisphere, the world's largest globe. To counter the outward forces at the equator, a tension ring was also built into the design, albeit with only 24 radial cables. The massive New York State pavilion's Tent of Tomorrow tension ring, with 96 Roebling cables attached, is shown as it appears today. The obvious through rust is on the nonstructural drainage troth, shown in the construction photographs. Without the fiberglass roof channeling rainwater into it or drainage pipes to carry it away, it no longer serves any purpose.

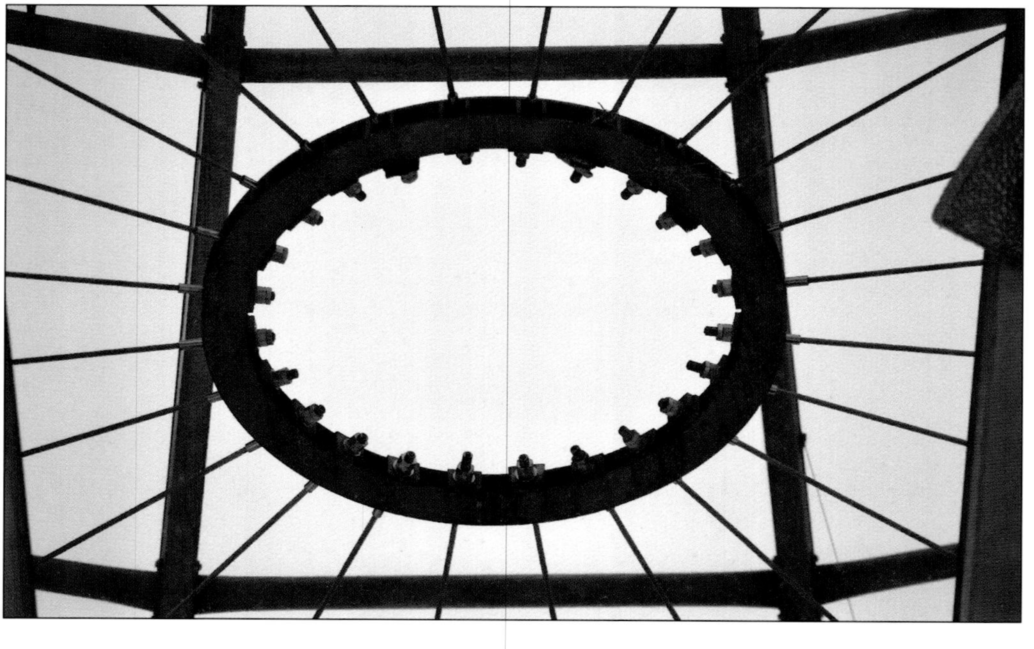

Four

THE OBSERVATION TOWERS

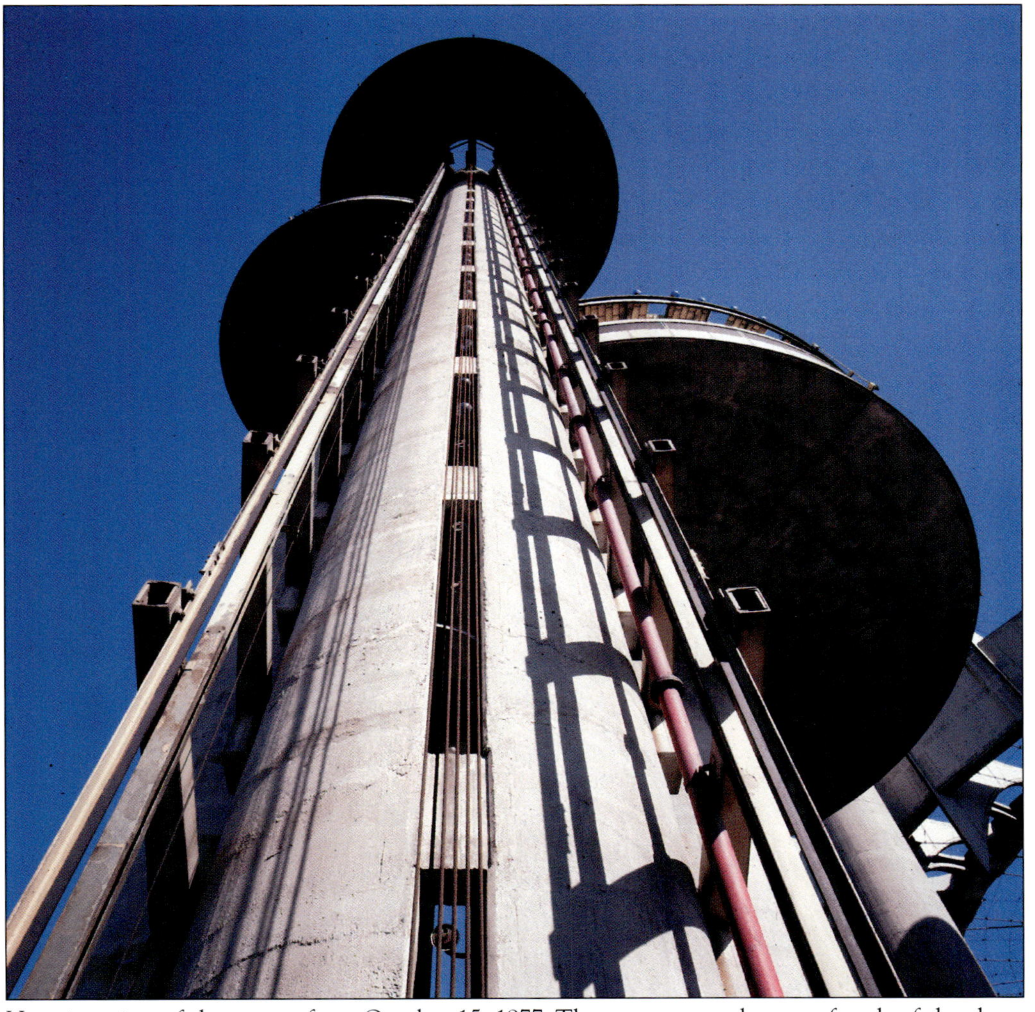

Here is a view of the towers from October 15, 1977. The concrete at the top of each of the three towers measures 240 feet, 11 inches; 194 feet, 7.5 inches; and 100 feet, 10.5 inches tall. Each tower has a 60-foot-diameter observation platform that hangs down from the top with cables, like a marionette. From the top platform, a secondary platform hangs 20 feet, 7.5 inches directly below.

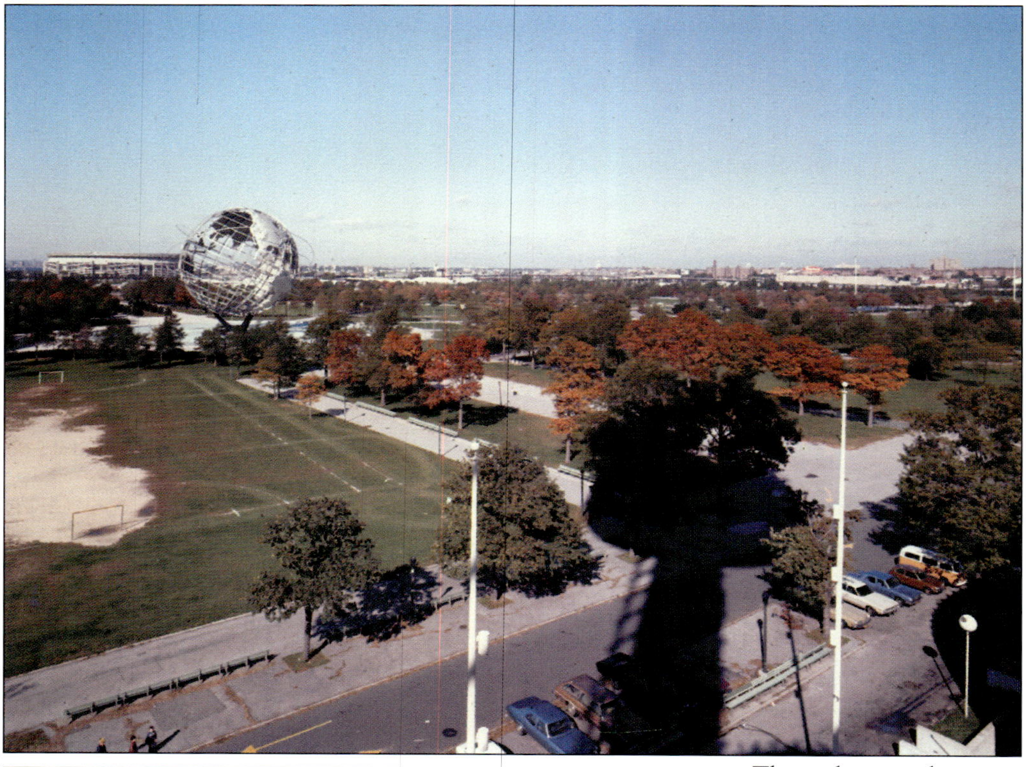

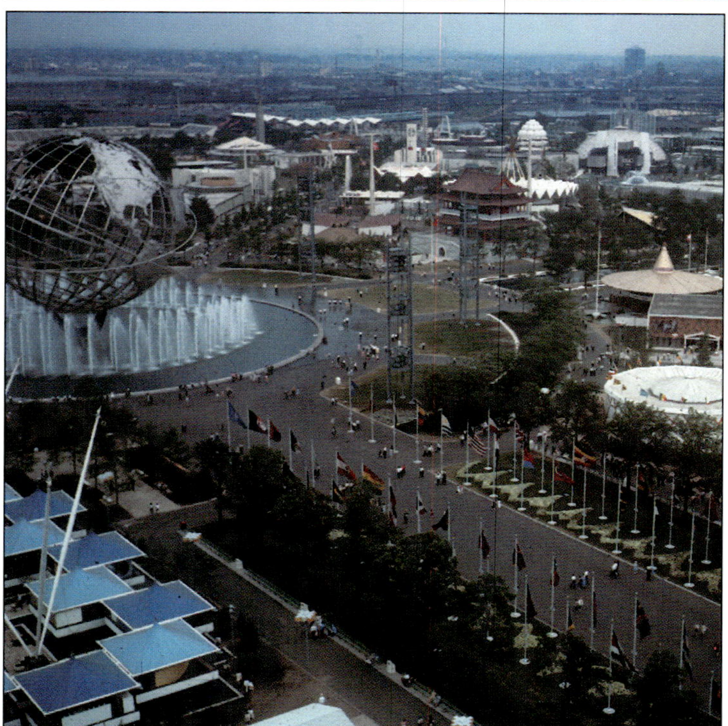

These photographs compare 1977 (above) and 1964 (left) views from the towers. Looking toward the Unisphere with the Court of the Nations running diagonally, international pavilions are on the far side and state exhibits are on the near side. Both photographs were taken from the lowest platform, at 81 feet, 7.5 inches off the ground. The towers cast a shadow across the intersection of the old Avenue of the United Nations and the Court of the Nations in the image taken on October 15, 1977. In the center of the horizon, the Whitestone Bridge can be seen in the world's fair–era photograph.

Here are two more photographs of the same view looking toward the Unisphere. The October 15, 1977, photograph was shot through the slots on the side of the tower column (a by-product of the slip-form concrete process used for all of the New York State pavilion columns) from a landing on stairs inside. The underside of the third 60-foot-diameter platform frames the top, which is 184 feet off the ground. Prominent in the world's fair photograph are the New Jersey pavilion, the United States pavilion (demolished shortly before the 1977 photograph), and Shea Stadium in the distance (demolished in 2009).

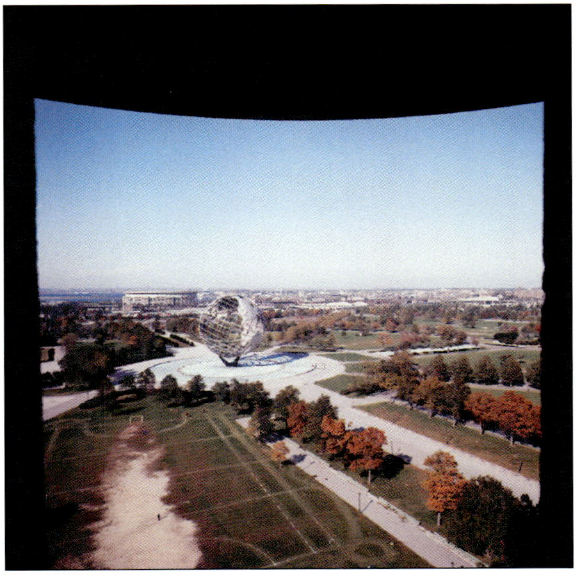

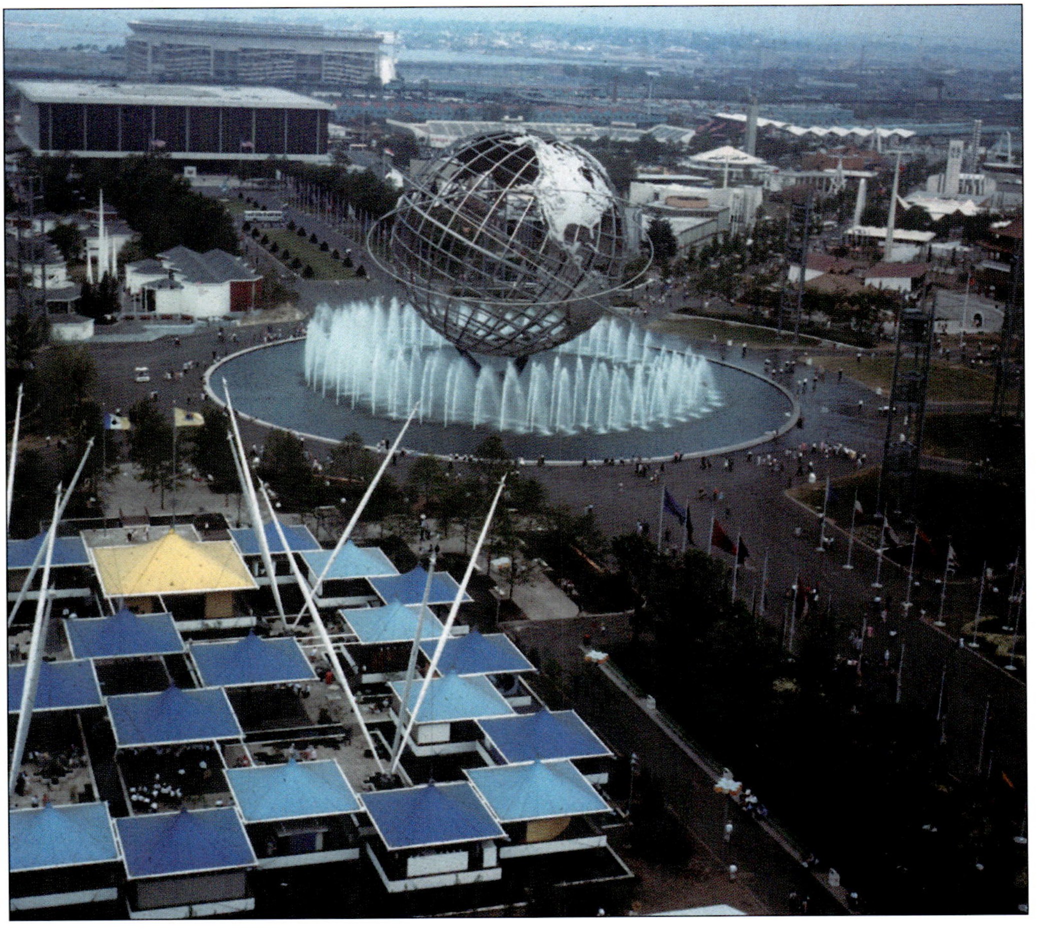

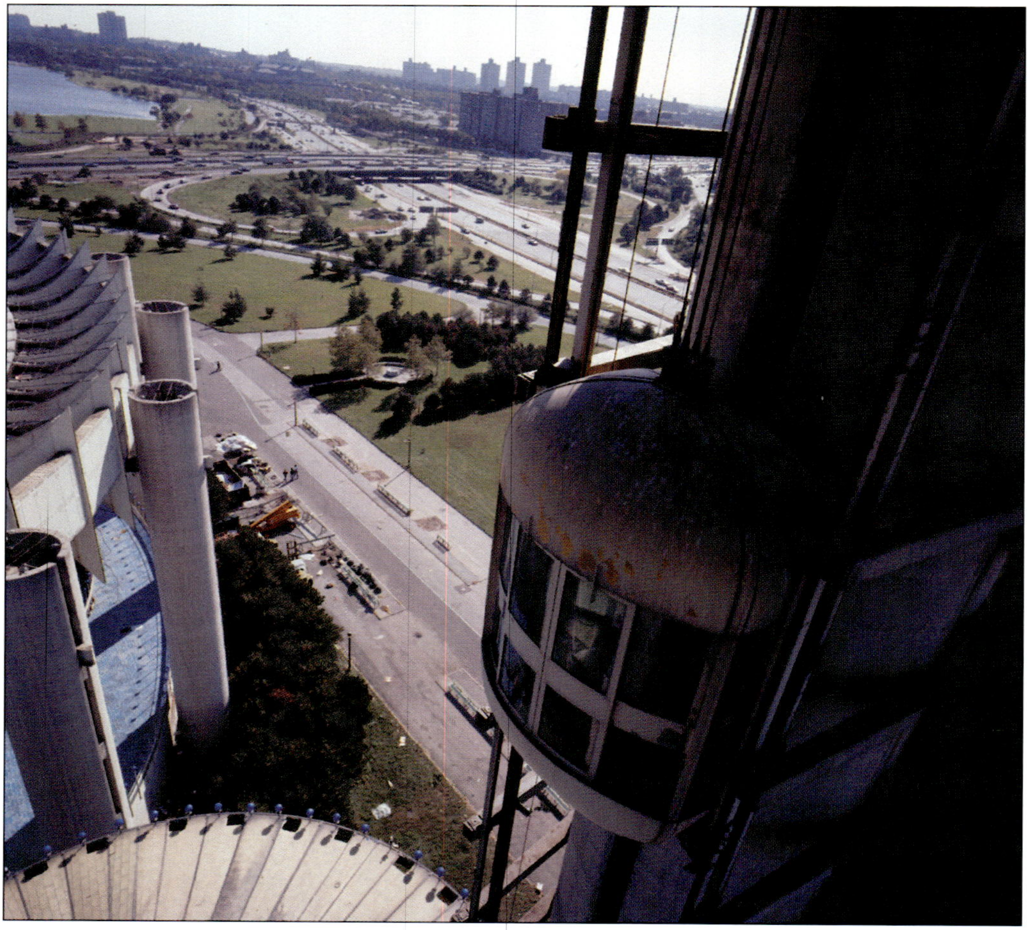

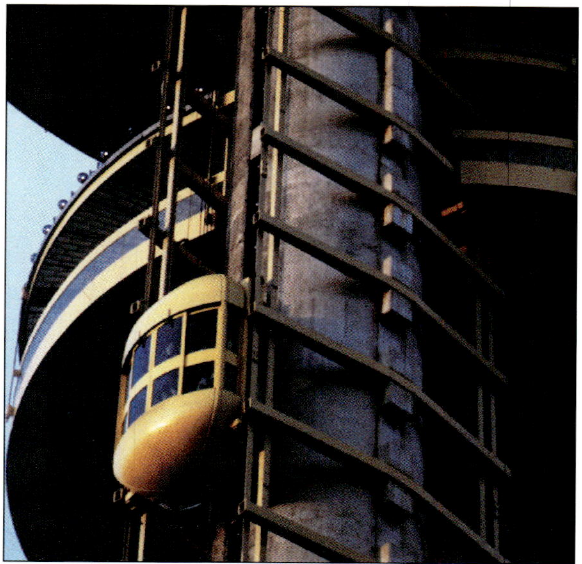

Pictured in October 1977 (above) and in September 1965 (left) are the famed Sky-Streak capsule elevators that once whisked passengers up 216 feet in 19 seconds. Since 1973, the Sky-Streak capsule elevator would remain frozen in this final resting position 140 feet above ground. The second elevator cab was left in the service pit; the elevators would never move again. This type of Otis capsule elevator is still in use at the 1965-built Skylon Tower in Niagara Falls and at the Seattle Space Needle, built for the 1962 world's fair. On May 19, 2007, the Space Needle welcomed its 45-millionth visitor.

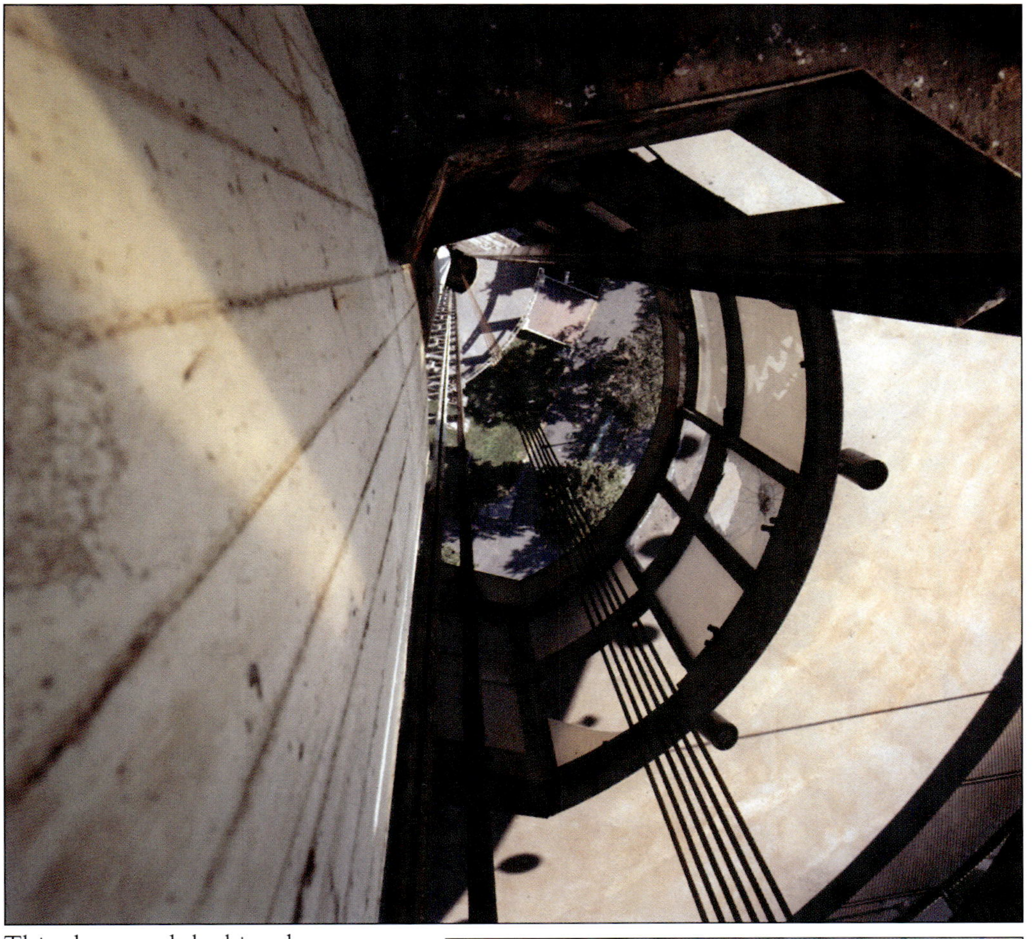

This photograph looking down on the elevator cables from the top platform is from October 15, 1977. During the fair, the elevator operators were often college students, and to put some humor into their job, they would tell Sky-Streak passengers that, due to air currents at the top, they would have to disembark facing backwards. Their gullibility would be met with laughter from passengers waiting for the trip down, who had fallen for the same routine earlier. The frames of the "Miniature Trip through New York" on the mezzanine appear like snowflakes. (Right, courtesy of Vincent P. Marchese.)

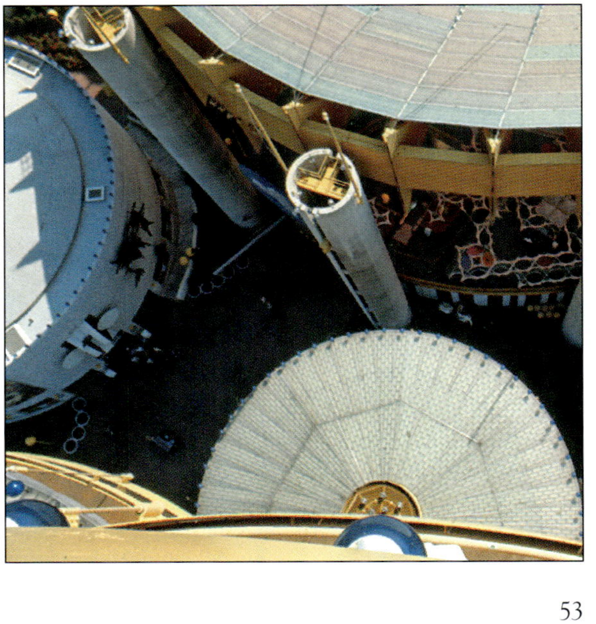

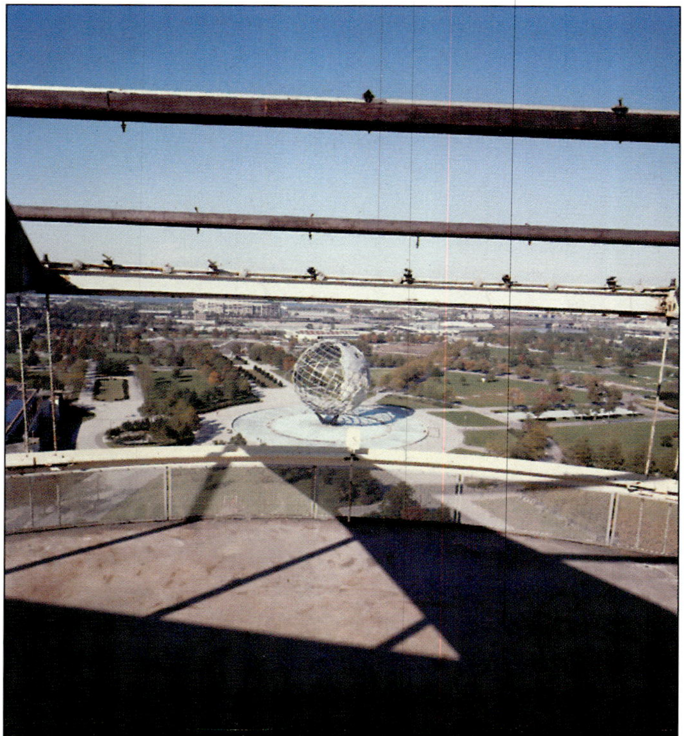

The photograph from the highest observation platform was taken on October 15, 1977 (left). The top covering of Kalwall panels were gone from all of the upper observation decks by then, although, they were still over the lower-level platform, as seen in this chapter's introduction photograph. The photograph below of the top observation platform, at 232 feet, 3 inches above the ground, is from September 1965. Both this deck and the matching deck that hangs 20 feet below are suspended from the same eight cable pairs that can be seen around the outer edge. The Whitestone Bridge appears to the right in the distance in the 1965 photograph. (Both, author's collection.)

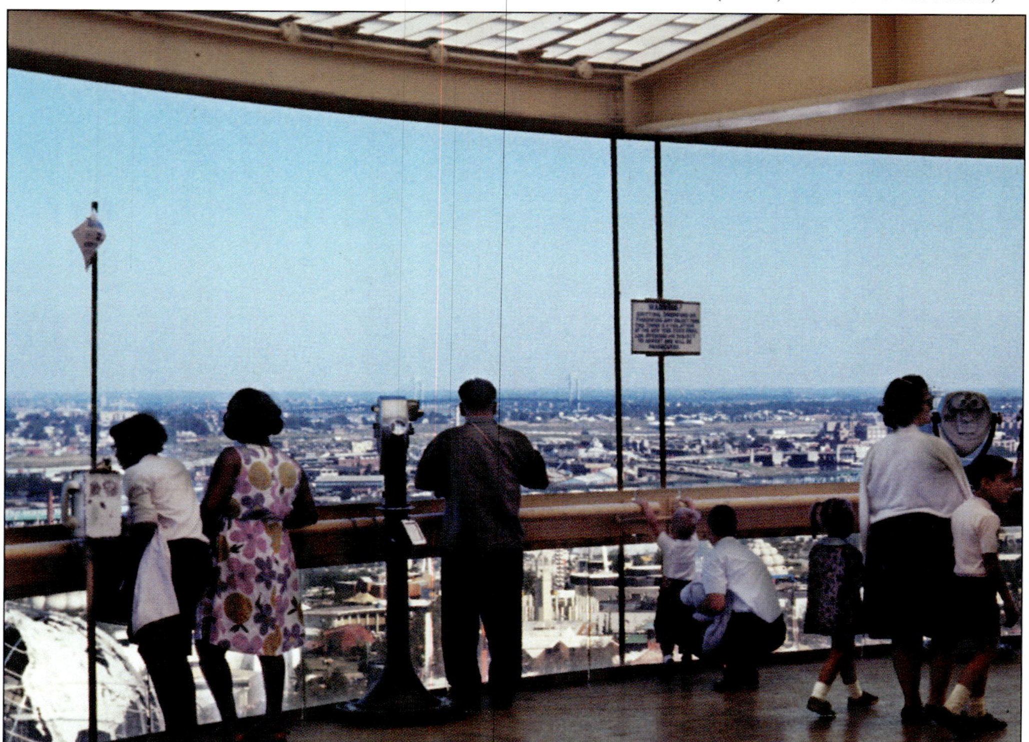

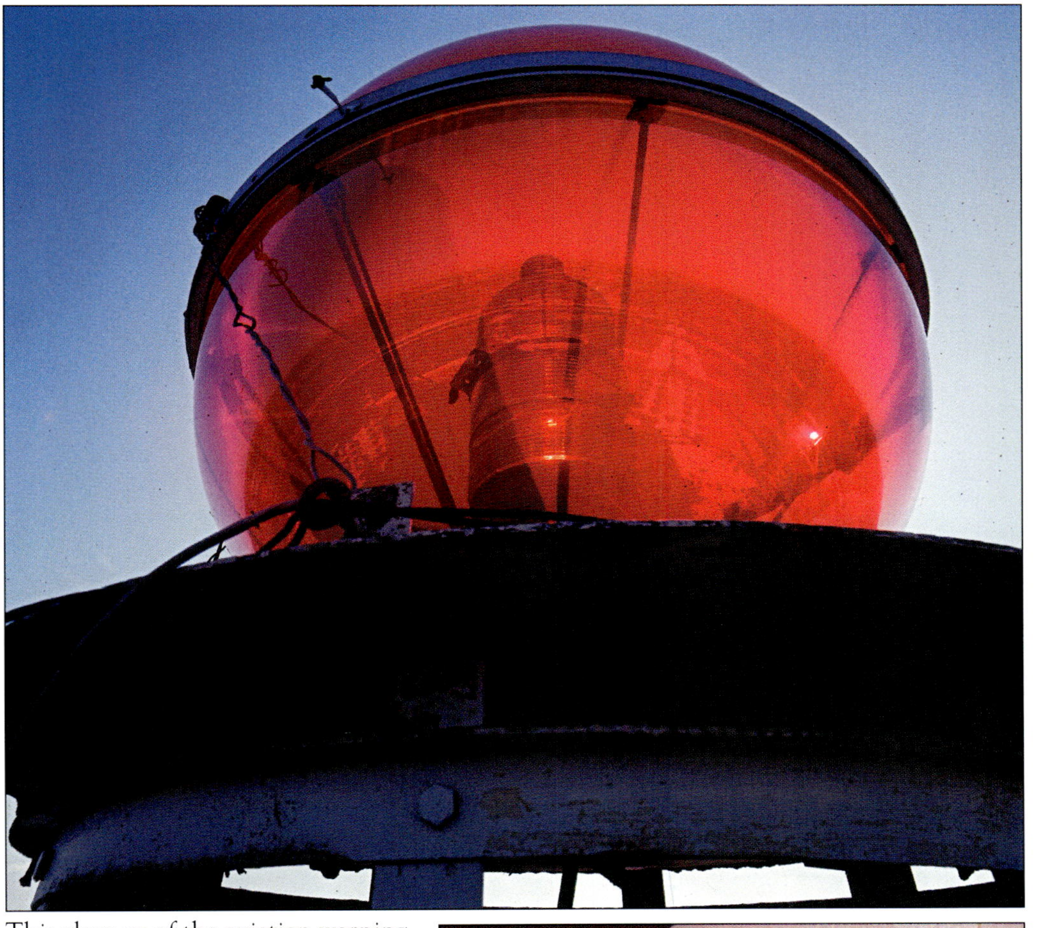

This close-up of the aviation warning light, with the park reflected across its surface, is from October 15, 1977. It is the tallest feature of the New York State pavilion at 252 feet above the ground. The light had to be replaced in 2006 by Vertical Access, an Ithaca-based mountain climbing firm; the company had to scale the tower from the outside, since much of the interior stairway had corroded away. Also on top of the tower was this Otis elevator flyball governor, a power-cutoff system that can still be found in some elevators that have worked for over 100 years.

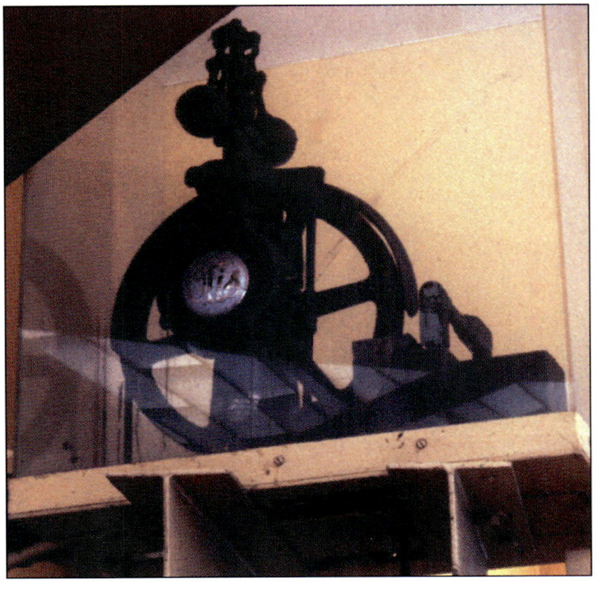

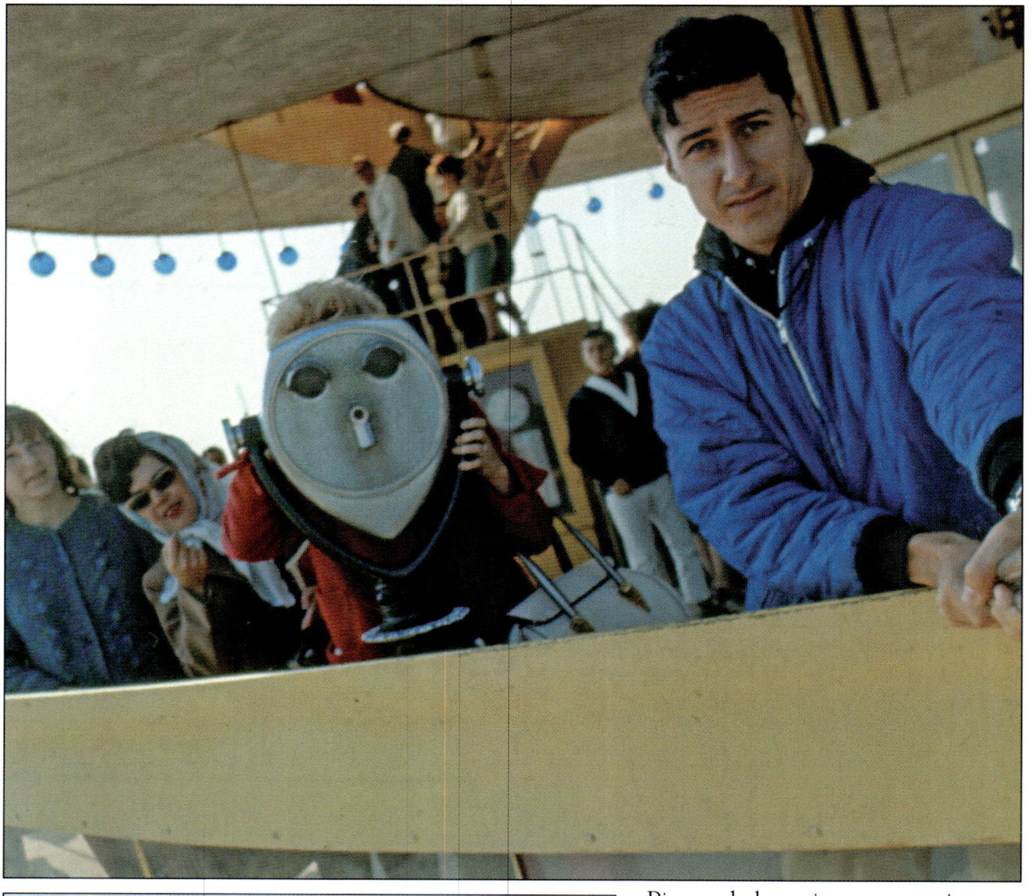

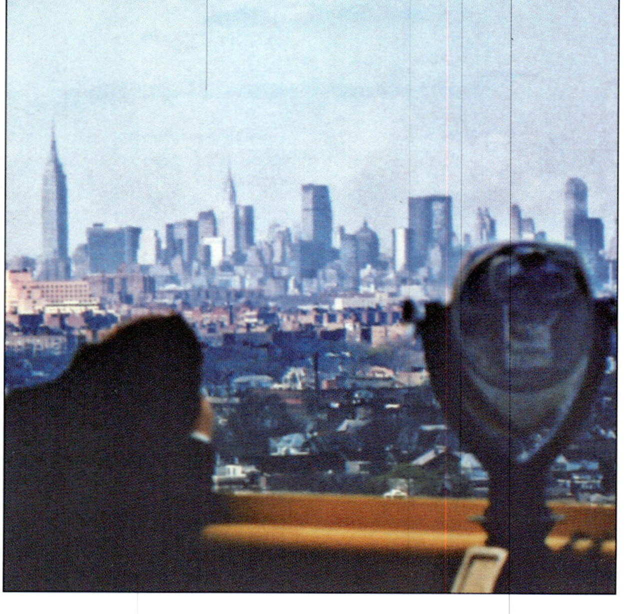

Pictured above is an expressive shot from the top observation platform. A timed self-portrait of Vince Marchese holding his camera out on a tripod 235 feet above the ground is both daring and creative. Marchese later became a well-skilled sky diver. He also took the skyline shot with a binocular stand; it is a telling image that underscores the relation of Manhattan to the world's fair and the borough of Queens. (Both, courtesy of Vincent P. Marchese.)

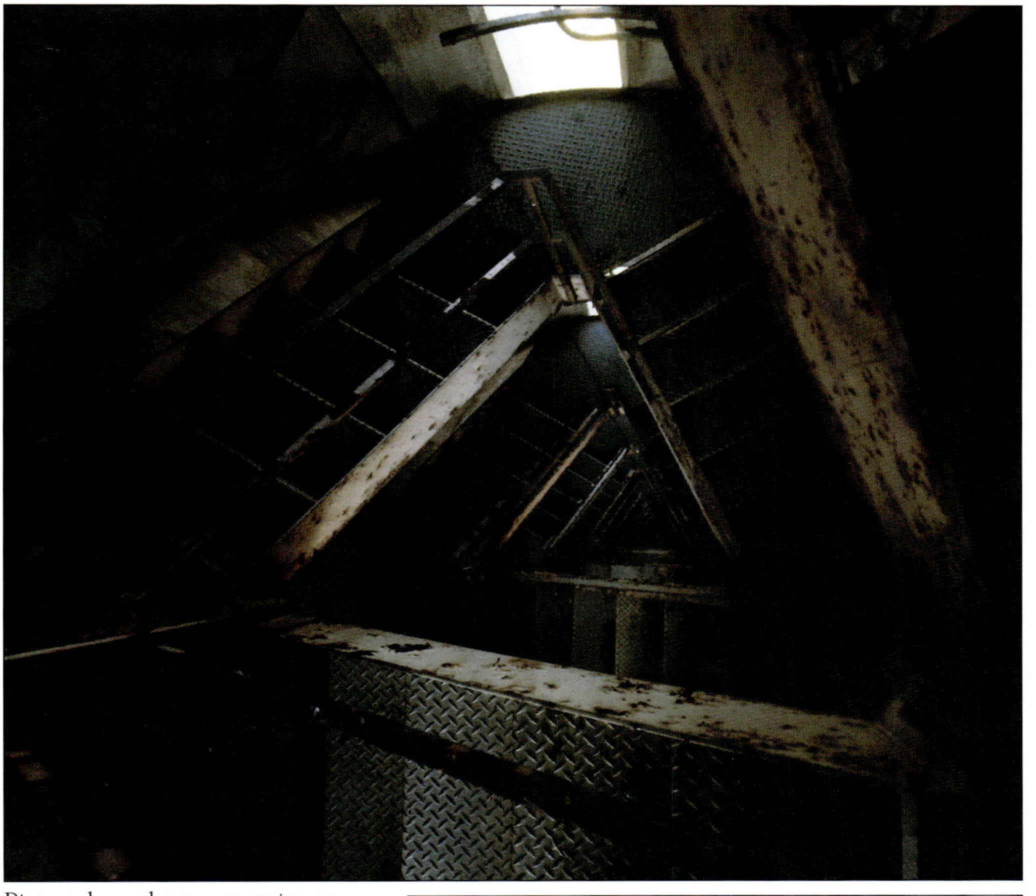

Pictured are the tower stairs on October 15, 1977. Taking the stairs to the top required ascending the first 185 feet, 4.5 inches with this triangular arrangement in Tower No. 2 and then crossing over to Tower No. 3 to climb another 31 feet, 3 inches (10 flights) to reach the penultimate platform. By October 2006, these steps had corroded to the extent that the tower had to be scaled by rope from the outside to replace the aviation light. A similar triangular stairway is found in one of the Tent of Tomorrow columns, providing for access to the roof. Without rust protection, its treads have also long since corroded away.

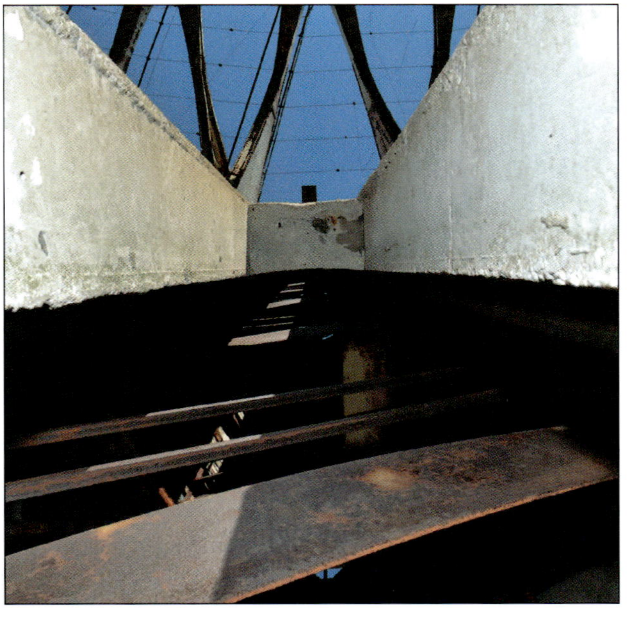

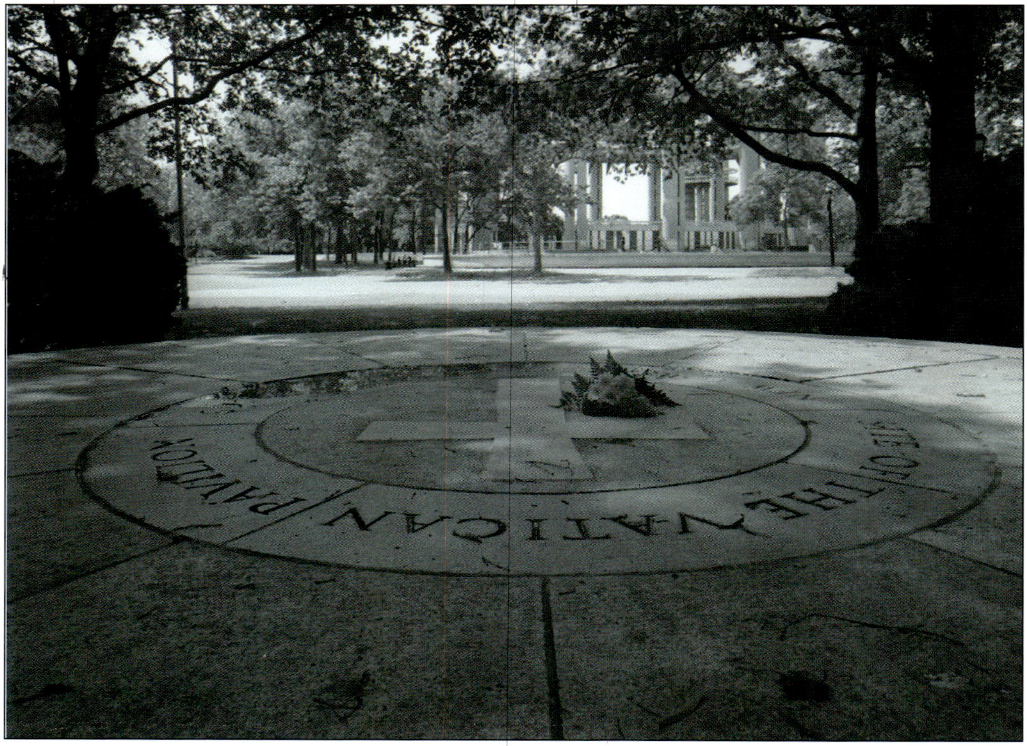

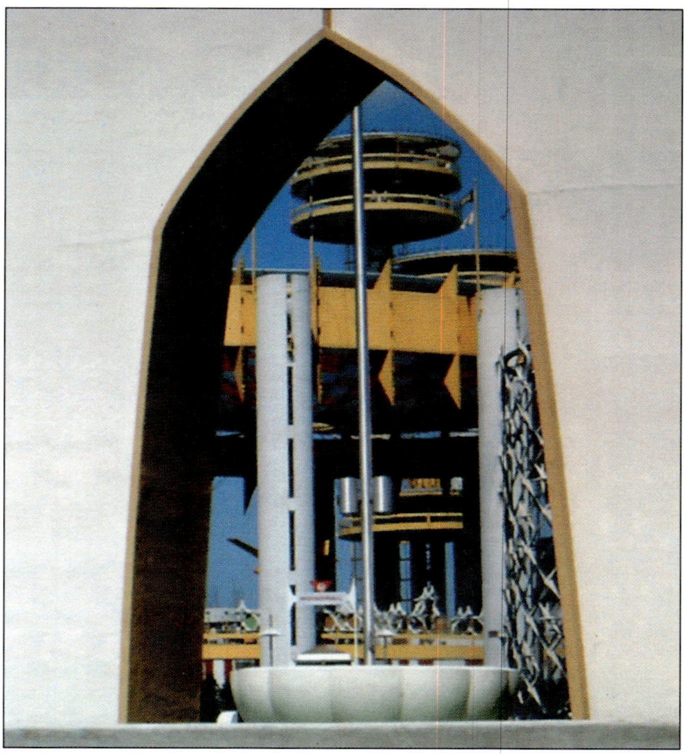

Today, a circular pad and a granite bench monument mark the site where the Vatican pavilion once stood; in the background is the New York State pavilion. The Maloof skateboard park replaced the Astral Fountain that was situated between the two pavilions. The skate park made its debut June 5–6, 2010, with a competition among top professional skateboarders from around the country. At left is an excellent composition of the New York State pavilion as seen through a portal in the Vatican pavilion, which was easily seen from the tower observation platforms. (Left, courtesy of Vincent P. Marchese.)

Note that there are not two elevators going up at the same time to a double observation platform. It is only a clever window-reflection shot of the towers, taken by Van Williams on April 25, 1964. Pictured at right in September 1965 is the tower group during the world's fair, with the Sky-Streak elevator disappearing below the top platform. At 252 feet tall to the top of its aviation light, it is still the tallest building for miles to this day. The eight-sided, glass-enclosed very-important-person (VIP) platform is the lowest platform at 65 feet above the ground. (Right, courtesy of the Queens Museum.)

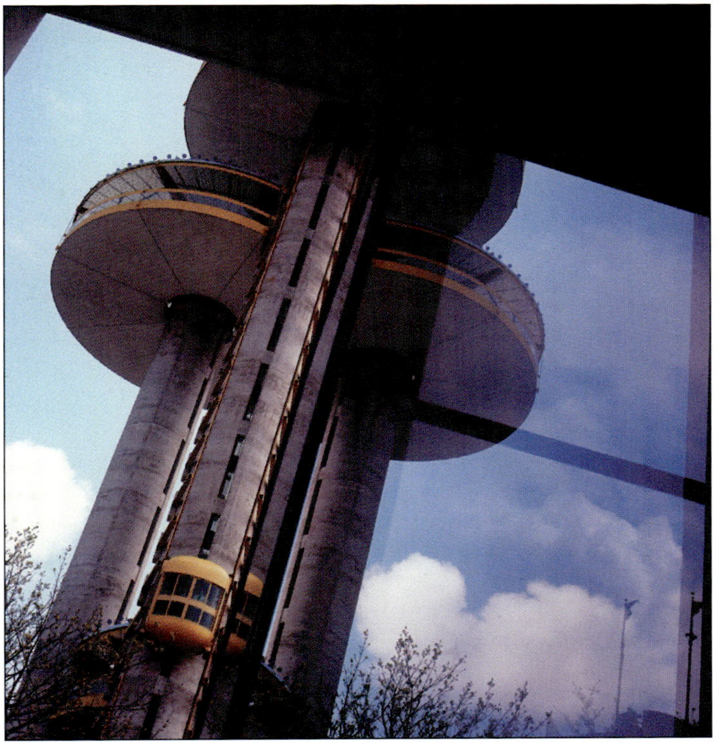

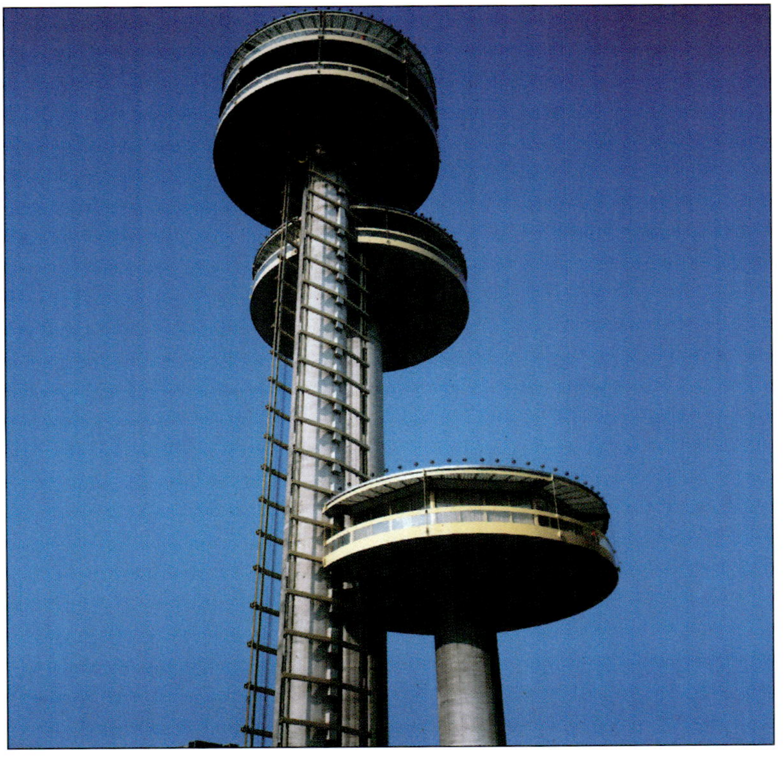

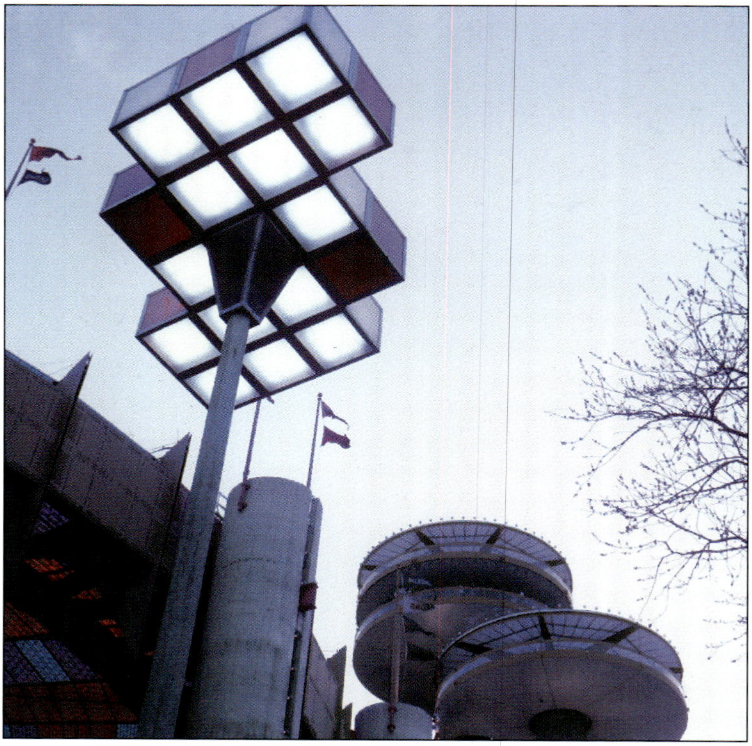

On April 25, 1965, Van Williams took this photograph of the towers at dusk with the tree branches still barren. A street luminaire's staggered arrangement of cubes with colored faces is an interesting contrast to the circular-themed New York State pavilion columns and platforms. The Sky-Streak elevator and a contrasting luminaire provide for a colorful view. These luminaires varied in color, shape, and number of cube elements for each area of the fair, each with a unique theme. (Left, courtesy of the Queens Museum.)

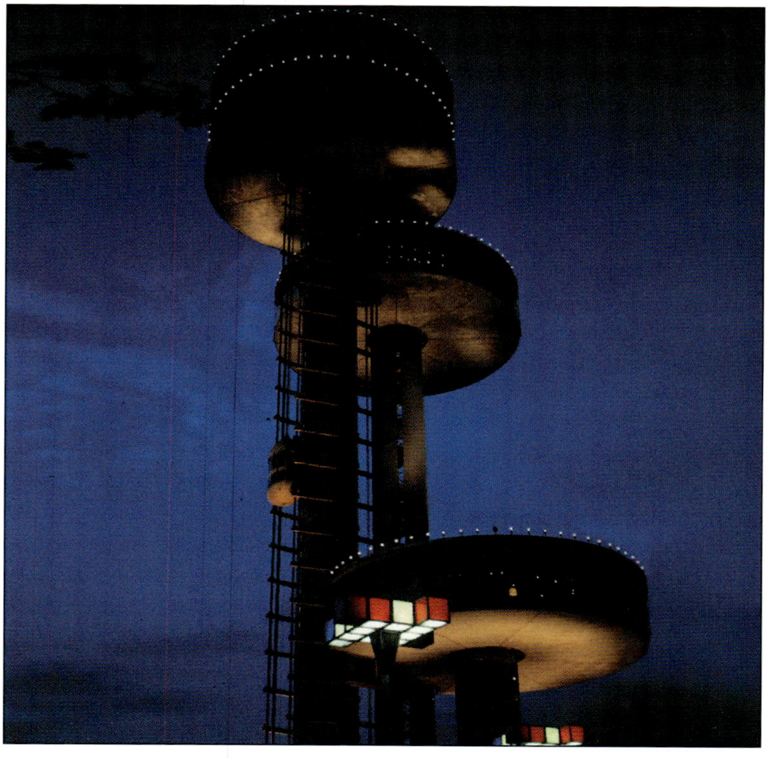

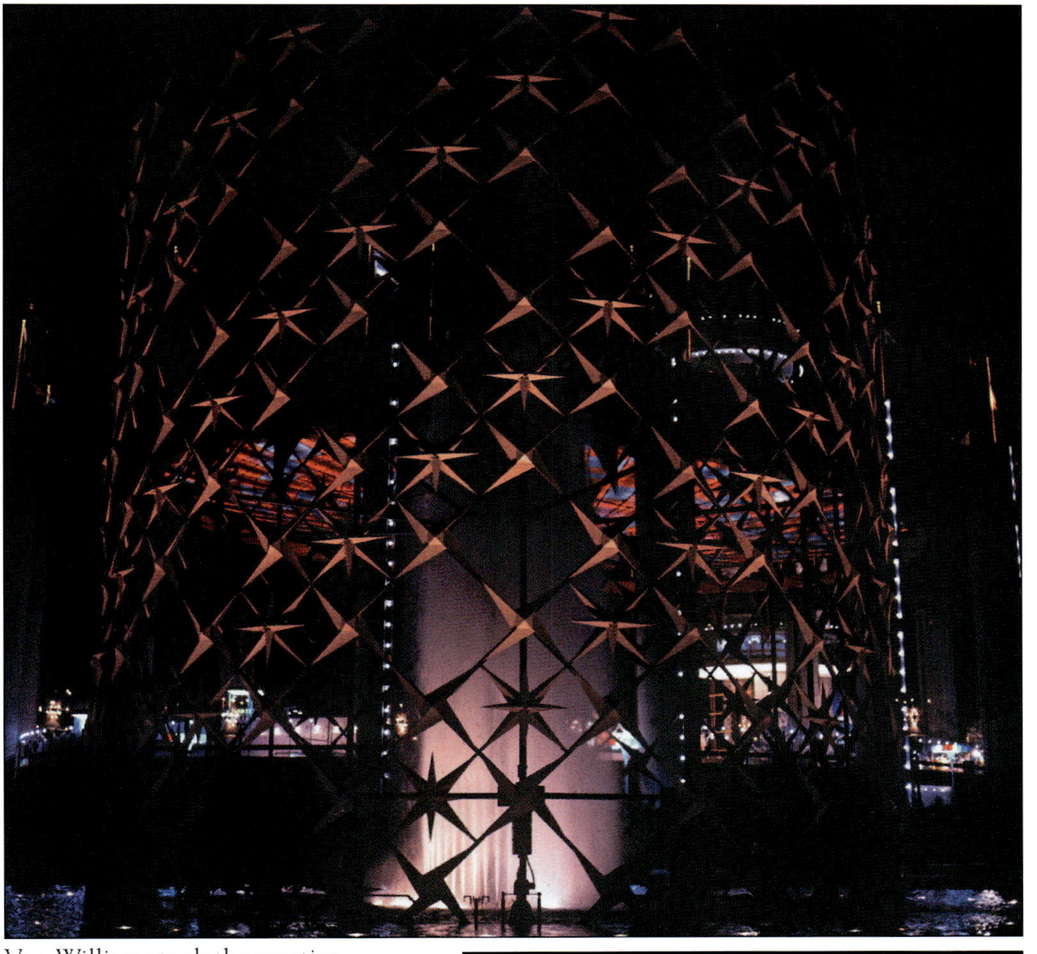

Van Williams took the creative photograph above through the Astral Fountain's decorative center sculpture with the New York State pavilion behind it. The towers at night stood out as a festival of lights, with up lights illuminating the platforms, globe lights ringing each platform, and strung lights the length of each column in the vertical slots. The Sky-Streak capsule elevator can be seen parked at the first deck of the top level, and the lower observation platform's VIP lounge is seen glowing behind its glass enclosure. The Tent of Tomorrow globe lights are actually blue, as seen in various daytime photographs. (Above, courtesy of the Queens Museum.)

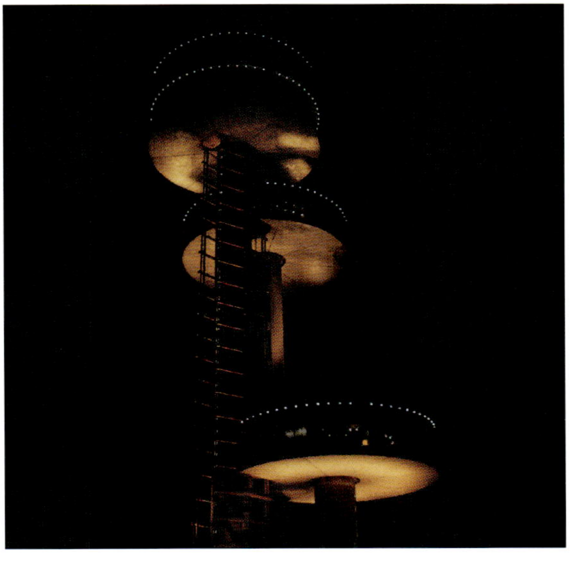

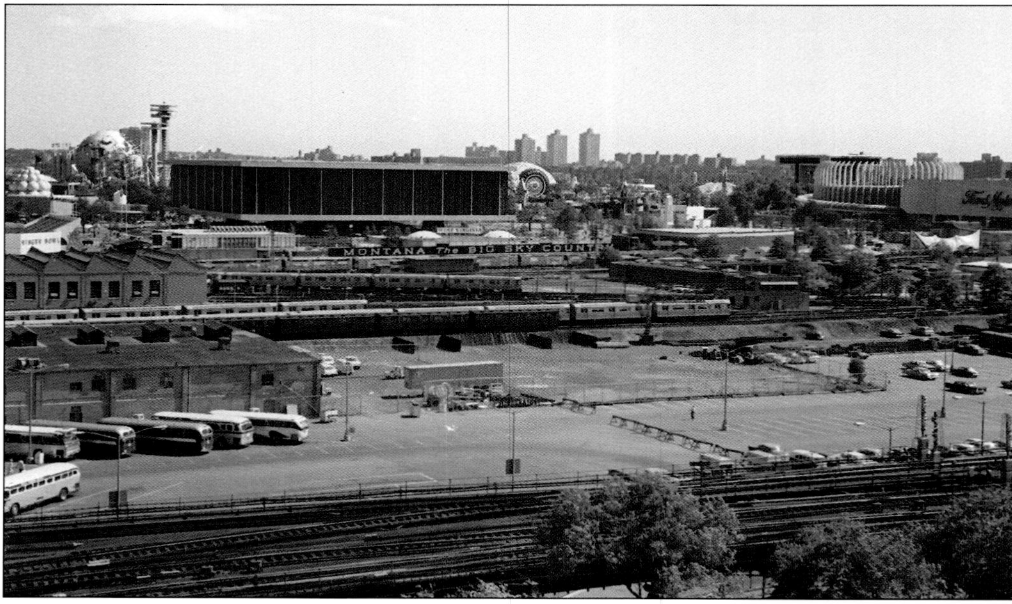

In this photograph, shot from Shea Stadium looking towards the fairgrounds, the New York State pavilion looks out between the Unisphere and the United States pavilion. The Singer Bowl, now reconfigured as the Arthur Ashe Tennis Stadium, appears at left, also a remnant of the fair. The tracks of the No. 7 subway, the main mode of public transportation to the fair, are in the foreground.

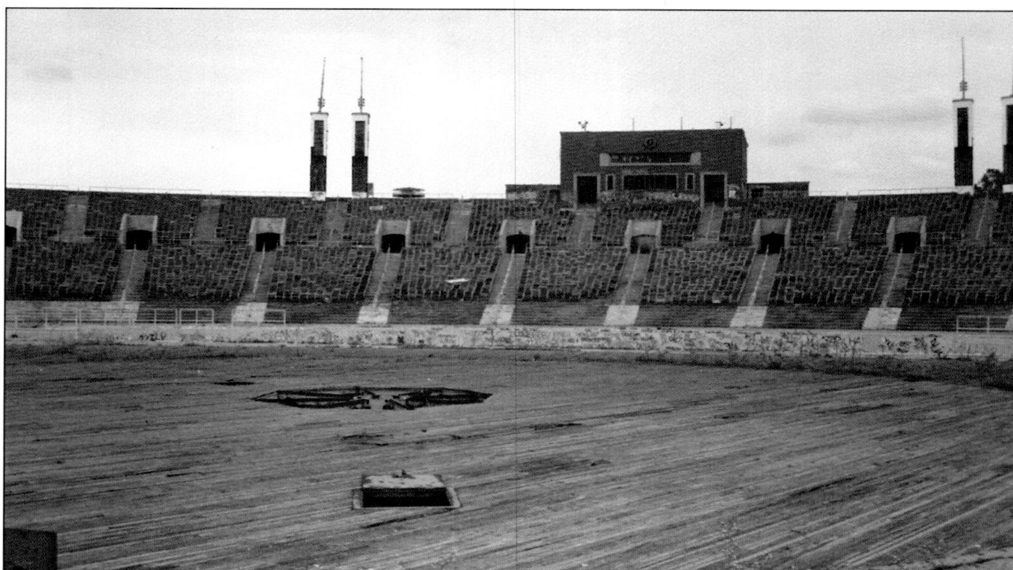

The tower observation platforms were even visible from the aquacade, seen here in October 1989. Another legacy structure that fell into disrepair, only this one was from the 1939 world's fair, was the Billy Rose Aquacade; it was demolished in 1996. The boathouse, restored in 2011, and the New York City pavilion, now the Queens Museum, are the only remaining buildings from the 1939 world's fair.

Five

Theaterama

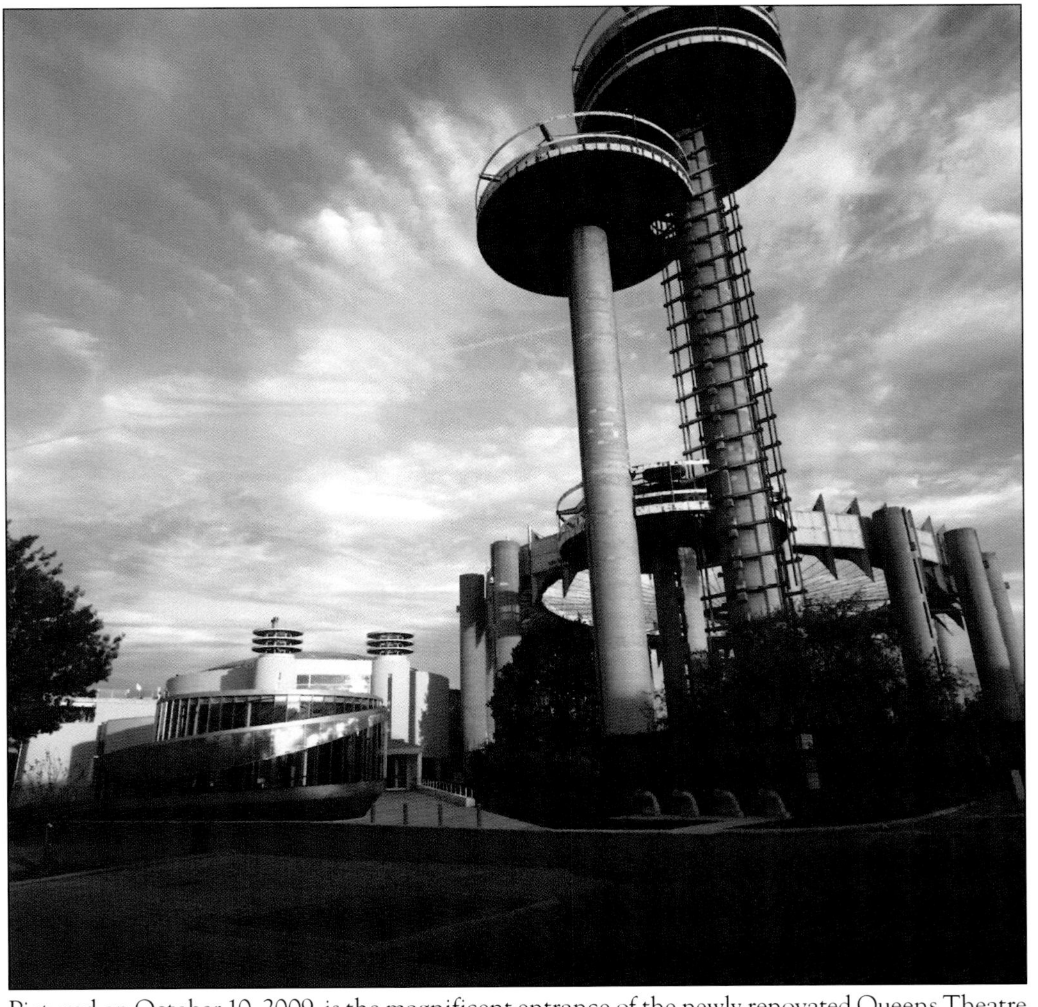

Pictured on October 10, 2009, is the magnificent entrance of the newly renovated Queens Theatre in the Park. In 1972, Theaterama was converted from its world's fair configuration to a performing arts venue. The Queens Theatre was officially established in 1989, after a $4 million renovation; it opened on October 16, 1993.

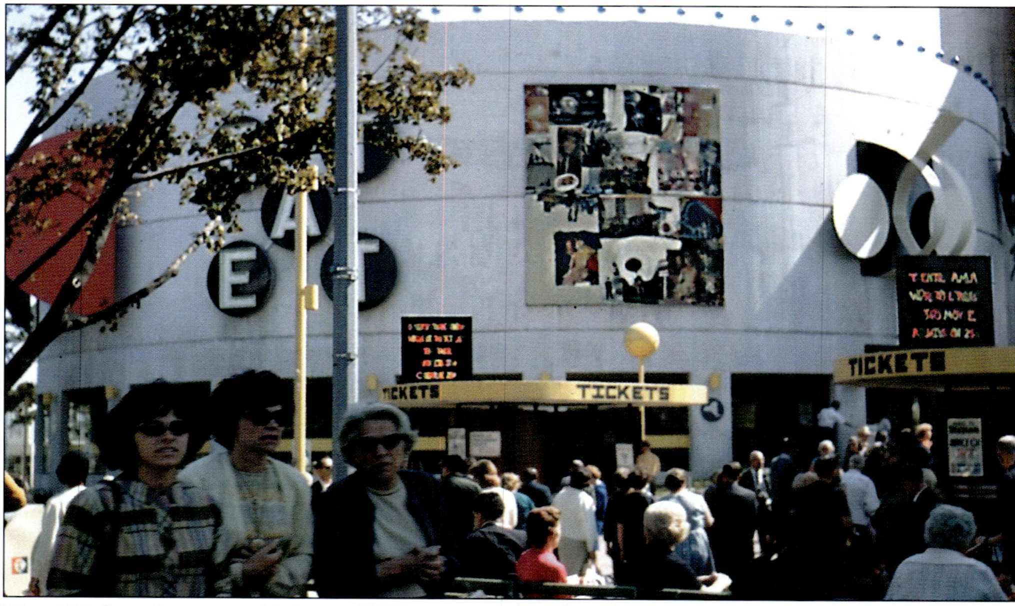

The 100-foot-diameter, 44-foot-tall Theaterama building featured a film tour of New York State, called *Round New York*, using the interior wall as a 360-degree screen. The building was known for its 10 large Pop Art displays, located on its facade, by emerging artists. All were commissioned by Philip Johnson himself who saw them as the perfect complement to the Googie architecture of the pavilion. (Courtesy of the Mike Kraus collection.)

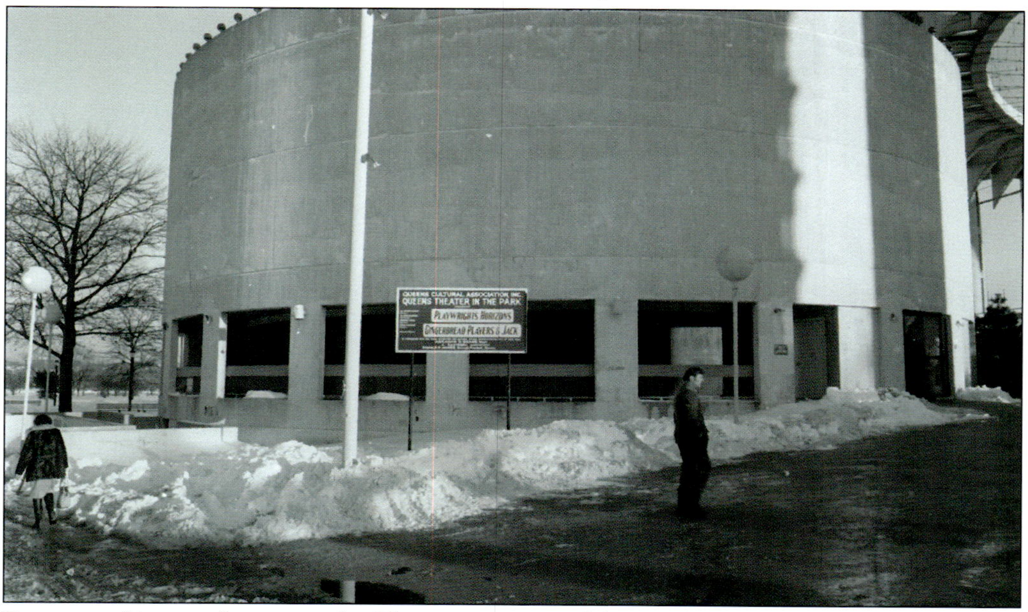

For most of its post-fair years, the Theaterama part of the pavilion has found reuse, operating as a playhouse since 1972. Taking the name Queens Theatre in the Park, after a 1993 remodel, it has grown to 464-seat theater, putting on 300 performances for 100,000 visitors per year. A second expansion in 2008 added a glass-walled, 3,000-square-foot lobby. This photograph was taken in January 1978.

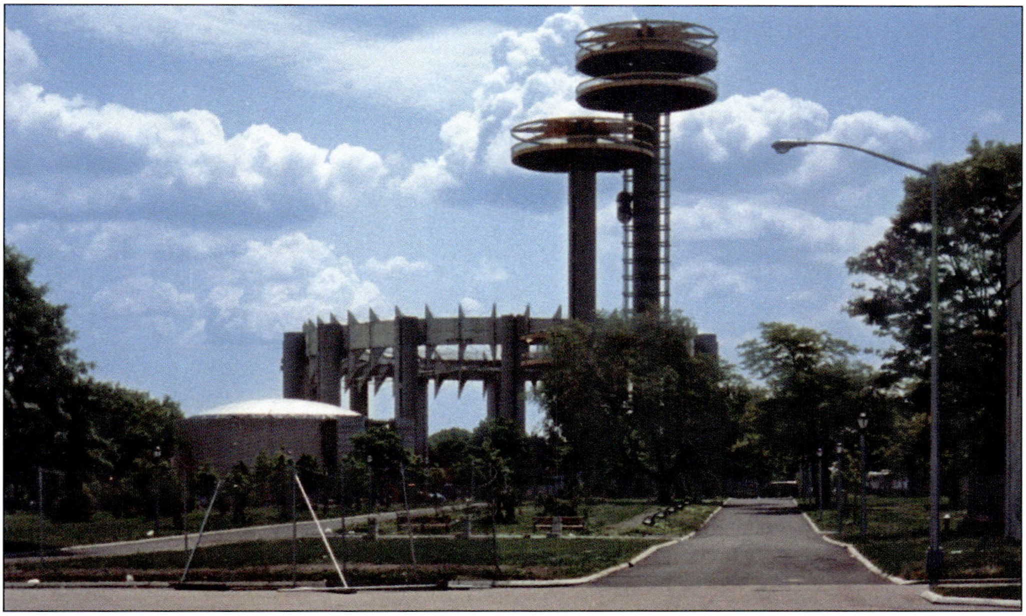

In these construction photographs from May 1992, work was under way for the theater's new entrance and box office. Two 44-foot-tall concrete columns were poured on either side of the entrance using the same slip-form method employed for the original pavilion. In the photograph above, one of the completed columns can be seen in relation to the Tent of Tomorrow columns. These entrance columns were then topped with a trio of disks, each on an eight-spoke steel fitting that mimics the observation tower platforms. The completed entrance was painted yellow to match the original color of the pavilion's crown.

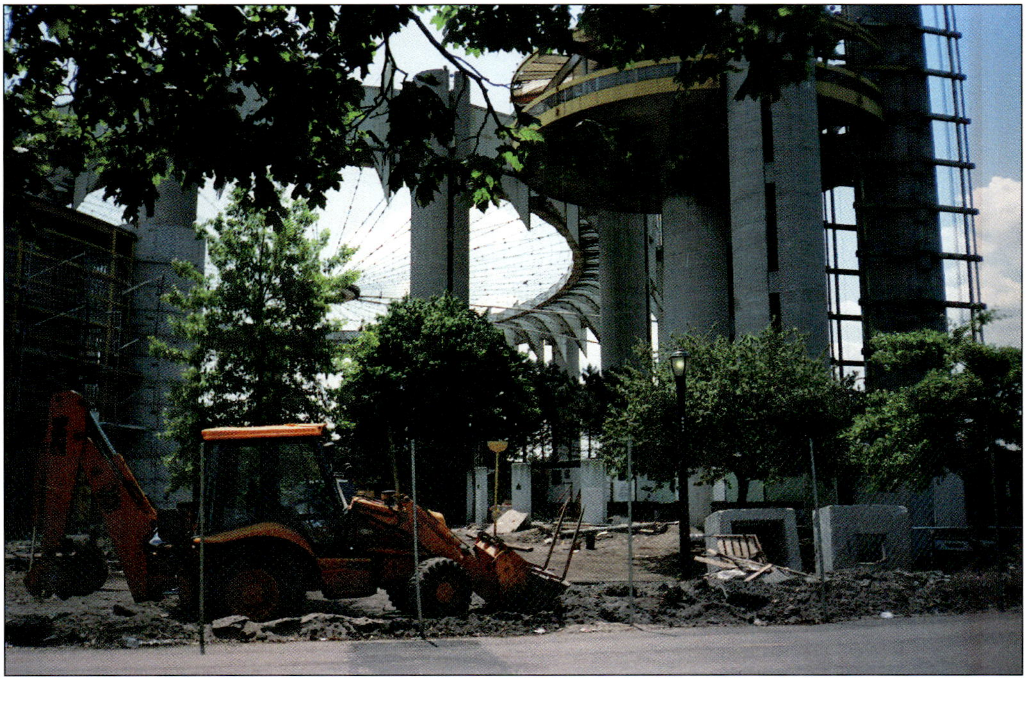

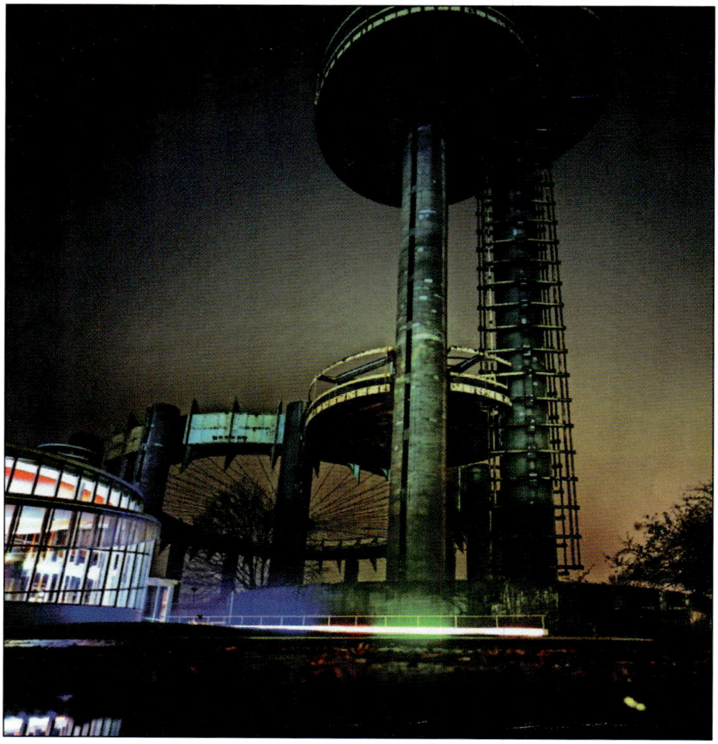

These nighttime views of Queens Theatre in the Park show the main entrance and ramp leading up to the new glass-walled reception lobby. With the colorful street luminaires of the fair long gone, the theater presents a welcoming sight that harkens back to the fair's festive atmosphere. Excellent interior lighting and accent paint on the ceiling combine with reflections after a rain to amplify the effect, and even the observation towers manage to catch some of the glow. The bright Queens Theatre in the Park stands in contrast to a darkened Tent of Tomorrow seen in the photograph below.

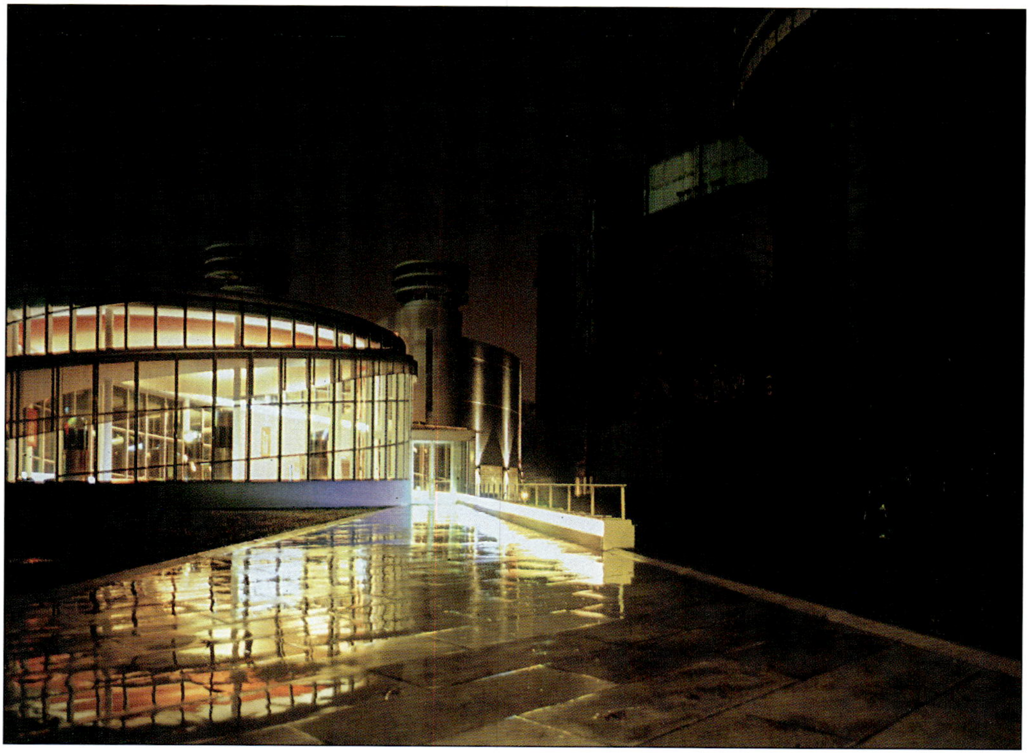

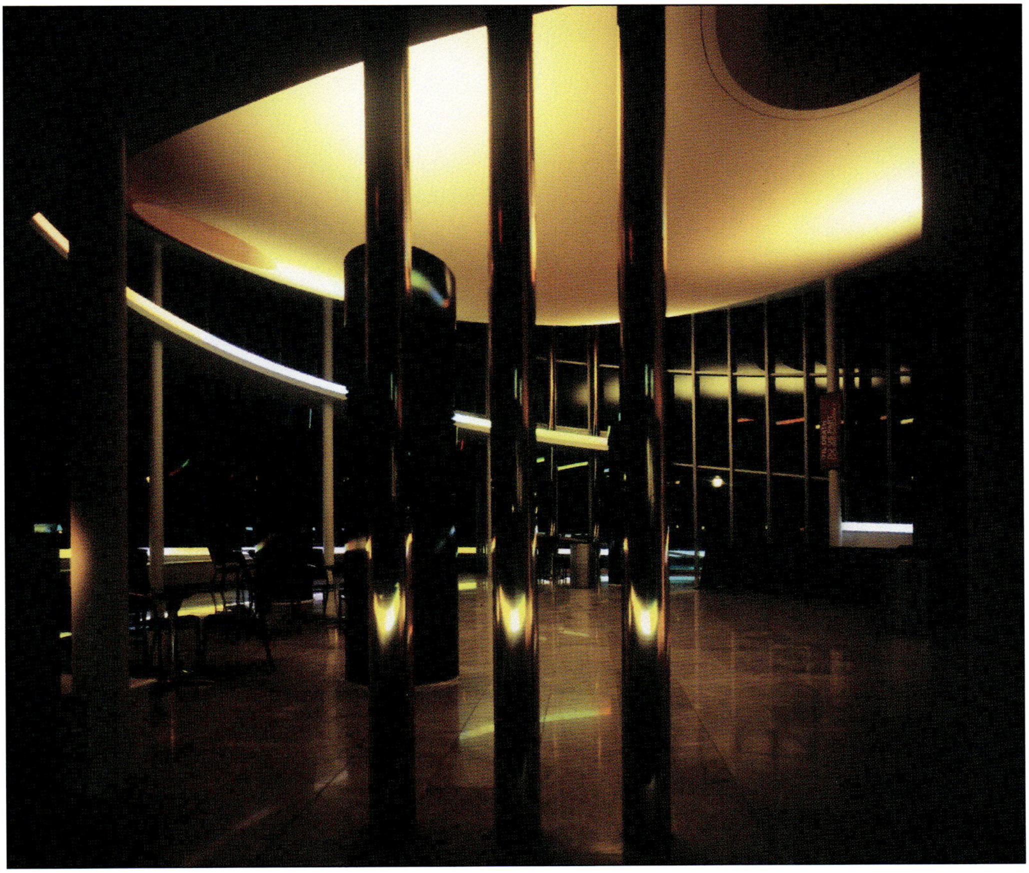

The interior lighting of the entrance lobby is enhanced by its reflection off the polished marble floor. A curved light fixture, chromed posts, oval skylight, and spiral-patterned exterior window frames highlight this unique space. It is interesting to note that this glass-walled reception area has a functional similarity to Philip Johnson's Glass House residence in New Canaan, Connecticut. The photograph at right shows that the building still retains the original rear-facing circular exterior wall. A darkened Tent of Tomorrow is partially illuminated by light shining through the glass blocks that now fill the openings around the lower wall.

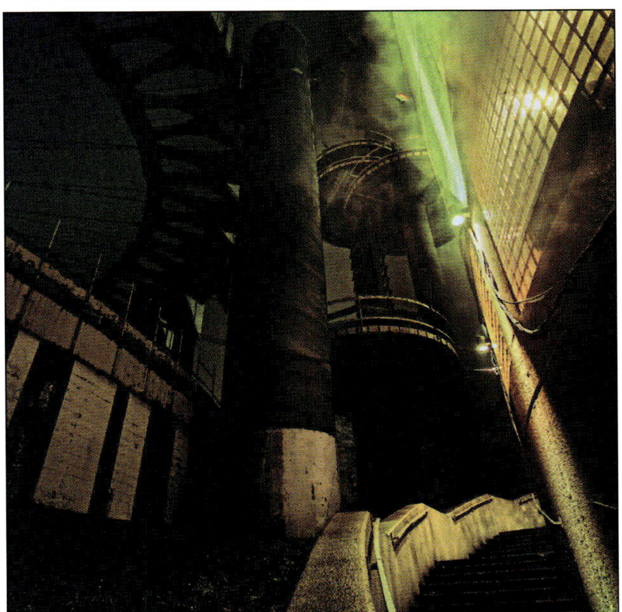

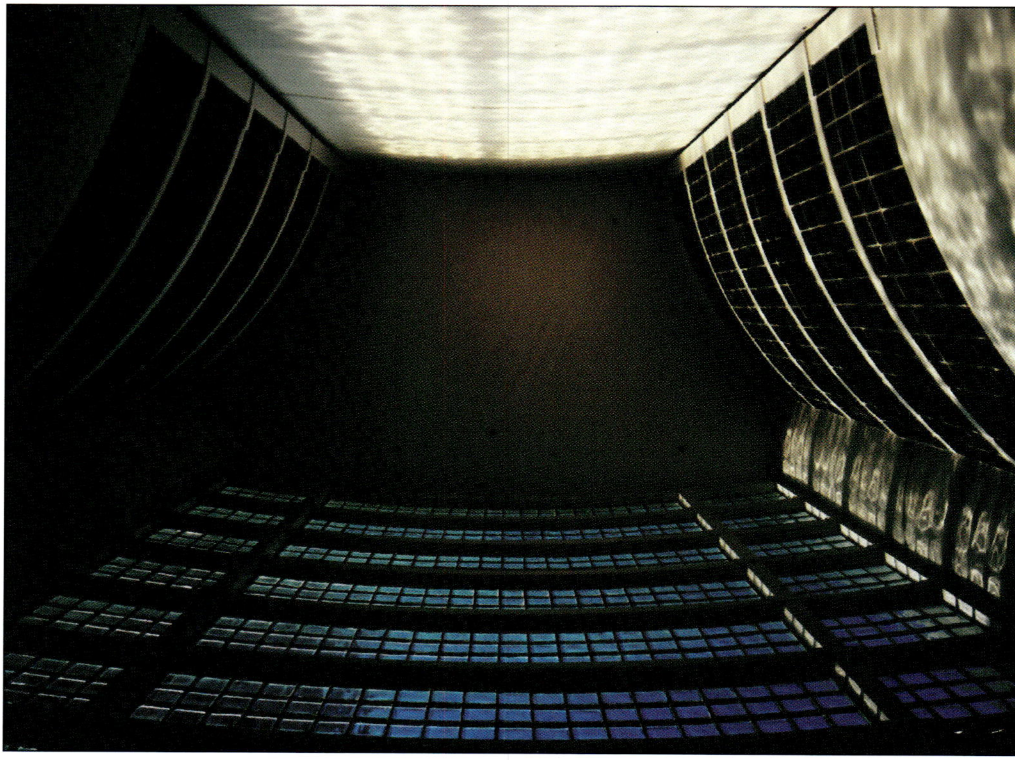

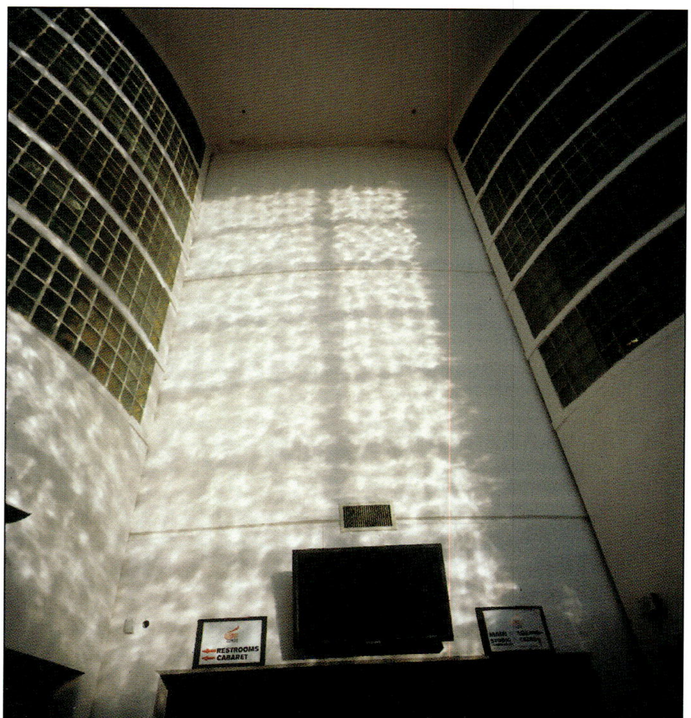

Once inside the Queens Theatre in the Park, walking through the lobby and past the box office, one can again see that the original circular exterior wall of Theaterama has been retained and integrated into the new design. Daylight streams through the outside glass blocks, forming a pattern on the wall where James Rosenquist's *Skyway* once hung. Note that the secondary inner walls curving out from the Theaterama exterior also have glass block. Taken together with a fishbowl-like lobby reception area, surrounded by glass, skylights, and glass blocks, this recent expansion has added many creative lighting enhancements to the theater.

The photograph at right, taken from the back of Queens Theatre in the Park's 464-seat auditorium, shows the stage being set up for a new show on October 10, 2009. Not generally known is the presence of a treasure trove of history in the form of props, set items, and ephemera dating back to the 1970s from the Queens Theatre in rooms under the mezzanine of the New York State pavilion's Tent of Tomorrow. In the photograph below is one such item. An urban archeology project in waiting; hopefully, they will be evaluated and cataloged one day.

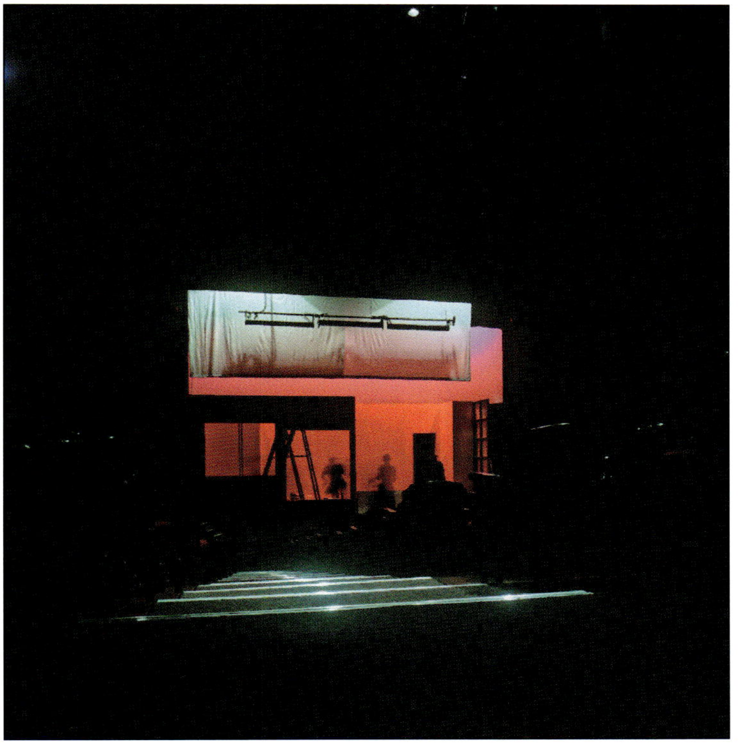

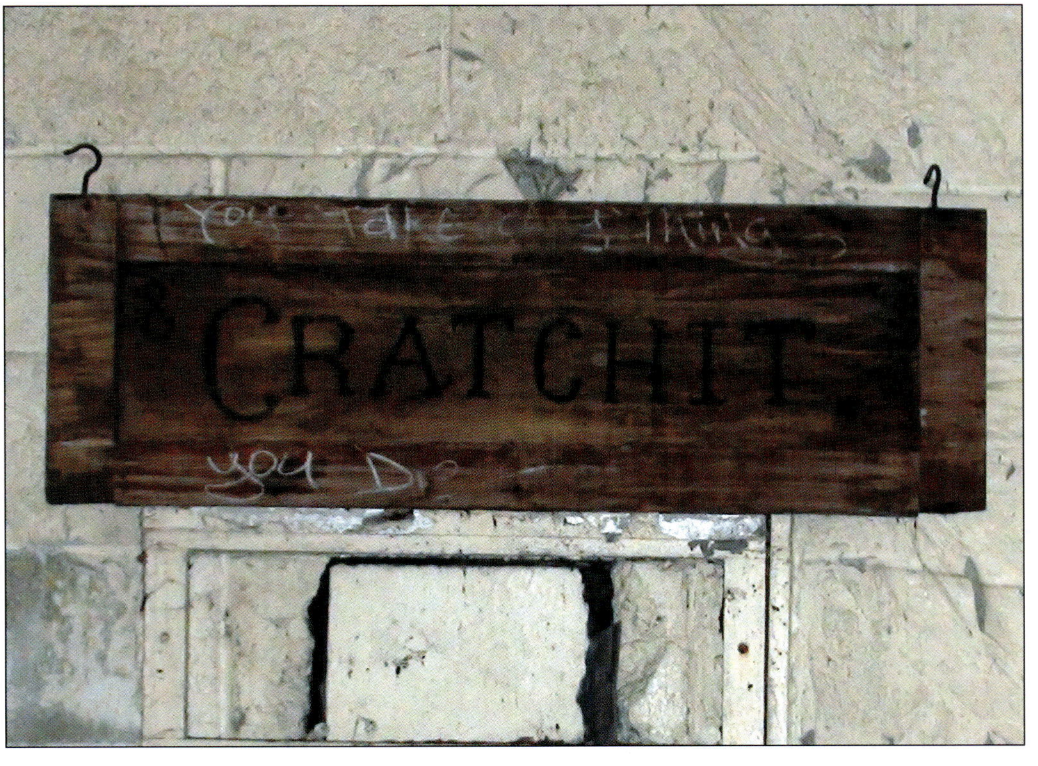

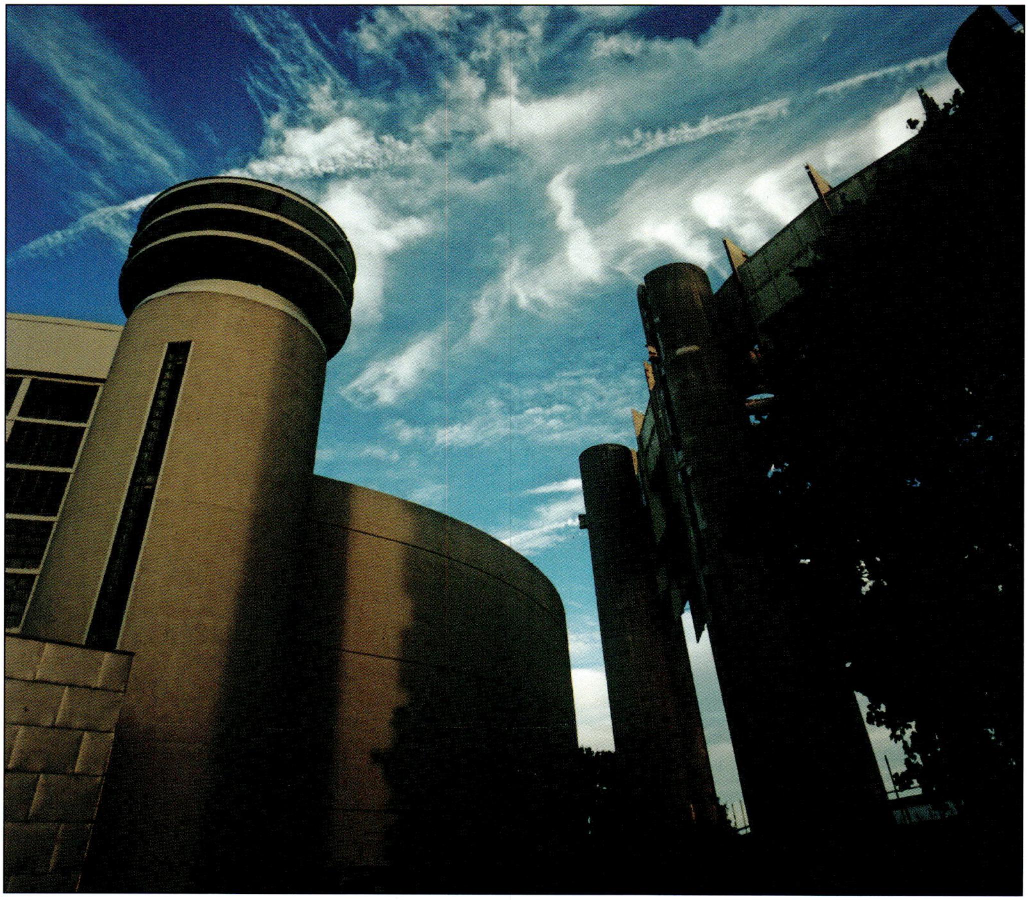

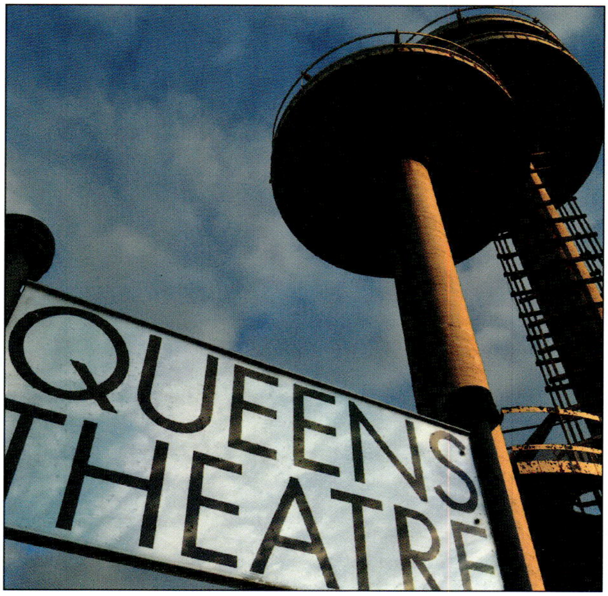

Above is another view from October 10, 2009, of the Queens Theatre in the Park in relation to the rest of the New York State pavilion. The original 44-foot-tall circular rear wall faces the Tent of Tomorrow, and one of the new accent columns can be seen. In a measure of attention to detail, as part of the theater's renovation, the "Queens Theatre" sign in front has a three-tier accent on top of its upright posts that mimic the tower observation platforms.

Six

10 Works of Pop Art on the New York State Pavilion

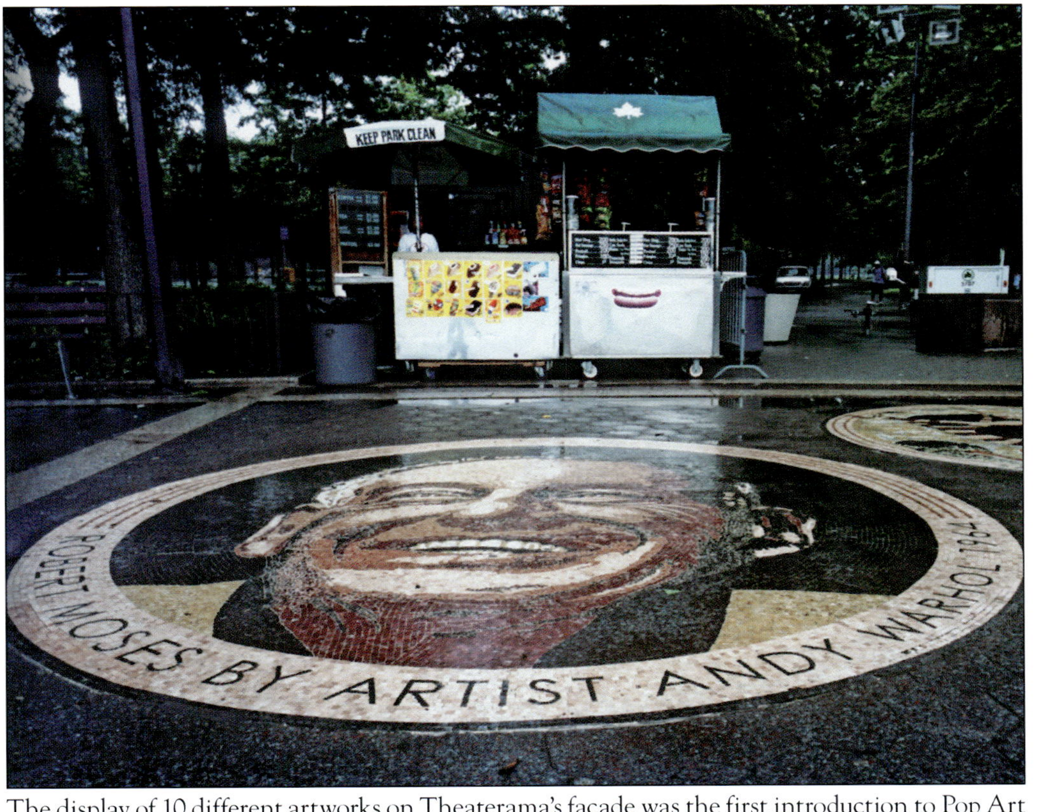

The display of 10 different artworks on Theaterama's facade was the first introduction to Pop Art for millions. When Andy Warhol's *Thirteen Most Wanted Men* was painted over, he proposed 25 Robert Moses portraits instead, an idea rejected by Philip Johnson, who had the political savvy to see the consequences. Ironically, the names of Andy Warhol and Robert Moses, who had no mutual admiration, are forever cemented together in this mosaic of Warhol's *Moses* mosaic by the entrance to Flushing Meadows Corona Park.

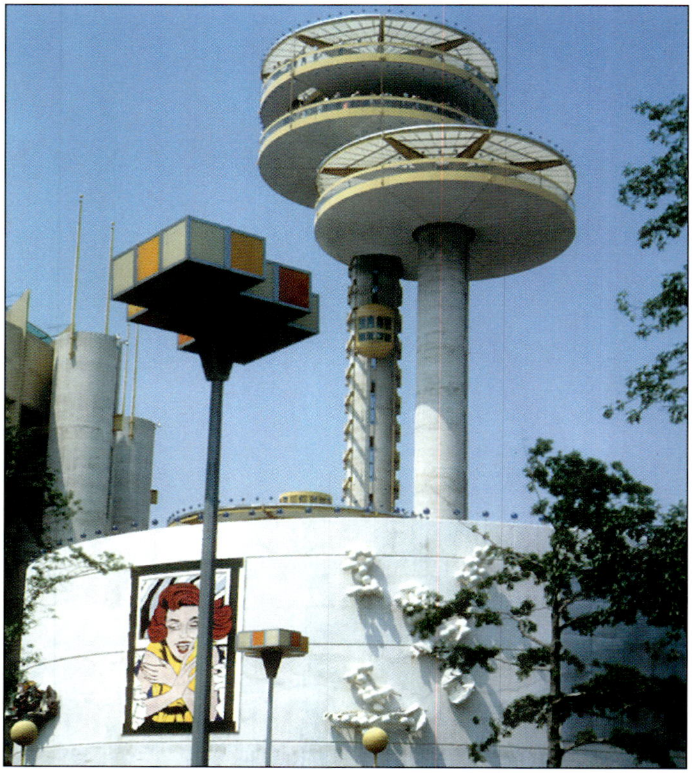

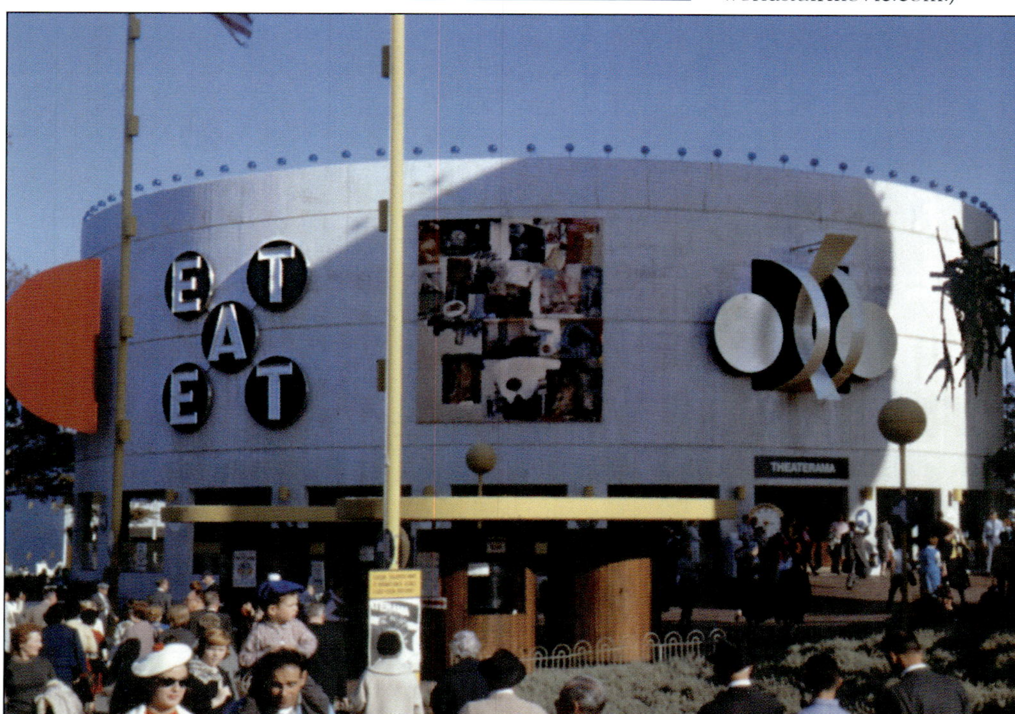

The Pop Art at left includes, from left to right, John Chamberlain's untitled work; Roy Lichtenstein's large version of *Girl in a Window*; Peter Agostini's *A Windy Autumn Day*; and Andy Warhol's *Thirteen Most Wanted Men*, which has been concealed with silver paint. James Rosenquist's *World's Fair Mural* is just out of view on the right. The Pop Art below includes, from left to right, Ellsworth Kelly's *Two Curves*; Robert Indiana's *EAT*; Robert Rauschenberg's *Skyway*; Alexander Liberman's *Prometheus*; and Robert Mallary's *Cliffhangers*. (Left, courtesy of the Bill Cotter collection; below, photograph by Alan Lovitch, courtesy of Ryan Ritchey for worldsfairmovie.com.)

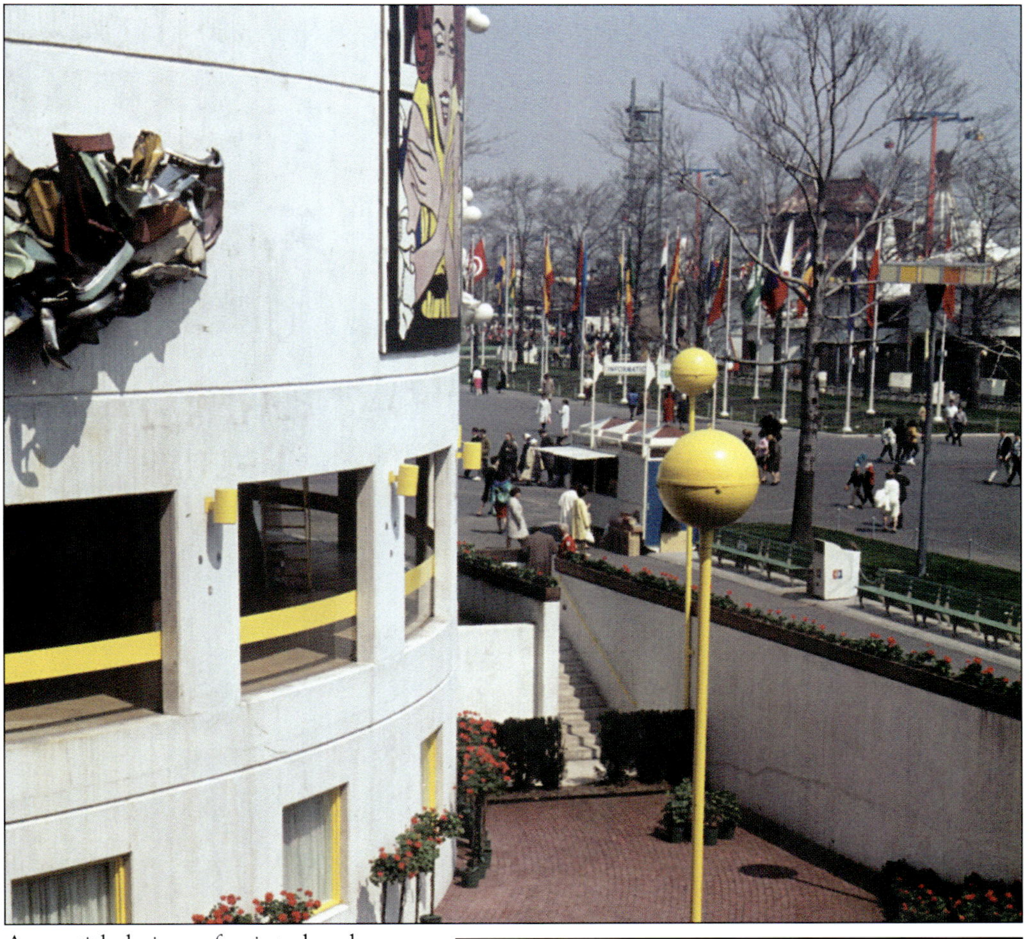

An untitled piece of painted and chrome crushed car parts by John Chamberlain was on loan from the Leo Castelli Gallery of New York City and lost after the fair. The late John Chamberlain was known as the artist of auto metal. He resided and worked on Shelter Island, New York. In 1964, he gained international recognition with exhibitions in Paris and at the Venice Biennale. Roy Lichtenstein's work, *Girl in the Window*, appears in the above photograph and at right. (Above, courtesy the Estate of Roy Lichtenstein; right, courtesy of the Bill Cotter collection.)

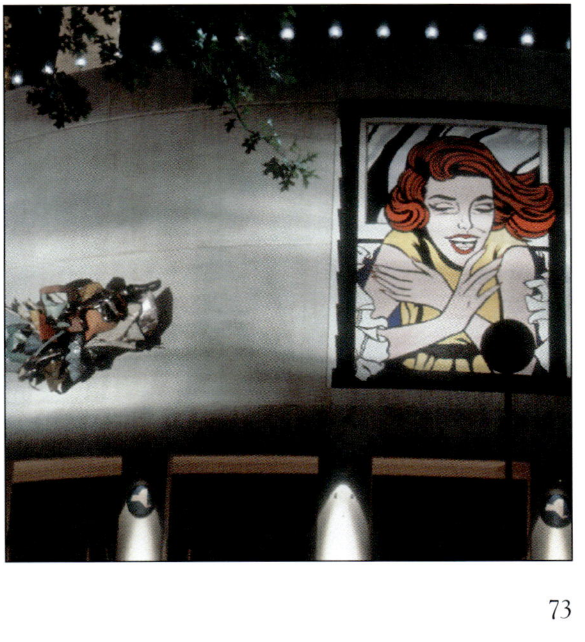

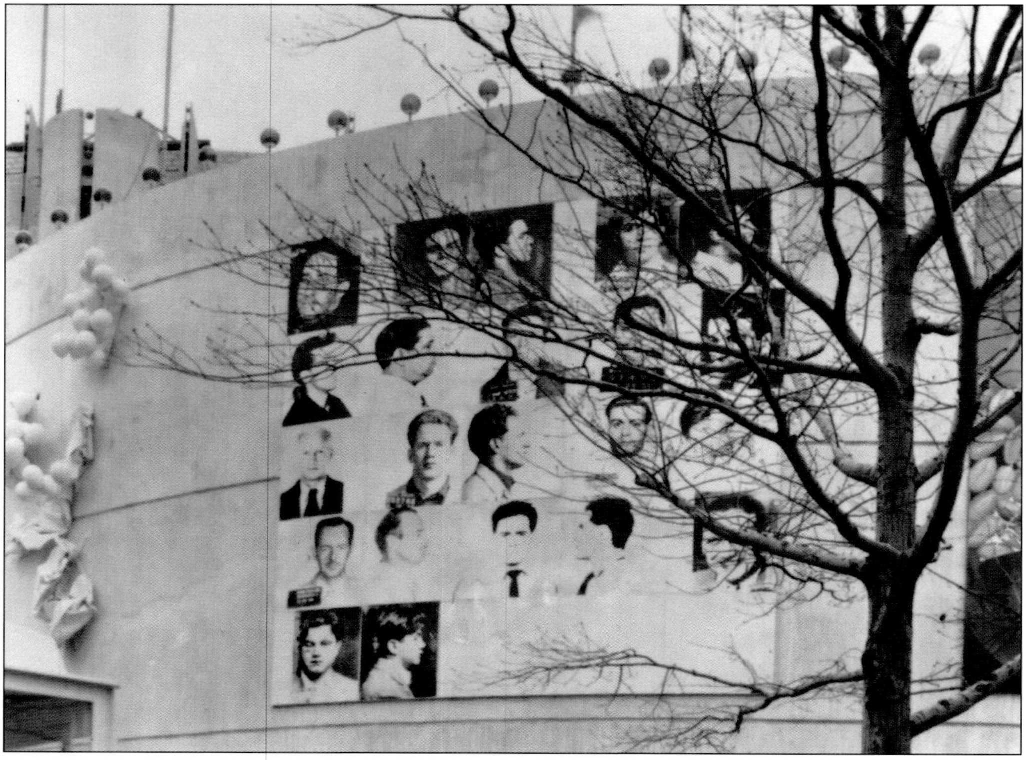

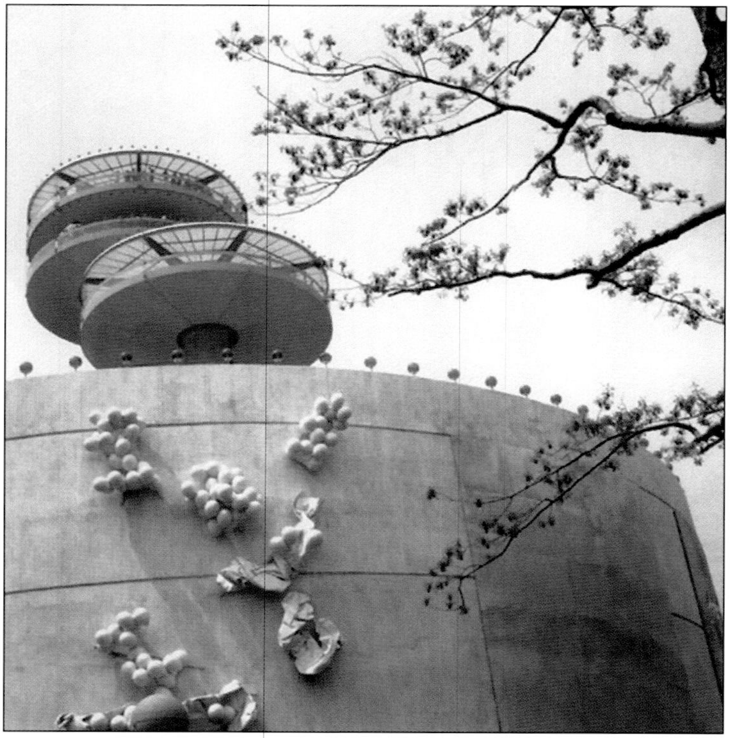

Thirteen Most Wanted Men by Andy Warhol was painted over with silver paint days before the fair opened. The 22 mug shots, silk-screened on 22 of the 25 square canvases that made up the 20-by-20-foot work, were scrapped after the fair. The painted over work is visible next to Peter Agostini's *A Windy Autumn Day* (currently in a Brooklyn storage facility). Unlike Warhol, Agostini got along well with Robert Moses (Above, copyright 2014 the Andy Warhol Foundation for the Visual Arts, Inc./Artists Rights Society, New York; left, courtesy of the Bill Cotter collection.)

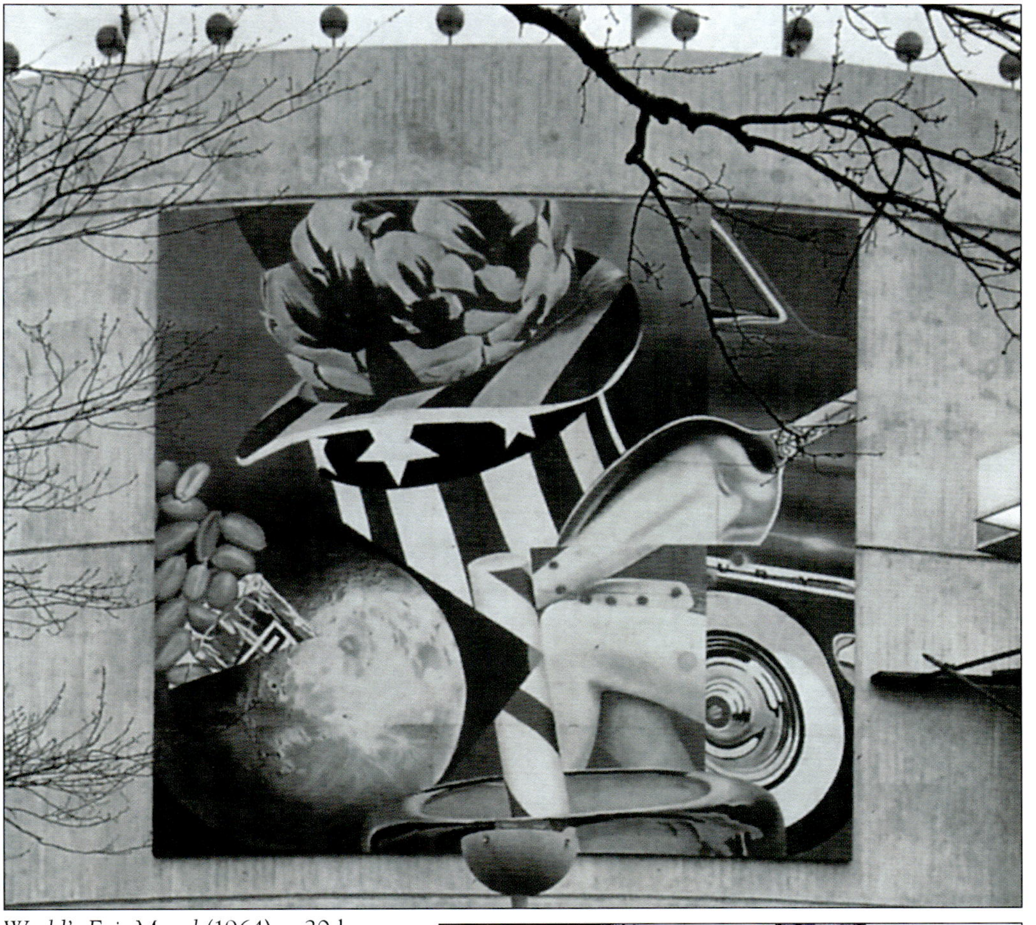

World's Fair Mural (1964), a 20-by-20-foot oil painting on Masonite by James Rosenquist, is now at the University of Minnesota Art Museum. It is interesting to note that this is listed on his website as part of a group show on Circarama, which was the original concept name for Theaterama. The colorful piece is hidden behind trees between the painted-over work by Andy Warhol and the Ellsworth Kelly's *Two Curves*, seen from the blue side. (Above, courtesy of Jim Strong, copyright James Rosenquist/VAGA New York 1988 www.vagarights.com.)

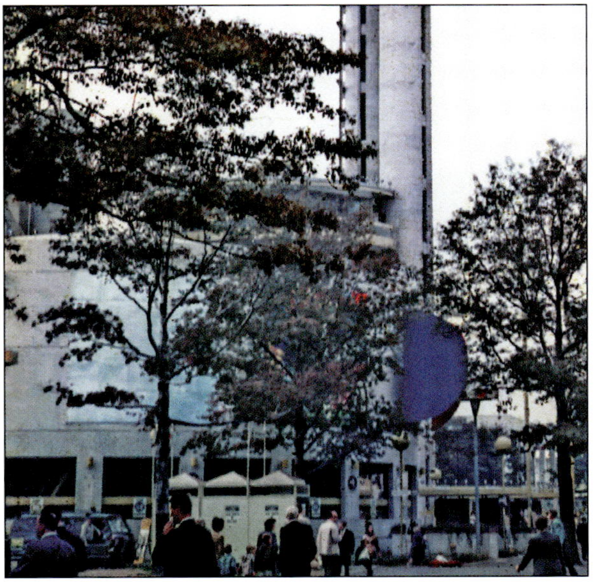

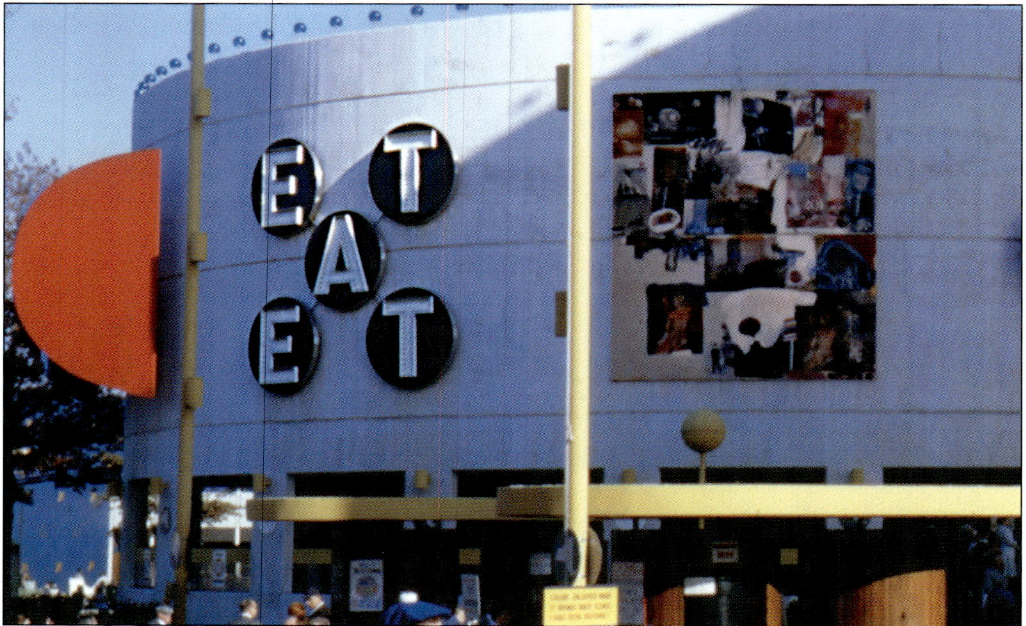

EAT by Robert Indiana, a sculpture of five aluminum discs with letters illuminated by a marquee-style outline of lightbulbs, has been displayed seasonally on the roof of the Farnsworth Art Museum in Maine since 2009. *Two Curves*, an 18-by-18-foot aluminum sculpture by Ellsworth Kelly, which appears to the left of the *EAT* sculpture, is now mounted on the Peabody Terrace Garage at Harvard University. (Above, photograph by Alan Lovitch, courtesy of Ryan Ritchey for worldsfairmovie.com, copyright 2014 Morgan Art Foundation/Artists Rights Society, New York; below, courtesy of the Farnsworth Art Museum.)

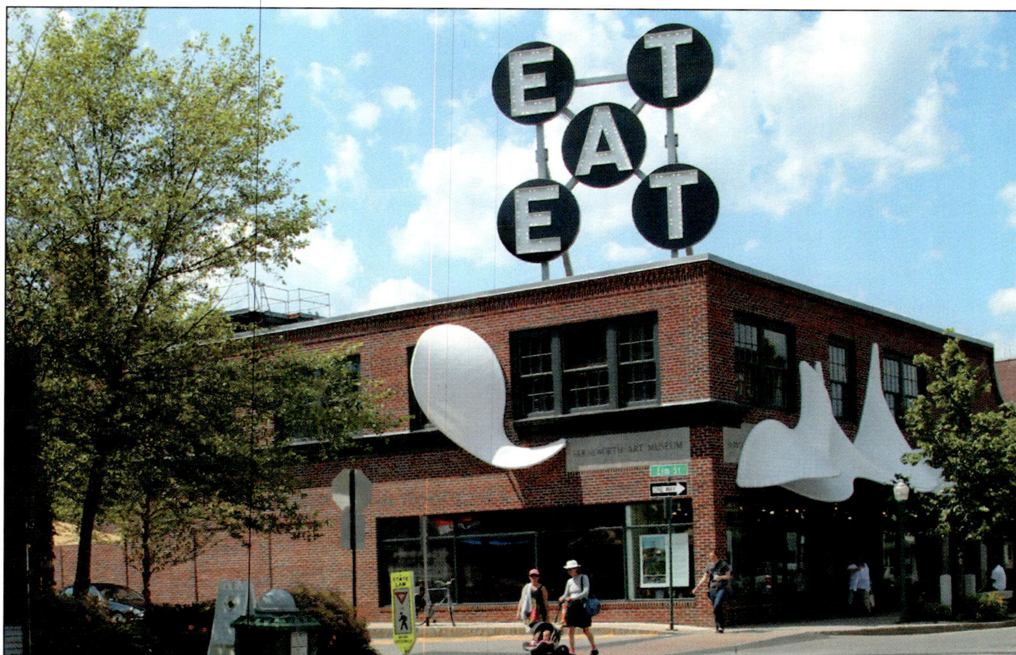

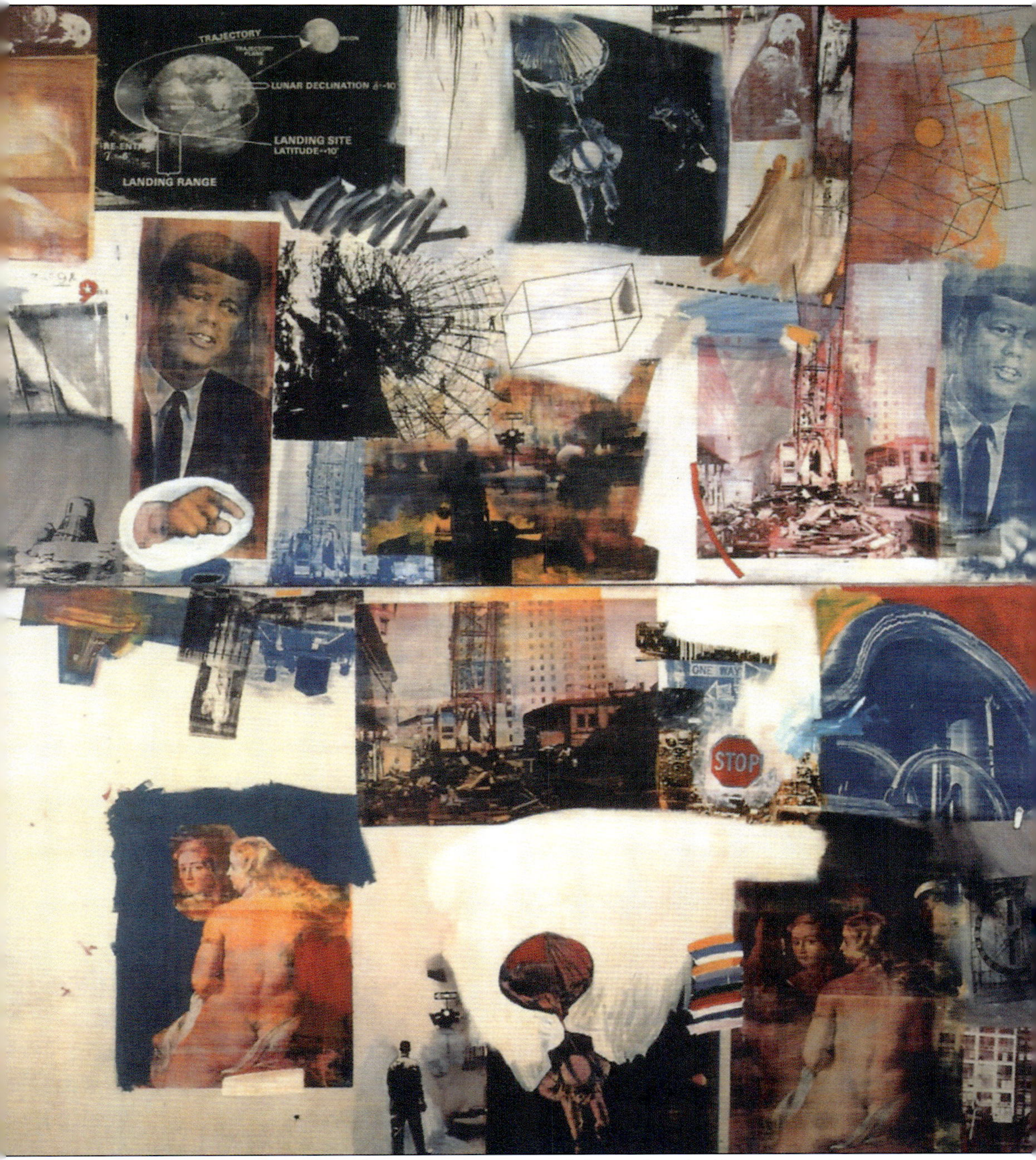

Skyway (1964) by Robert Rauschenberg is an 18-by-16-foot oil and silkscreen work on canvas, located today at the Dallas Museum of Art. It is an eclectic collage of images, from an iconic Pres. John Kennedy to Peter Paul Ruben's *Toilet of Venus*, each appearing twice but in different colors. Like all of the 10 Pop artworks, Philip Johnson commissioned it. Rauschenberg's decision to include Kennedy's image was done before the assassination. (Copyright VAGA New York www.vagarights.com.)

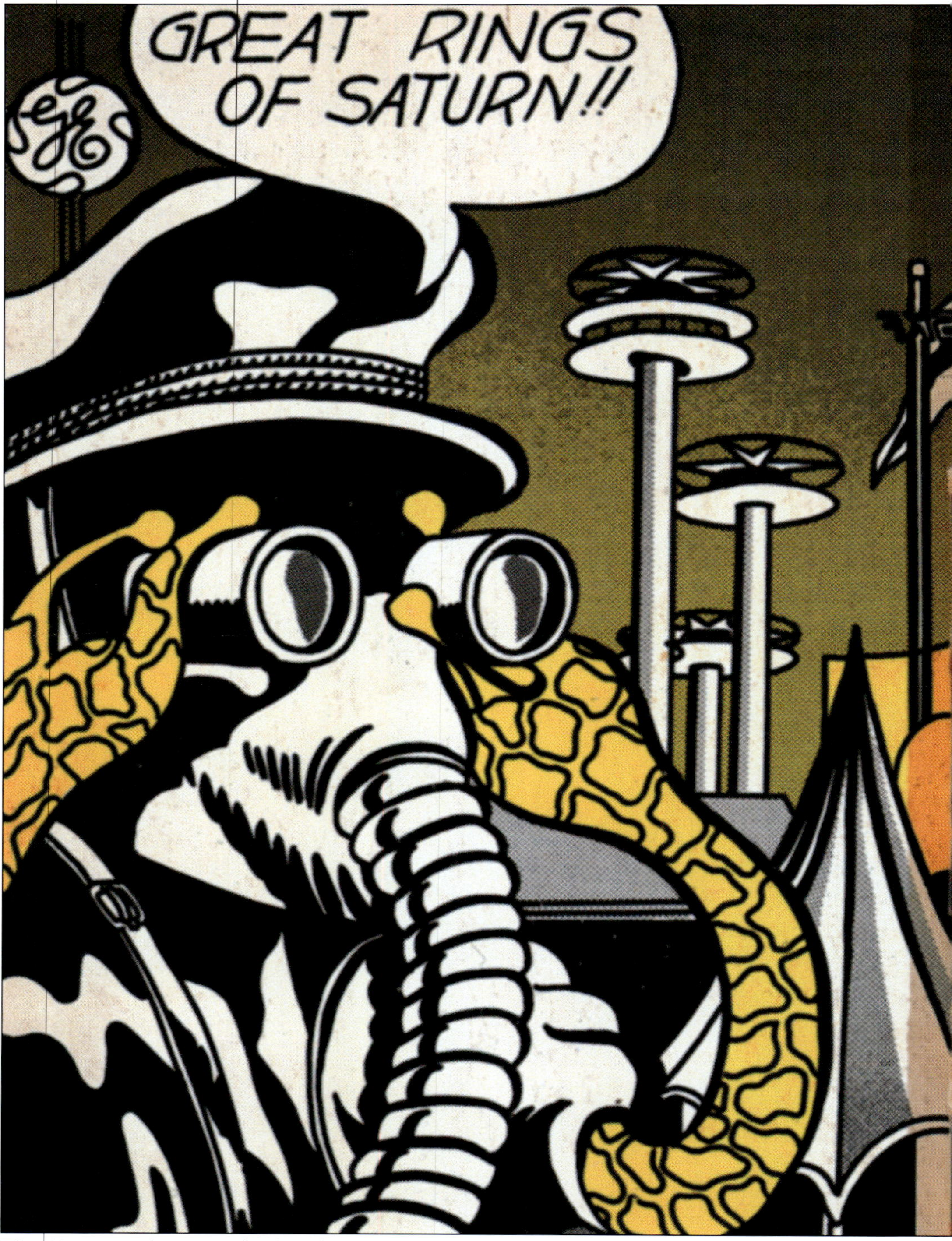

The 10 pieces of Pop Art displayed outside of Theaterama served to highlight the contemporary artistic tastes of its architect, Philip Johnson, and the state's governor, Nelson Rockefeller. The artwork went with the Googie style of the New York State pavilion. The above painting is a

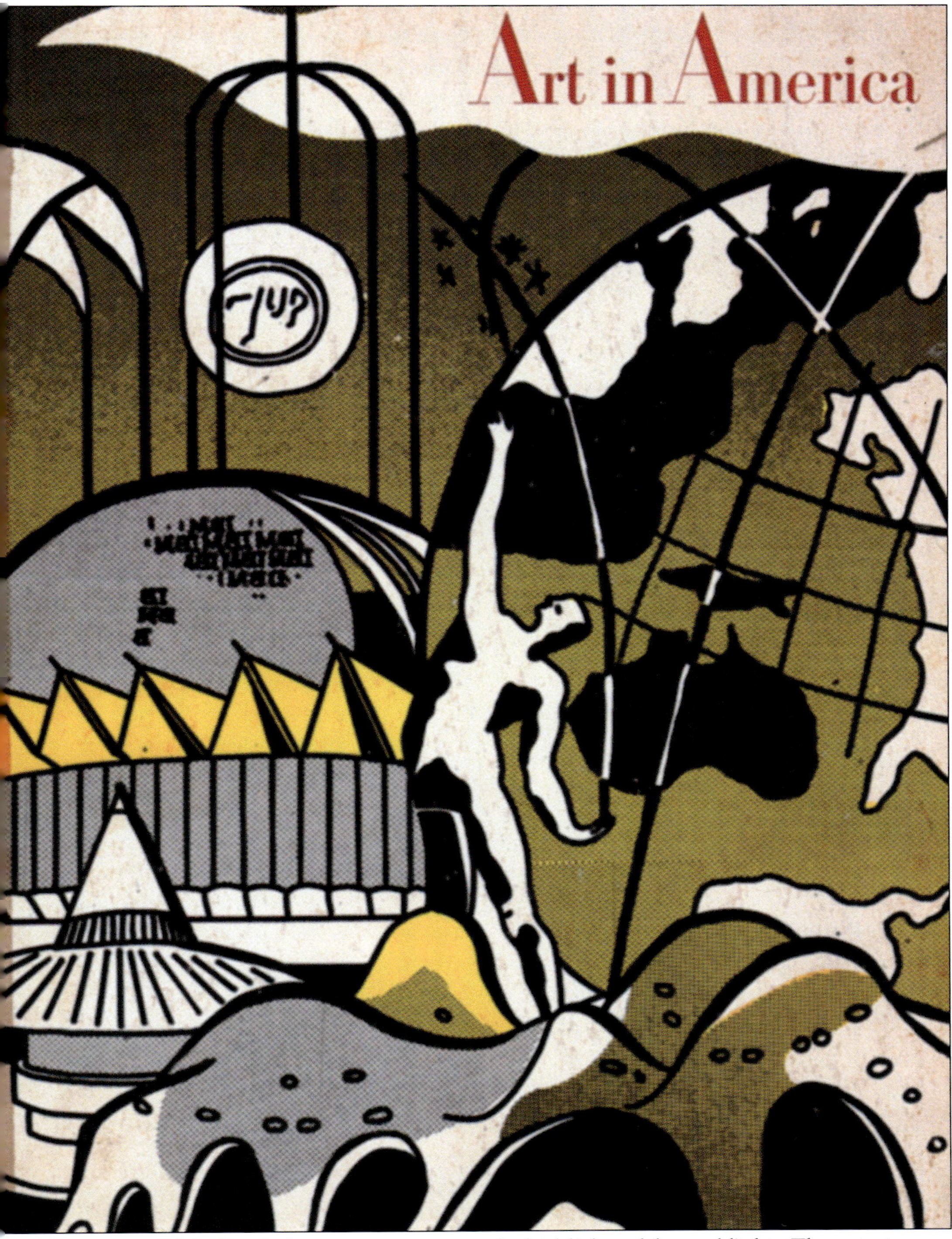

separate work by Roy Lichtenstein; it captures the highlights of the world's fair. The painting was used for the cover of the April 1964 issue of *Art in America*. (Copyright the Sterling and Francine Clark Art Institute with permission from the Estate of Roy Lichtenstein.)

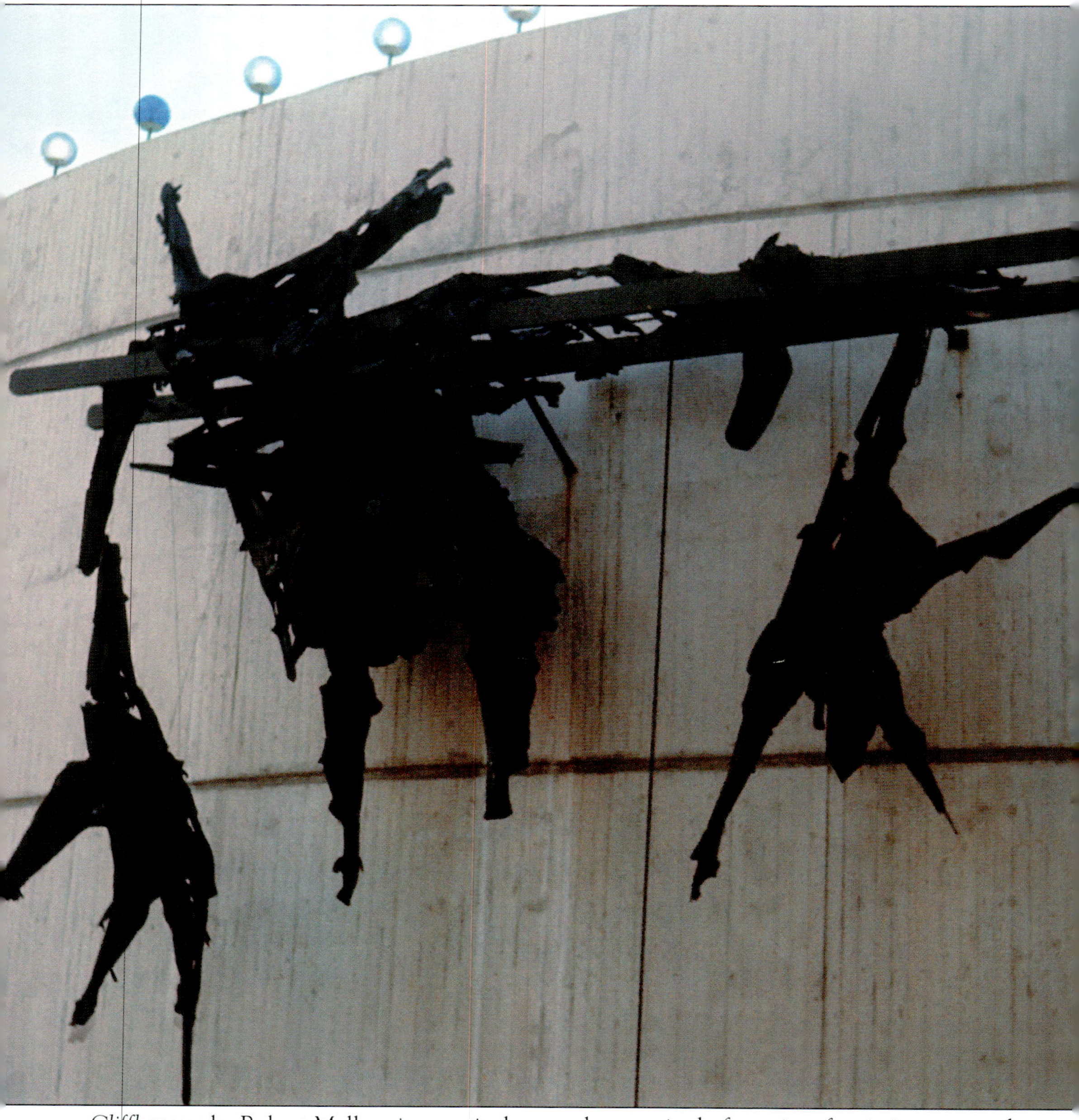

Cliffhangers by Robert Mallary is a meticulous work comprised of a series of resin-impregnated tuxedos, hanging from a steel ladder and a cable. The best description of this work comes from Robert's son Mike: "It is an incredible work that encapsulates the Tuxedo series for which Bob is mainly known. He and I are obsessed with the potential and actual loss of the value that the human endeavor has created and frittered away (in many cases) and outright destroyed (in many cases) and the fact that we are witnessing the beginning of what may be a self-inflicted death spiral. As an artist, Bob had a prophetic insight into these issues and stuck them in our face. *Cliffhangers* did this in spades. (Courtesy of the Bill Cotter collection.)

Seven

Post-Fair Adaptive Reuse

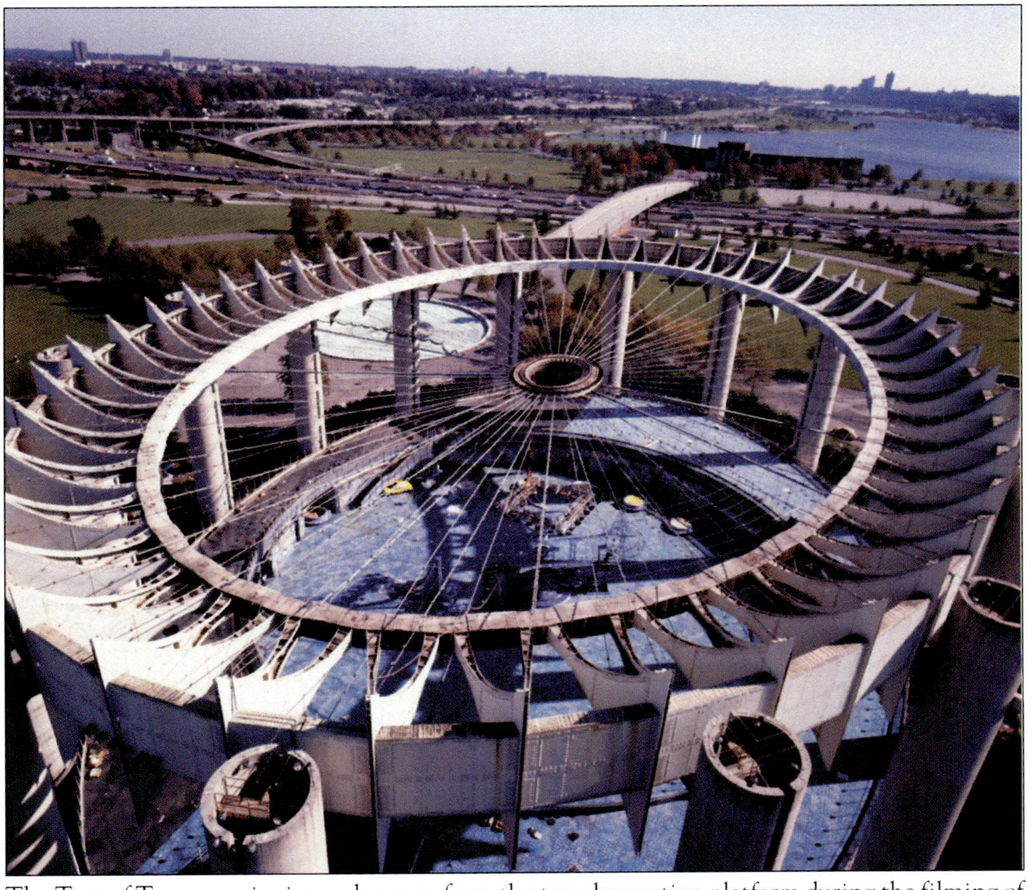

The Tent of Tomorrow is pictured as seen from the top observation platform during the filming of *The Wiz* on October 15, 1977. The map of New York State and mezzanine are covered with blue mats for the evening scenes, and a square overhead lighting fixture hangs down from the center tension ring. In the distance are the Billy Rose Aquacade and Meadow Lake.

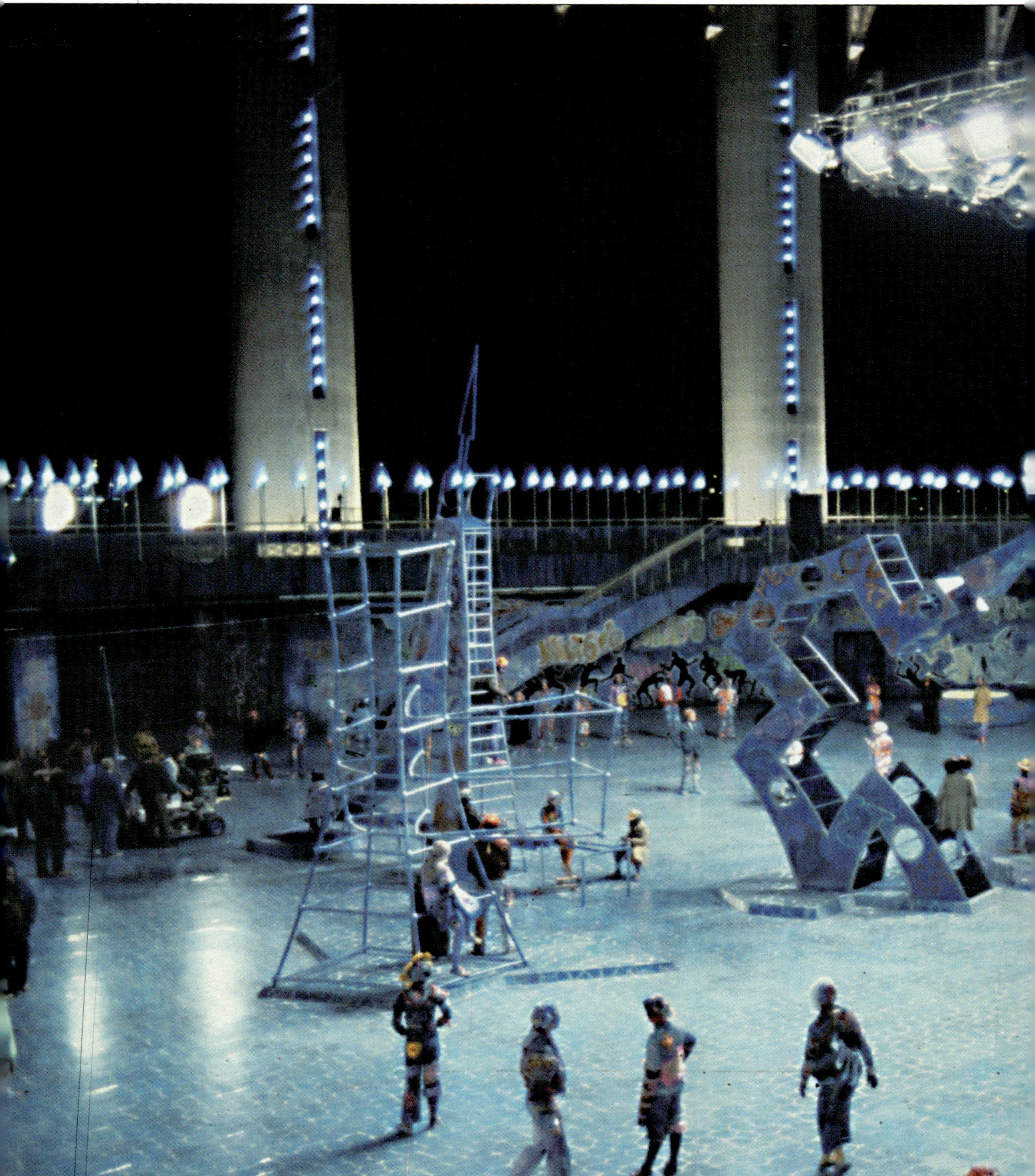

The pavilion again found use for filming as the set of *The Wiz*, a remake of the *Wizard of Oz*, starring Diana Ross as Dorothy, in early October 1977. The scenes were shot in a refurbished Tent of Tomorrow; power was brought in and all the globe lights were replaced with a frosted blue glass version. The mezzanine wall was adorned with graffiti art character outlines, from which actors

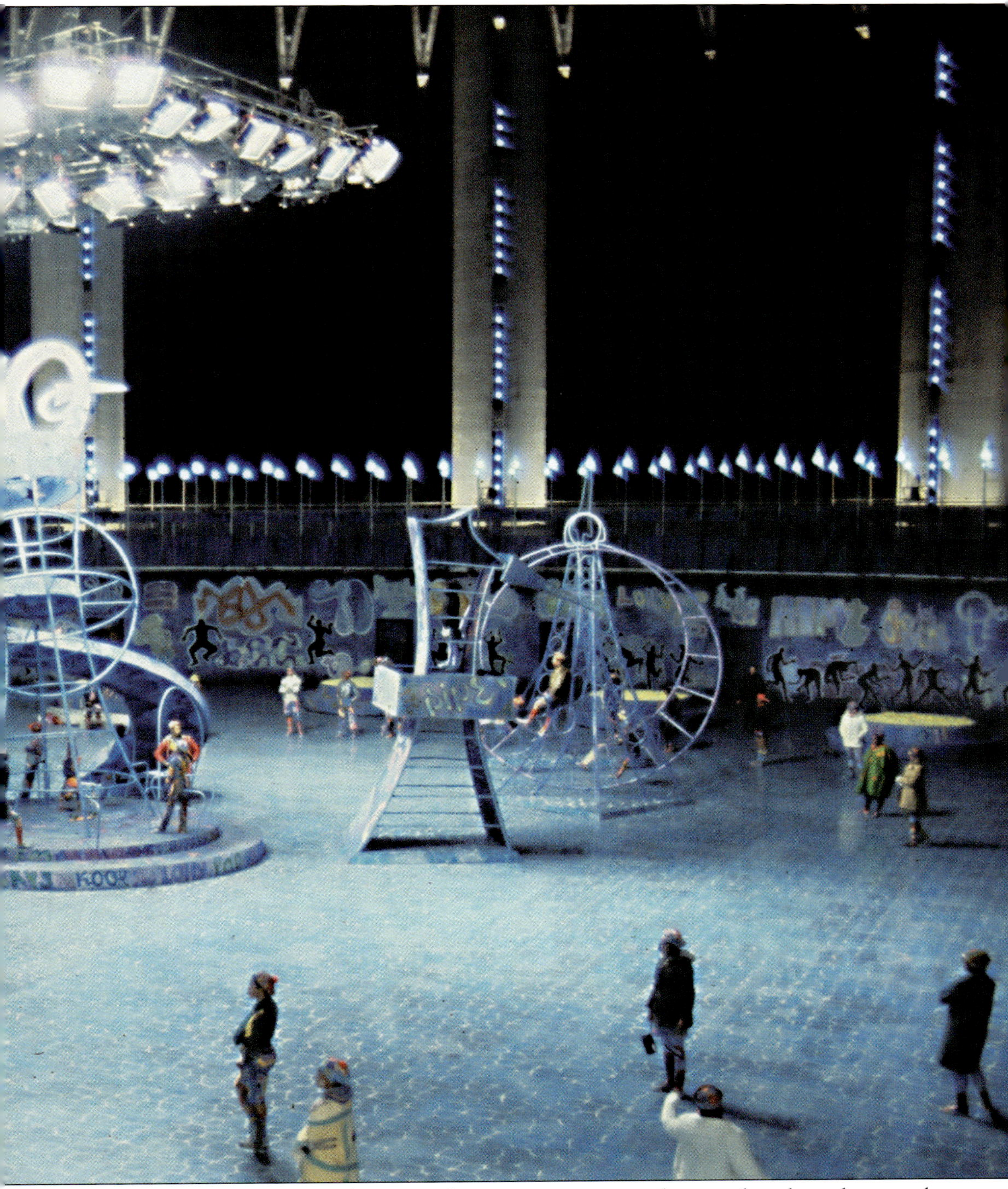

would appear to emerge. Dorothy enters the set on a trajectory that smashes through an oval panel inscribed with "OZ" in the center of the tension ring, landing in a mock-up "planter" filled with plastic balls (to match the four large existing concrete planters to the side of the terrazzo rotunda). (Copyright Universal Studios.)

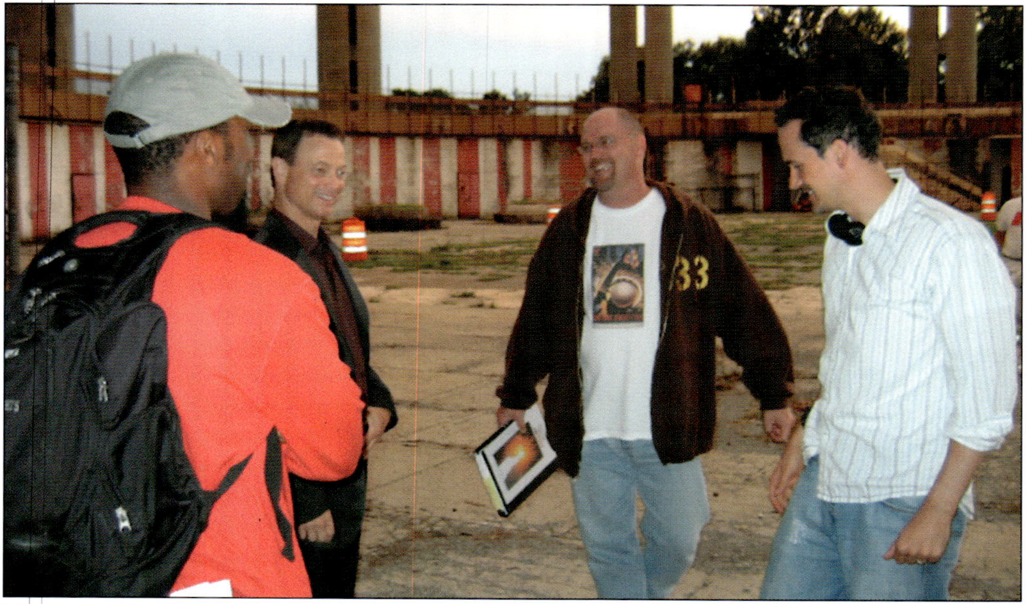

More recently, the pavilion appeared in two episodes of *Crime Scene Investigation: New York*, which aired on November 17 and 25, 2009. Since trucks were not allowed on the terrazzo, the camera had to be mounted on a telescopic boom that could extend out to the center of the rotunda. In the photograph above, scriptwriter Trey Calloway is in the center (script in hand), and actor Gary Sinise is on the left. (Both, courtesy of John Piro.)

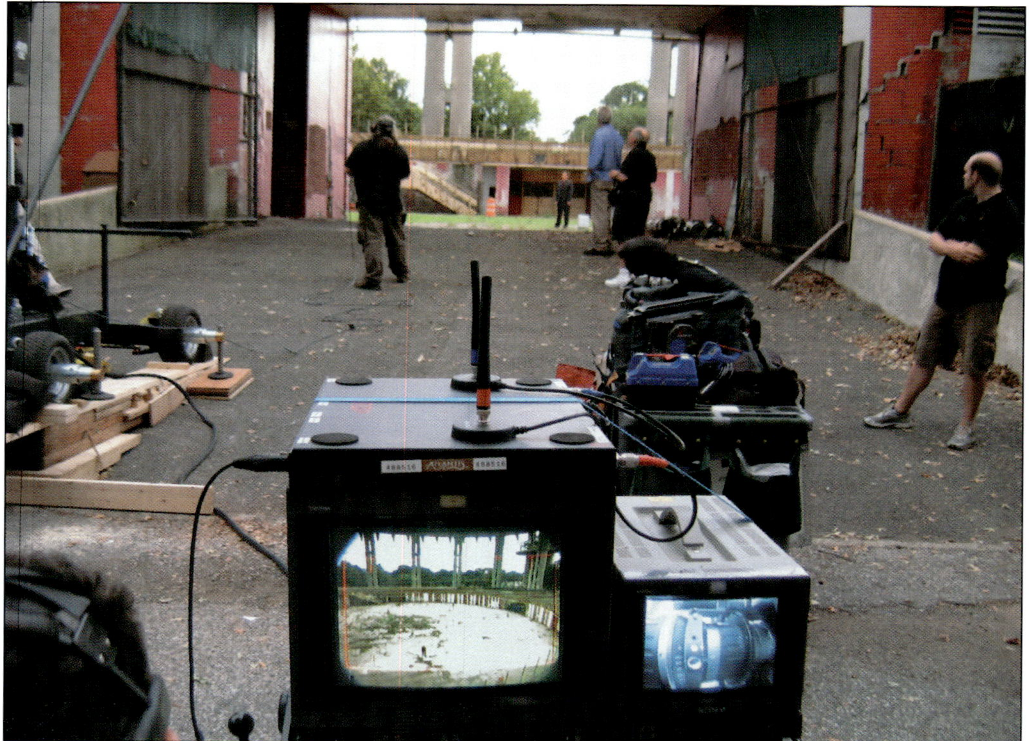

In 1972, an episode of the television detective series *McCloud*, with Dennis Weaver in the title role, was shot at the pavilion, including a scene of McCloud rappelling down the towers. Titled "Showdown at the End of the World," it aired on January 7, 1973. The same translucent white Kalwall panels seen behind Dennis Weaver in the photograph at right are visible in the world's fair–era picture below. (Right, copyright Universal Studios.)

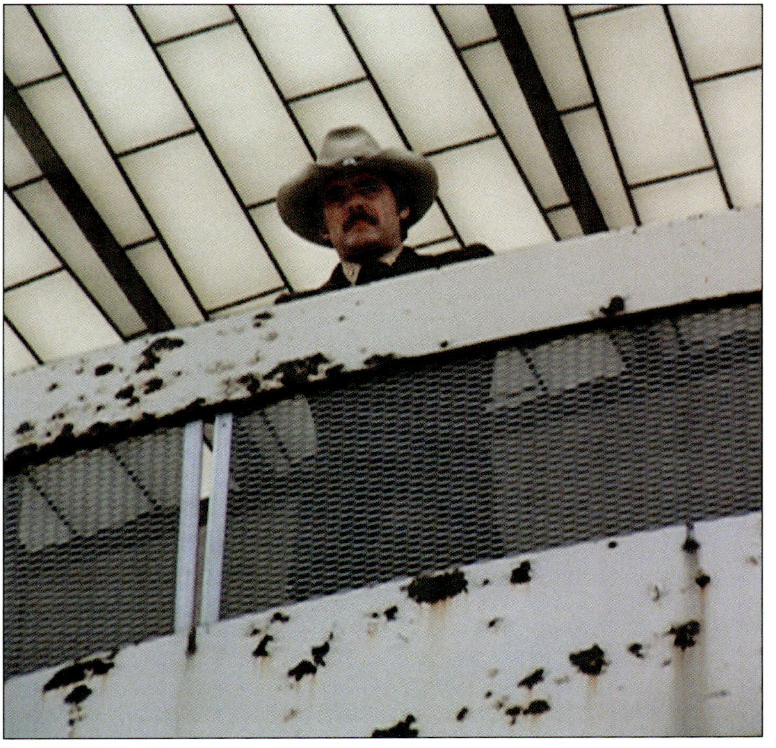

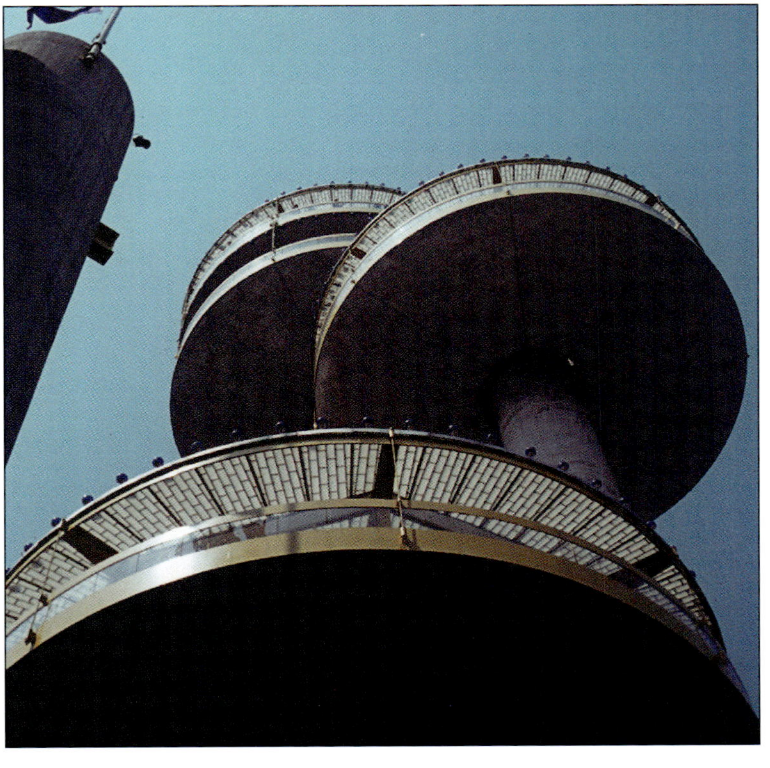

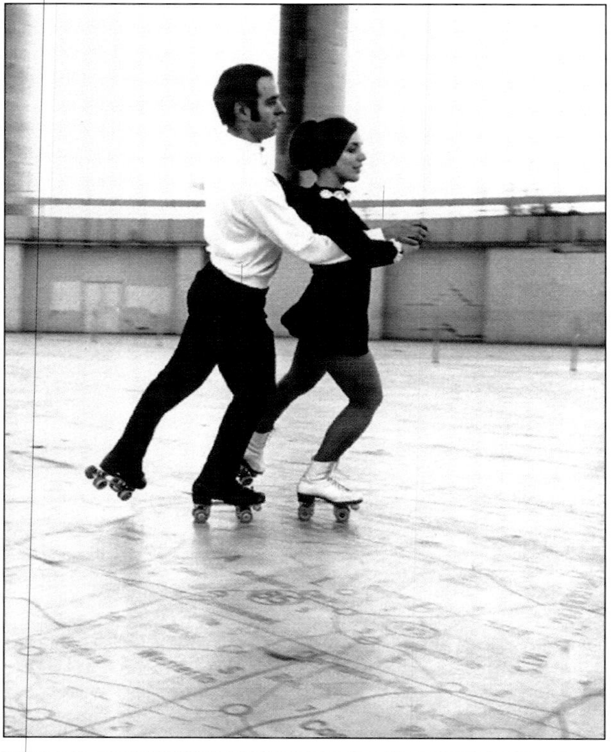

The Tent of Tomorrow's rotunda was leased as a roller skate rink, opening on St. Patrick's Day 1970. The successful venture helped to attract up to 100,000 visitors per year to the pavilion, but the rink was shut down in July 1974 amid concerns that some of the 1,488 colorful translucent roof panels had become too loose after a few of them blew off onto Grand Central Parkway during a windstorm. At first, there were reservations about skaters damaging the map, which now seems irrelevant. Pictured at left are Chris and Bob Jelin in a pair's routine; pictured below is a group skating session. (Both, courtesy of Christine Rafalke.)

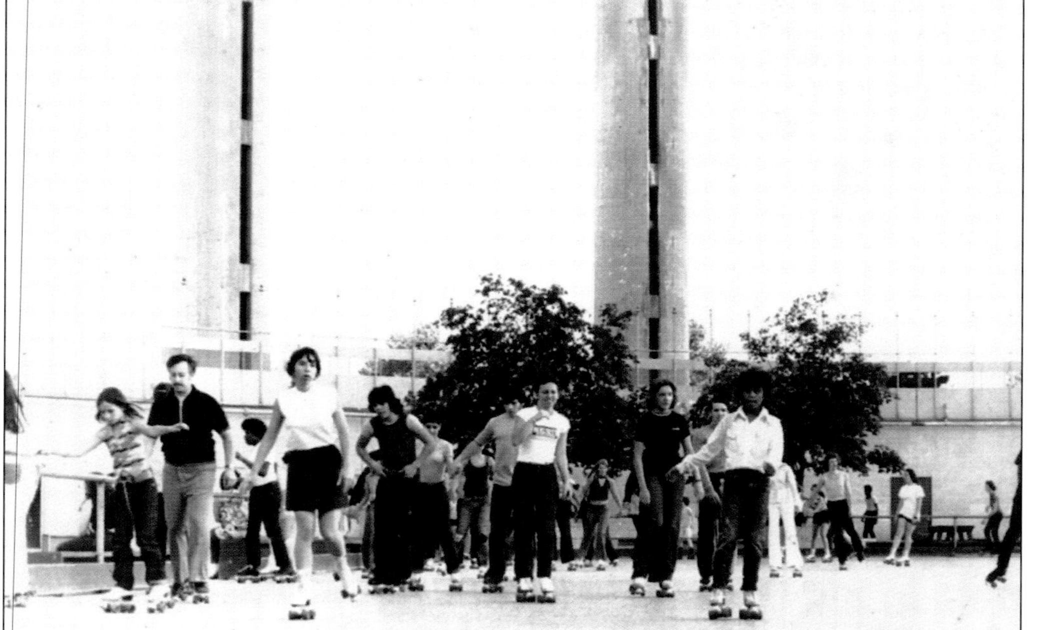

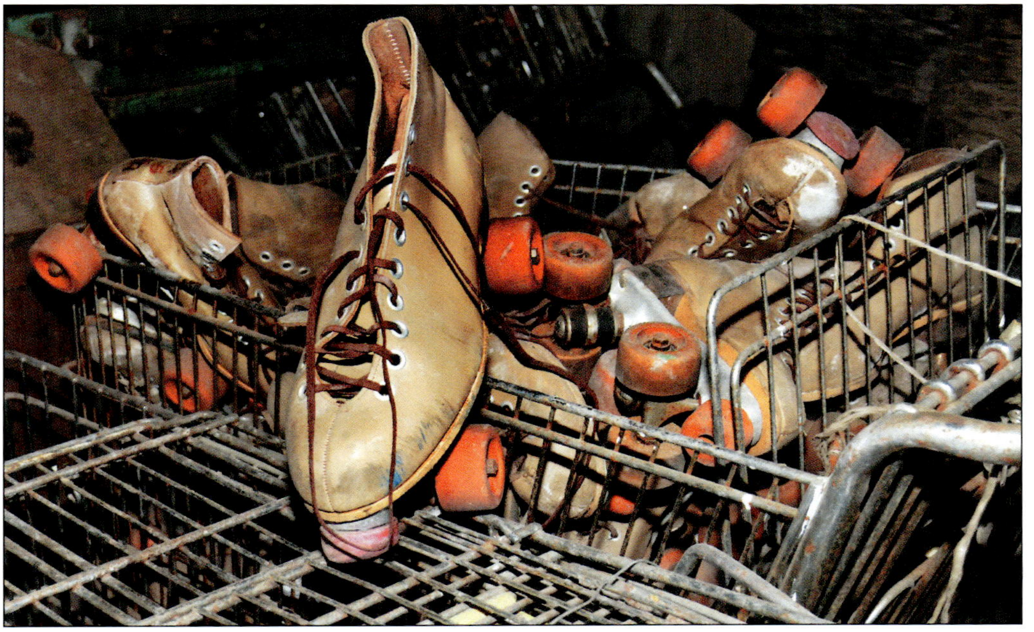

Here are some sad images of the remains of the roller rink. The photographs were taken where patrons got their skate rentals. A painted sign by the women's side of the rental counter implores that skates be returned with laces placed inside and that there were no half sizes. There were 600 pairs of indoor skates with low-durometer hardness wheels. (Some skates are still there today.) A protective coat covering the terrazzo ensured that skaters would not have an impact on the map. Ironically, it would be disuse and removal (instead of repair) of the roof that what would ultimately destroy the terrazzo map.

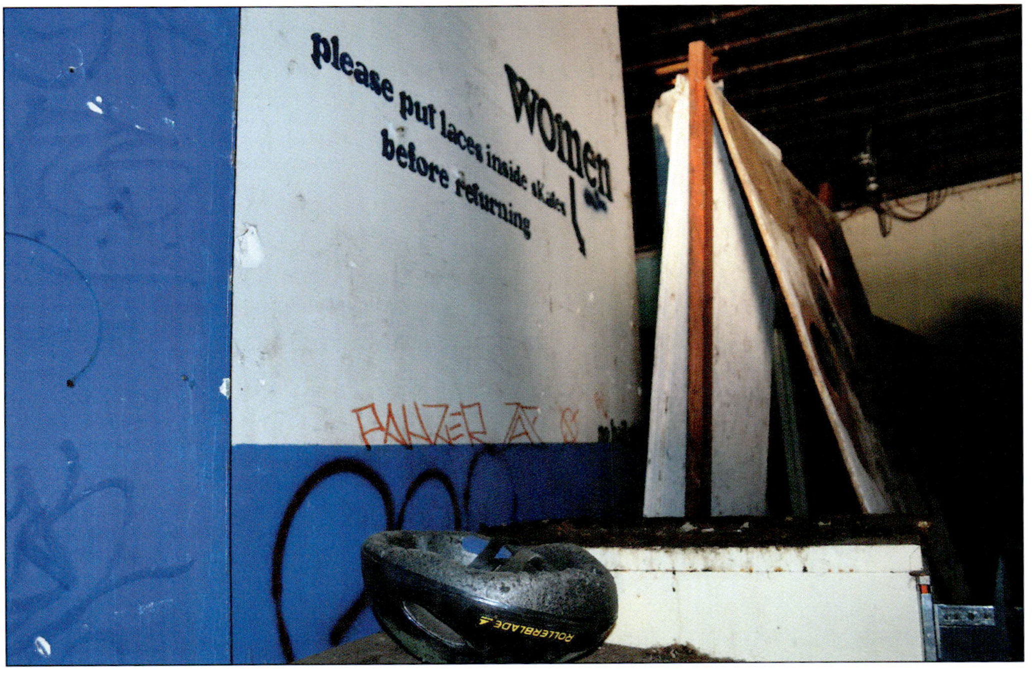

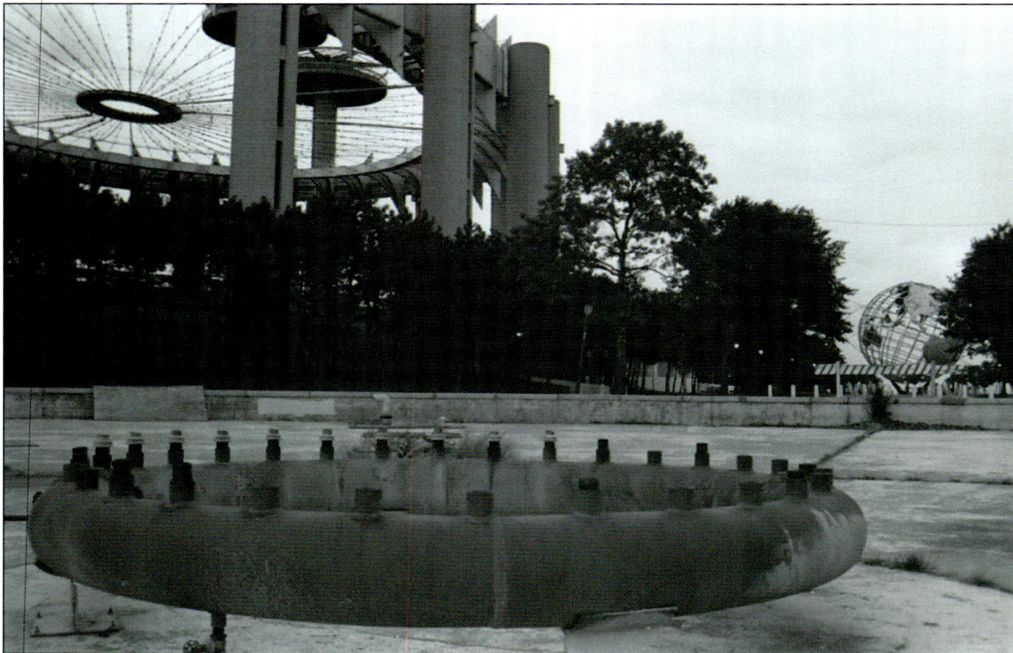

This photograph looking toward the New York State pavilion by the Astral Fountain is from October 1989. By then, the fountain was no longer used. The Astral Fountain was a ring of 40 jets that could shoot water at the rate of 5,600 gallons per minute; the jets were surrounded by a fretwork of stars. The fountain was cut up and replaced by the Maloof skateboard park in 2010, which remains popular.

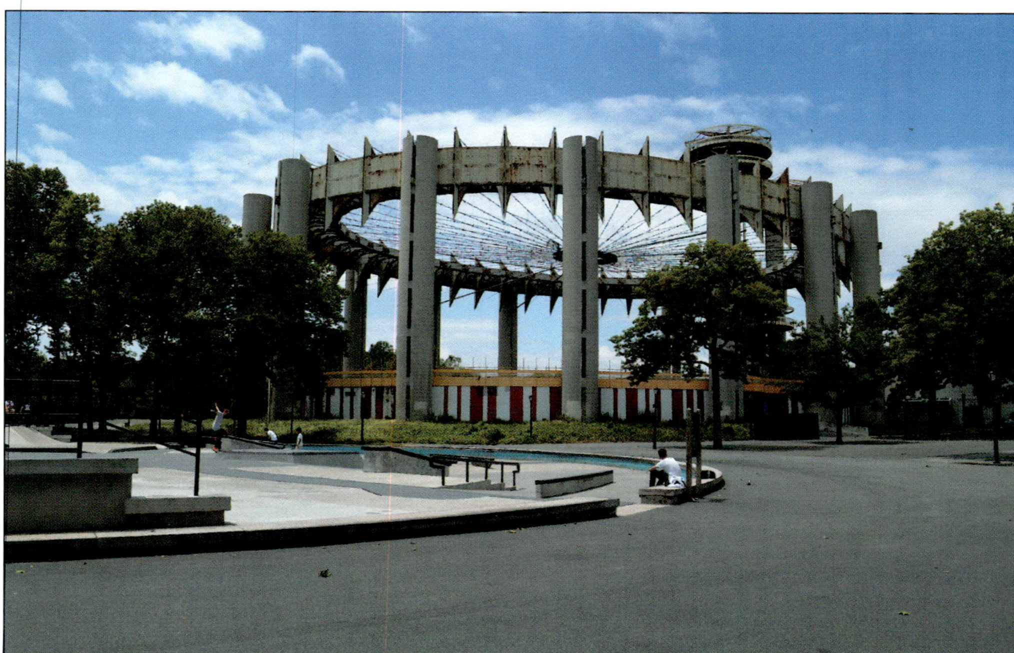

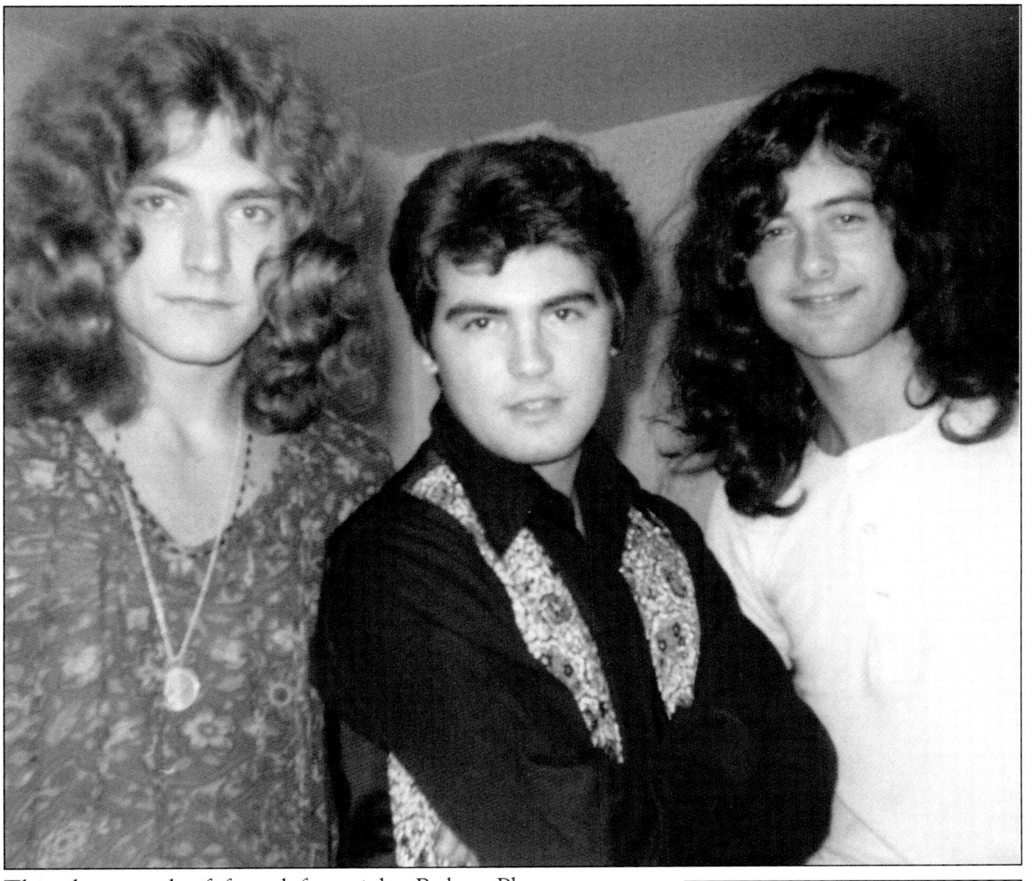

This photograph of, from left to right, Robert Plant, Ron Kellerman, and Jimmy Page, taken in a mezzanine room of the New York State pavilion, is from their concert appearance there on August 29, 1969. The late Ron Kellerman, a musician and producer from Perth Amboy, New Jersey, had an extraordinary friendship and long-running correspondence with Jimmy, well before fame, going all the back to 1963. When his sister Denise took this photograph, they knew that Led Zeppelin had achieved stardom, but at the concert, they realized they were also already well into the stratosphere of rock and roll legend status. (Above, courtesy of Denise Kelly.)

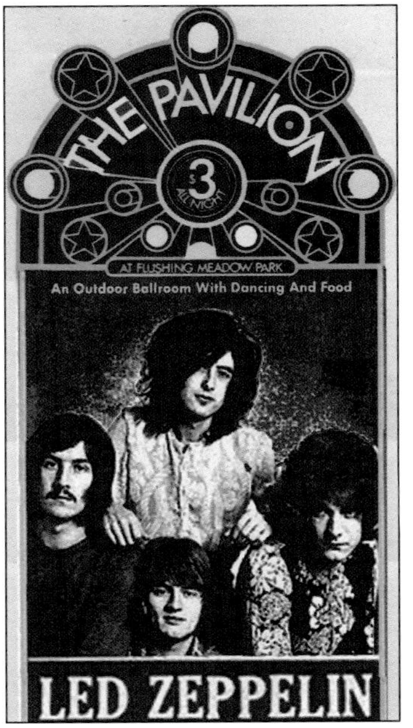

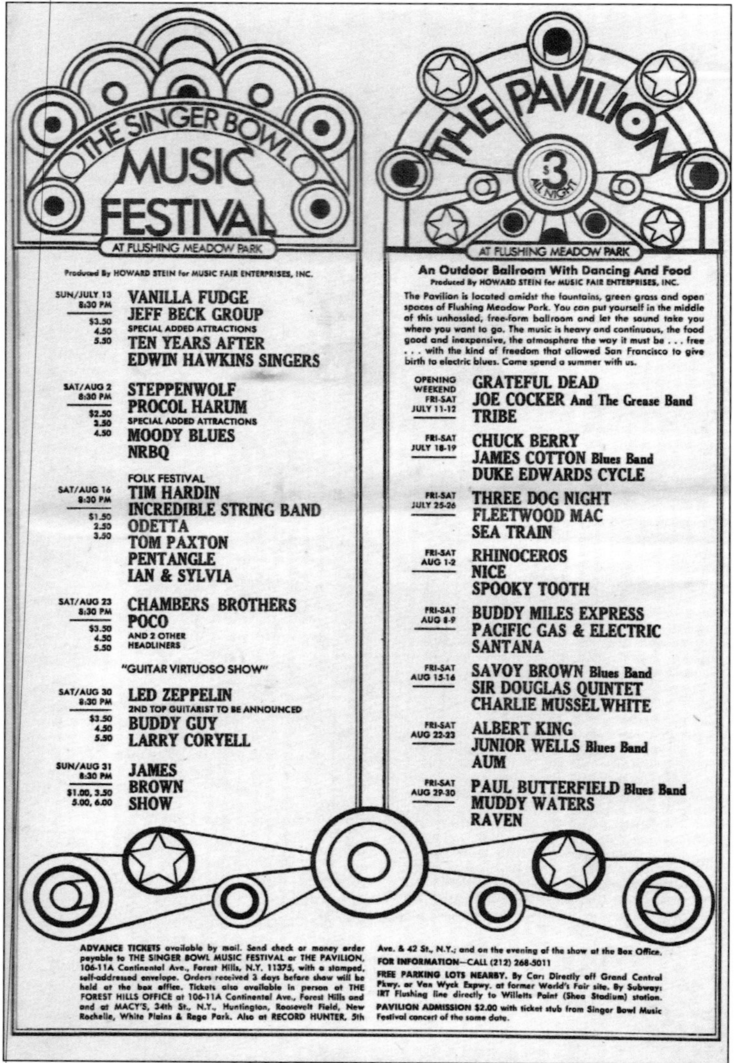

The Led Zeppelin concerts were originally planned for the Singer Bowl but were later moved to the New York State pavilion. They were held on August 29 and 30 to a sold out crowd of 10,500 for each night, with 2,500 fans being turned away at the door. By January 1978, when this photograph was taken, plans were under way to convert the world's fair–era Singer Bowl into the US Tennis Association National Tennis Center.

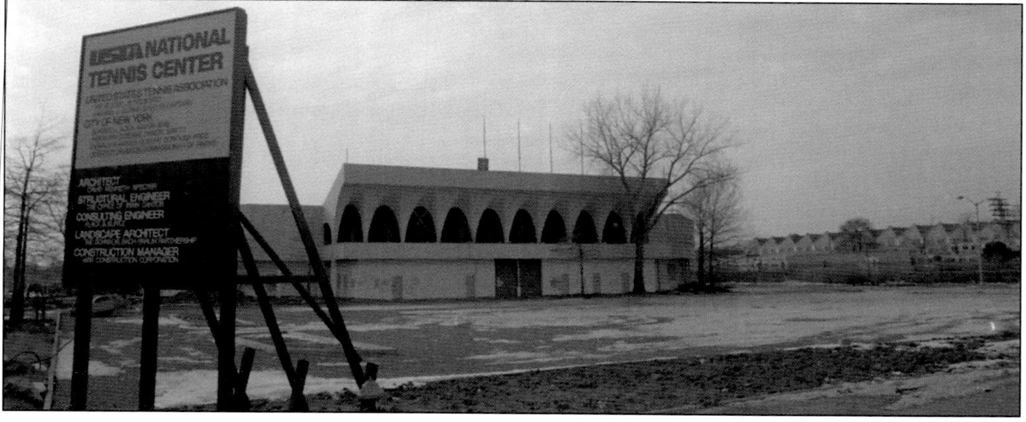

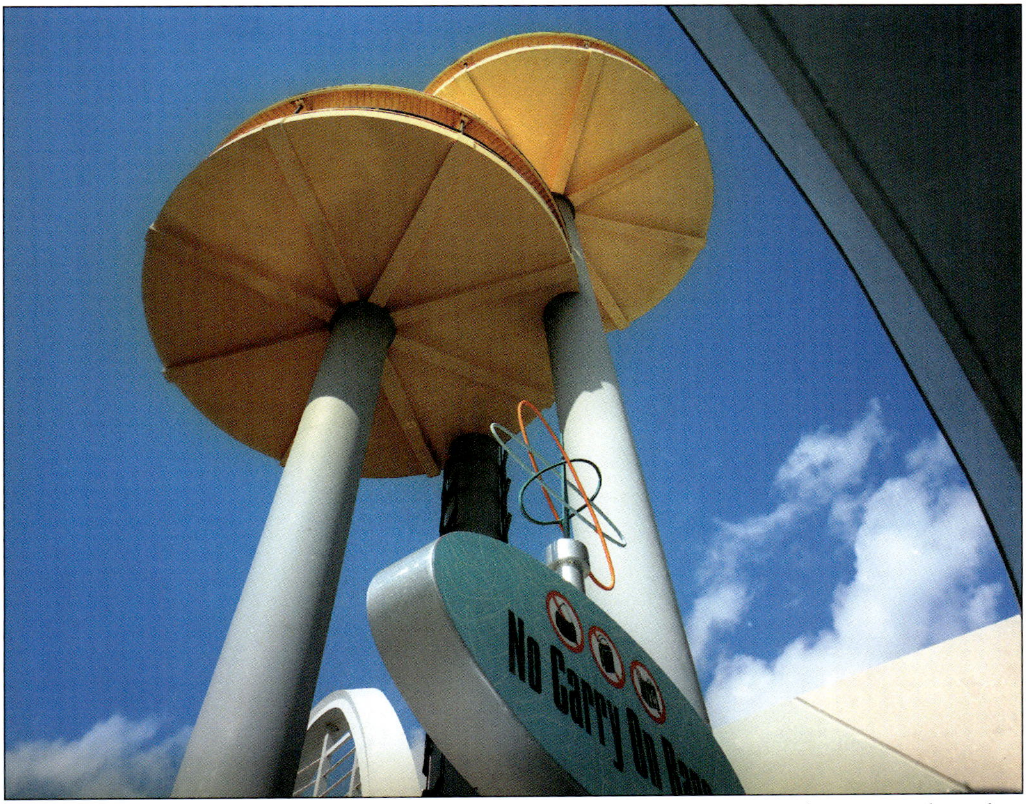

The *Men in Black* movie, featuring a mock-up of the New York State pavilion, was released in 1997. Planning for a *Men in Black* ride began shortly after the film at the Theme Parks at Universal Orlando Resort. The ride has guests enter a *Men in Black* training facility disguised as a "pavilion" and participate in a spinning "shoot in the dark" laser-tag game. Construction of the scaled-down version of the pavilion towers and show building began in 1998; it houses the largest theme ride ever built in a Universal Studio park, opening to the public on April 14, 2000.

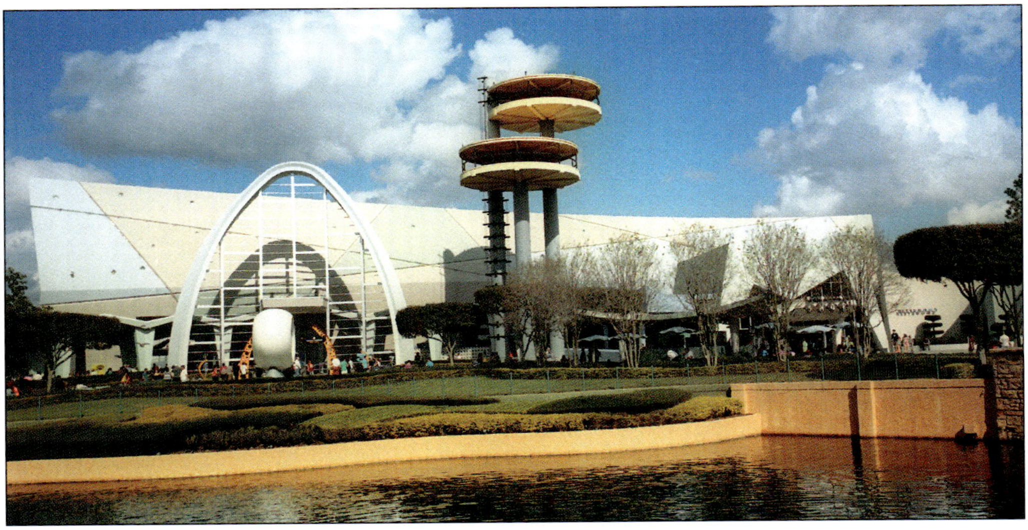

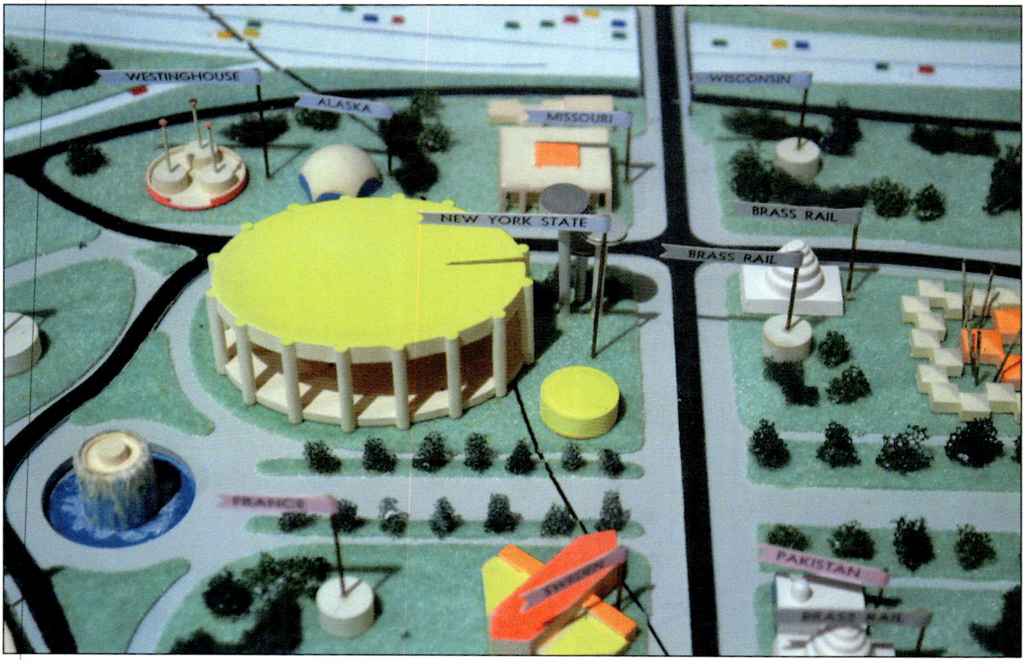

Two models of the New York State pavilion are in the Queens Museum. One is part of the "Panorama of the City of New York," and another is part of a tabletop world's fair site scale model. The panorama is a 1-inch-equals-100-feet scale model of the entire city, including the buildings in Flushing Meadow Corona Park. It is the world's largest scale model at 9,335 square feet. Visitors can walk over parts of the model around the perimeter on a Plexiglas walkway. The photograph below was taken at the closest approach to the New York State "Mini Pavilion."

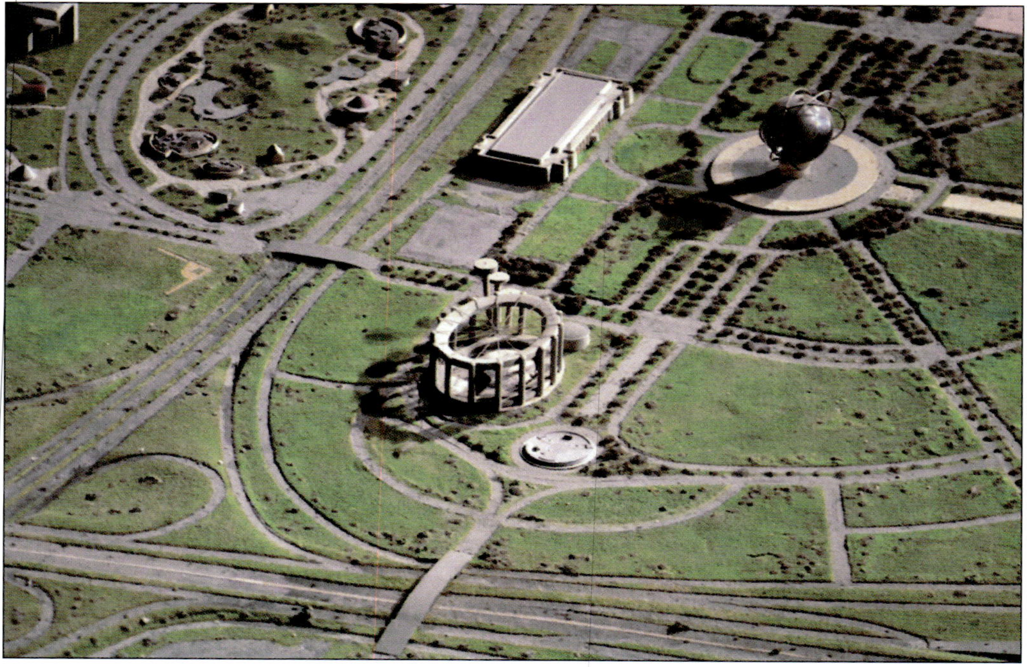

The photograph at right of the pavilion is from October 15, 1977, when the Tent of Tomorrow was being used (repurposed) for the set of *The Wiz* and the mezzanine and terrazzo were covered with blue patterned pads. The photograph below is from June 22, 2013, showing the newly painted mezzanine; the repurposing of its appearance was designed to call attention to the pavilion's potential and its plight. This effort has proved to be successful in focusing both media and political attention on the pavilion, particularly in connection with the 50th anniversary of the world's fair's opening on April 22, 2014.

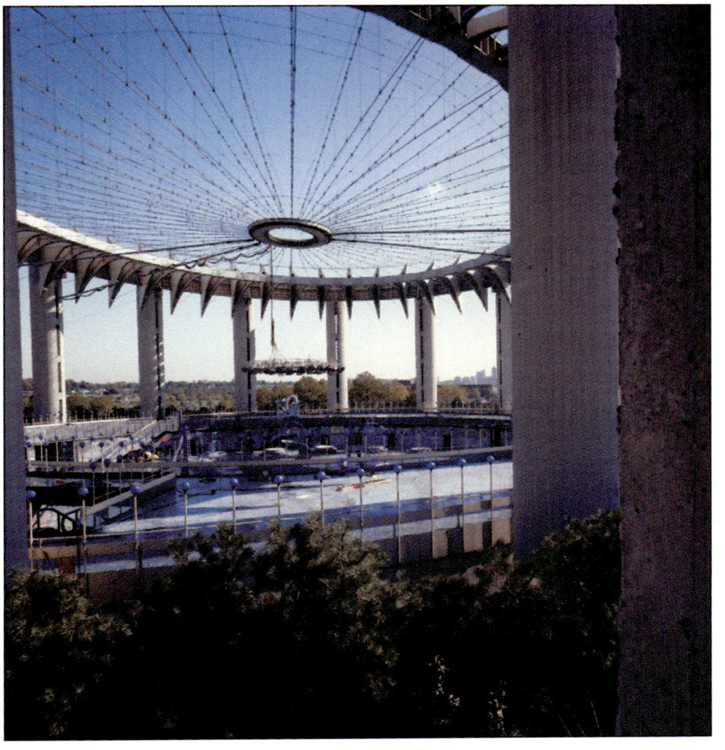

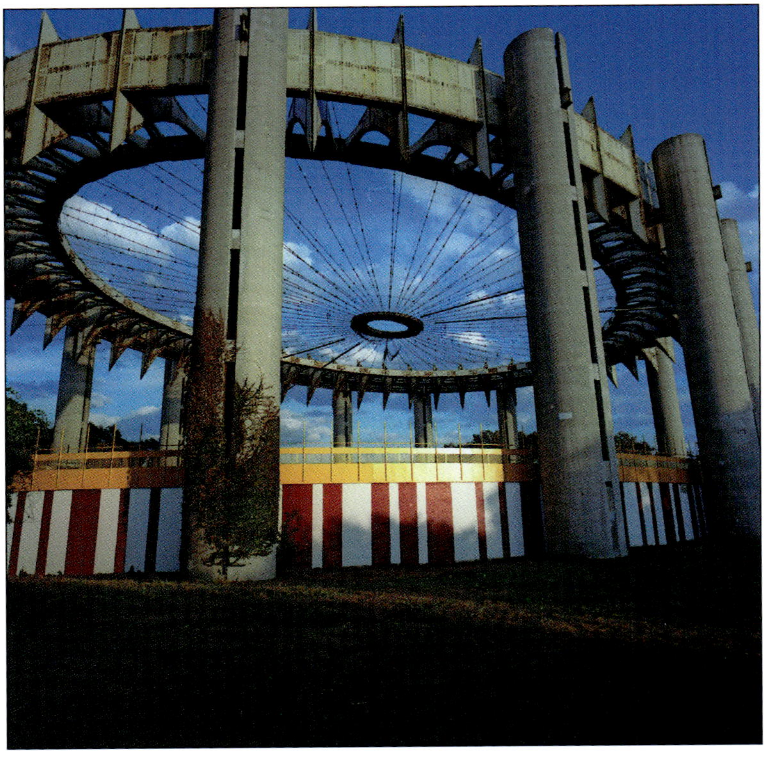

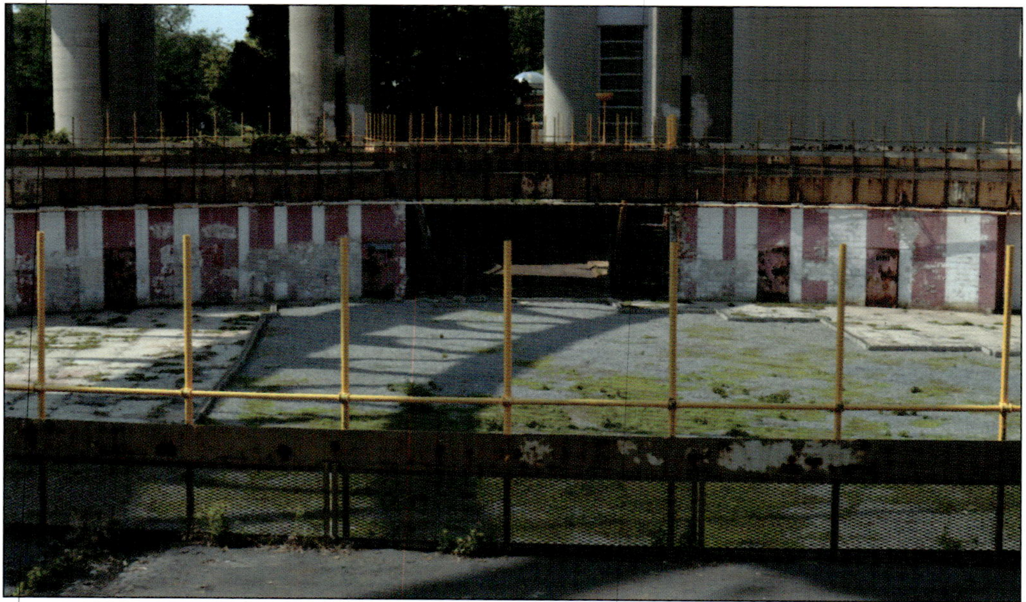

The all-volunteer effort to paint the mezzanine began in September 2009. Late in 2011, then parks commissioner Adrian Benepe visited the pavilion and was so impressed with the outcome of the mezzanine exterior painting that he encouraged the work to continue on the inside of the rotunda. Nothing speaks louder to the repainting effort's dramatic visual impact than comparative photographs. These were taken on June 22, 2013, when the interior walls of the mezzanine rotunda were halfway complete. They are facing opposite sides of the rotunda showing the old fading and peeling section versus the newly painted section.

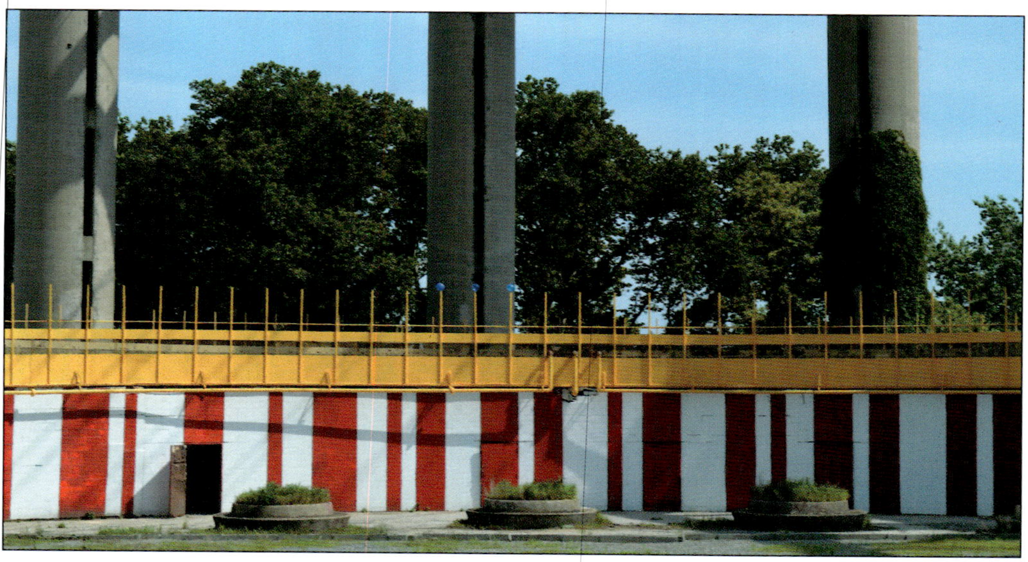

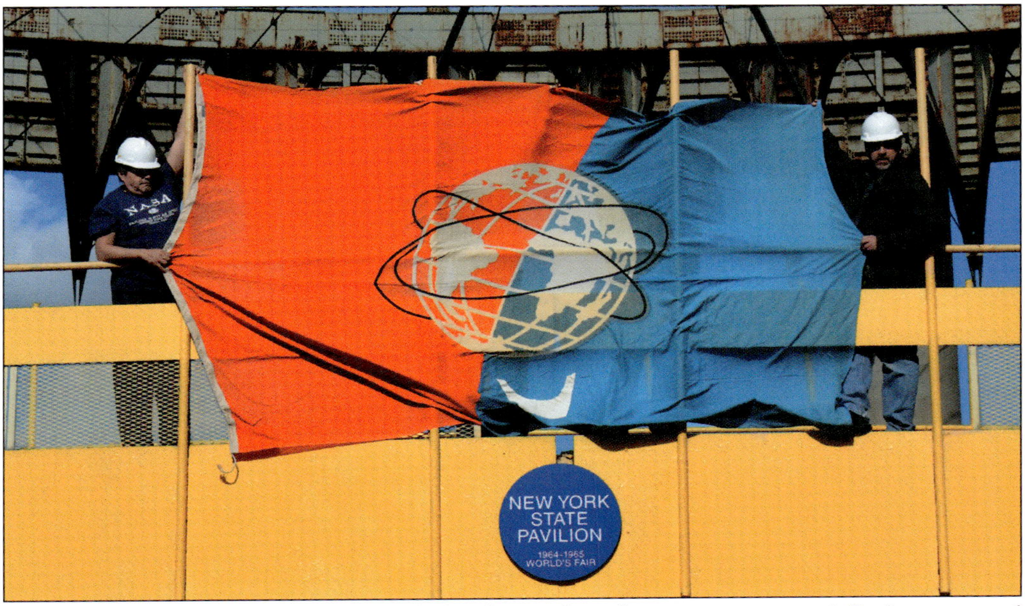

The late Ray Dasher donated this world's fair flag to the volunteer paint crew. A Pinkerton guard had rescued it from a storage locker in the GM pavilion at the end of the fair. It last flew in May 1964 but was taken down because it was too large and could be reached on a windless day. By coincidence, the same guard attended a 2009 commemorative in Chicopee, Massachusetts, for the 60th anniversary marking the end of the Berlin Blockade, where Dasher gave a speech about organizing food donations for the airlift when he was a Chicopee High School student. After discussing events of the day, including the world's fair, the guard presented Ray with this flag. The painters pictured below are, from left to right, (first row) the author, Mitch Silverstein, and John Piro; (second row) Olga Fernandez, Stephanie Bohn, Gary Miller, Thomas Bleuzen, Jim Brown, and Ed Gossett.

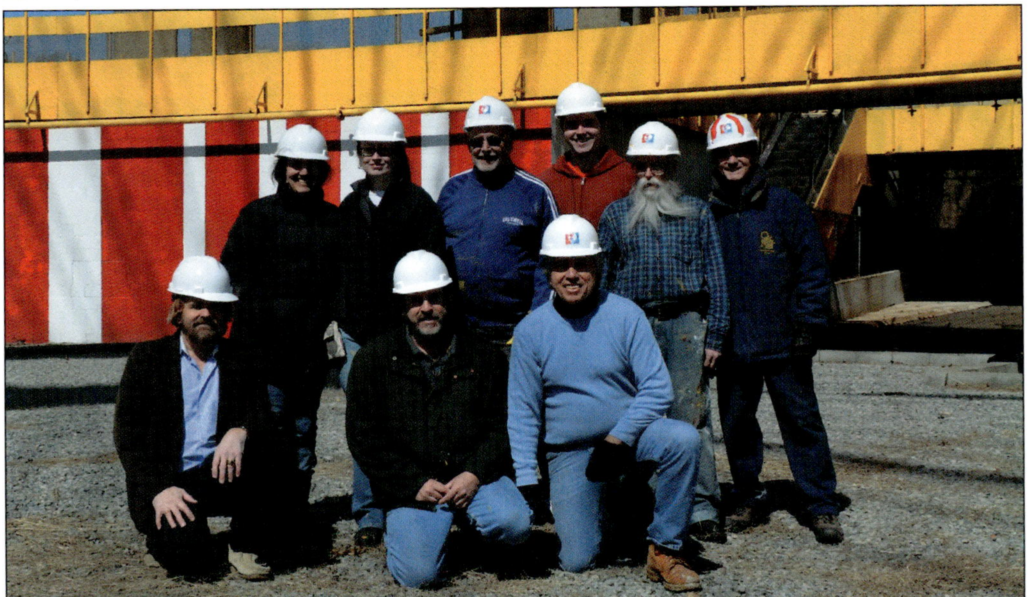